常用针灸取穴汉英对照图解

CHINESE-ENGLISH ILLUSTRATION OF COMMONLY USED METHODS OF LOCATING THE ACUPOINTS

张登部　王金玲　编著
路玉滨　张　伟　译

Written By Zhang Dengbu　Wang Jinling
Translated By Lu Yubin Zhangwei

山东科学技术出版社
SHANDONG SCIENCE AND TECHNOLOGY PRESS

前　言

　　针灸学是中国医药学的一个重要组成部分。腧穴是针灸学的重要内容。应用针刺和艾灸的方法治疗疾病，必须做到取穴准确、针刺深浅适度以及恰当地运用补泻手法，才能达到预期的效果。其中，取穴准确是重要环节。要做到取穴准确，必须熟练掌握各种取穴方法，了解腧穴所在部位的结构特点等，此书即是为达到这个目的而编绘的。

　　本书以彩图为主，文字说明为辅，共分两个部分。第一部分为腧穴总论，主要介绍腧穴的基本知识；第二部分为经络腧穴各论，共介绍常用经穴和奇穴287个，一穴一图，并按"取穴法"、"功效与主治"、"操作"及"备注"逐项介绍，以使读者进一步掌握该穴的结构特点。

　　本书内容简明扼要，图文并茂，适合于中外广大初学针灸者及临床针灸医生参考学习。由于我们水平有限，书中缺点、错误在所难免，恳切希望广大读者批评指正。

PREFACE

Acupuncture-moxibustion is an important component part of traditional Chinese medicine, and acupoint constitutes an important content of the acupuncture and moxibustion. When disease is to be treated with acupuncture and moxibustion, it is imperative to locate acupoint correctly, puncture at proper depth and apply such manipulations as reducing and reinforcing appropriately in order to achieve the expected therapeutic effects. In doing so, locating an acupoint correctly is of particular significance. To correctly locate an acupoint, one must master well various kinds of method of locating acupoints and know the structural features of the areas where the acupoints are located. This is just the purpose of the book which mainly introduces the locating method of points and the structural features of the areas.

This book, with colorful pictures and literal descriptions, consists of two parts. General Introduction to Acupoints, the first part of the book, is aimed at introduction of the basic knowledge of acupoints, while Acupoints of Meridians, the second part, introduces 287 commonly used acupoints and extra acupoints, each of which is described by a picture, locating method, actions and indications, manipulation and notes, with an aim to help readers to master the structural feature of the acupoints.

Being concise and brief with both pictures and literal explanations, this book is suitable for both learners and clinical practitioners of acupuncture and moxibustion.

目 录

腧穴总论

经络腧穴各论

2

CONTENTS

General Introduction to Acupoints

Acupoints of Meridians

1. The Lung Meridian of Hand-Taiyin
   Zhongfu (LU 1)   Chize (LU 5)   Kongzui (LU 6)   Lieque (LU 7)   Jingqu (LU 8)   Taiyuan (LU 9)   Yuji (LU 10)   Shaoshang (LU 11)

2. The Large Intestine Meridian of Hand-Yangming
   Shangyang (LI 1)   Erjian (LI 2)   Sanjian (LI 3)   Hegu (LI 4)   Yangxi (LI 5)   Pianli (LI 6)   Xialian (LI 8)   Shanglian (LI 9)   Shousanli (LI 10)   Quchi (LI 11)   Zhouliao (LI 12)   Binao (LI 14)   Jianyu (LI 15)   Futu (LI 18)   Yingxiang (LI 20)

3. The Stomach Meridian of Foot-Yangming
   Sibai (ST 2)   Juliao (ST 3)   Dicang (ST 4)   Jiache (ST 6)   Xiaguan (ST 7)   Touwei (ST 8)   Renying (ST 9)   Rugen (ST 18)   Burong (ST 19)   Liangmen (ST 21)   Tianshu (ST 25)   Guilai (ST 29)   Biguan (ST 31)   Futu (ST 32)   Yinshi (ST 33)   Liangqiu (ST 34)   Dubi (ST 35)   Zusanli (ST 36)   Shangjuxu (ST 37)   Tiaokou (ST 38)   Xiajuxu (ST 39)   Fenglong (ST 40)   Jiexi (ST 41)   Neiting (ST 44)   Lidui (ST 45)

4. The Spleen Meridian of Foot-Taiyin
   Yinbai (SP 1)   Taibai (SP 3)   Gongsun (SP 4)   Shangqiu (SP 5)   Sanyinjiao (SP 6)   Lougu (SP 7)   Diji (SP 8)   Yinlingquan (SP 9)   Xuehai (SP 10)   Jimen (SP 11)   Fujie (SP 14)   Daheng (SP 15)   Dabao (SP 21)

5. The Heart Meridian of Hand-Shaoyin
   Jiquan (HT 1)   Shaohai (HT 3)   Lingdao (HT 4)   Tongli (HT 5)   Yinxi (HT 6)   Shenmen (HT 7)   Shaofu (HT 8)   Shaochong (HT 9)

6. The Small Intestine Meridian of Hand-Taiyang
   Shaoze (SI 1)   Houxi (SI 3)   Wangu (SI 4)   Yanglao (SI 6)

Zhizheng (SI 7) Xiaohai (SI 8) Jianzhen (SI 9) Naoshu (SI 10) Tianzong (SI 11) Bingfeng (SI 12) Quyuan (SI 13) Jianwaishu (SI 14) Jianzhongshu (SI 15) Tianchuang (SI 16) Tianrong (SI 17) Quanliao (SI 18) Tinggong (SI 19)

7. The Bladder Meridian of Foot-Taiyang

Jingming (BD 1) Zanzhu (BD 2) Quchai (BD 4) Tongtian (BD 7) Yuzhen (BD 9) Tianzhu (BD 10) Dazhu (BD 11) Fengmen (BD 12) Feishu (BD 13) Jueyinshu (BD 14) Xinshu (BL 15) Geshu (BL 17) Ganshu (BL 18) Danshu (BL 19) Pishu (BL 20) Weishu (BL 21) Sanjiaoshu (BL 22) Shenshu (BL 23) Qihaishu (BL 24) Dachangshu (BL 25) Guanyuanshu (BL 26) Xiaochangshu (BL 27) Pangguangshu (BL 28) Ciliao (BL 32) Chengfu (BL 36) Yinmen (BL 37) Weiyang (BL 39) Weizhong (BL 40) Gaohuang (BL 43) Shentang (BL 44) Yixi (BL 45) Geguan (BL 46) Weicang (BL 50) Zhishi (BL 52) Zhibian (BL 54) Heyang (BL 55) Chengjin (BL 56) Chengshan (BL 57) Feiyang (BL 58) Fuyang (BL 59) Kunlun (BL 61) Shenmai (BL 62) Shugu (BL 65) Zhiyin (BL 67)

8. The Kideny Meridian of Foot-Shaoyin

Yongquan (KI 1) Rangu (KI 2) Taixi (KI 3) Dazhong (KI 4) Zhaohai (KI 6) Fuliu (KI 7) Jiaoxin (KI 8) Zhubin (KI 9) Yingu (KI 10) Dahe (KI 12) Qixue (KI 13) Shiguan (KI 18) Youmen (KI 21) Shufu (KI 27)

9. The Pericardium Meridian of Hand-Jueyin

Tianchi (PC 1) Quze (PC 3) Ximen (PC 4) Jianshi (PC 5) Neiguan (PC 6) Daling (PC 7) Laogong (PC 8) Zhongchong (PC 9)

10. The Sanjiao Meridian of Hand-Shaoyang

Guanchong (SJ 1) Yemen (SJ 2) Zhongzhu (SJ 3) Yangchi (SJ 4) Waiguan (SJ 5) Zhigou (SJ 6) Huizong (Sj 7) Sanyangluo (SJ 8) Tianjing (Sj 10) Qinglengyuan (Sj 11)

3

Naohui (SJ 13)　Jianliao (Sj 14)　Tianliao (SJ 15)　Tianyou (SJ 16)　Yifeng (SJ 17)　Luxi (SJ 19)　Jiaosun (SJ 20)　Ermen (SJ 21)　Erheliao (SJ 22)　Sizhukong (SJ 23)

11. The Gallbladder Meridian of Foot-Shaoyang

Tongziliao (GB 1)　Tinghui (GB 2)　Shangguan (GB 3)　Hanyan (GB 4)　Xuanlu (GB 5)　Xuanli (GB 6)　Qubin (GB 7)　Shuaigu (GB 8)　Tianchong (GB 9)　Wangu (GB 12)　Yangbai (GB 14)　Toulinqi (GB 15)　Fengchi (GB 20)　Jianjing (GB 21)　Riyue (GB 24)　Jingmen (GB 25)　Daimai (GB 26)　Wushu (GB 27)　Weidao (GB 28)　Juliao (GB 29)　Huantiao (GB 30)　Fengshi (GB 31)　Xiyangguan (GB 33)　Yanglingquan (GB 34) Yangjiao (GB 35)　Waiqiu (GB 36)　Guangming (GB 37)　Yangfu (GB 38)　Xuanzhong (GB 39)　Qiuxu (GB 40)　Zulinqi (GB 41)　Xiaxi (GB 43)　Zuqiaoyin (GB 44)

12. The Liver Meridian of Foot-Jueyin

Dadui (LR 1)　Xingjian (LR 2)　Taichong (LR 3)　Zhongfeng (LR 4)　Ligou (LR 5)　Xiguan (LR 7)　Ququan (LR 8)　Zhangmen (LR 13)　Qimen (LR 14)

13. The Ren Meridian

Huiyin (RN 1)　Qugu (RN 2)　Zhongji (RN 3)　Guanyuan (RN 4)　Shimen (RN 5)　Qihai (RN 6)　Yinjiao (RN 7)　Shenque (RN 8)　Shuifen (RN 9)　Xiawan (RN 10)　Jianli (RN 11)　Zhongwan (RN 12)　Shangwan (RN 13)　Juque (RN 14)　Jiuwei (RN 15)　Danzhong (RN 17)　Xuanji (RN 21)　Tiantu (RN 22)　Lianquan (RN 23)　Chengjiang (RN 24)

14. The Du Meridian

Changqiang (DU 1)　Yaoshu (DU 2)　Yaoyangguan (DU 3)　Mingmen (DU 4)　Jinsuo (DU 8)　Zhiyang (DU 9)　Lingtai (DU 10)　Shendao (DU 11)　Shenzhu (DU 12)　Taodao (DU 13)　Dazhui (DU 14)　Yamen (DU 15)　Fengfu (DU 16)

Naohu (DU 17) Houding (DU 19) Baihui (DU 20) Qianding (DU 21) Shangxing (DU 23) Shenting (DU 24) Suliao (DU 25) Shuigou (DU 26) Duiduan (DU 27) Yinjiao (DU 28)

15. Extra acupoints
SishengSong (Ex-HV 1) Yintang (Ex-HV 3) Yuyao (Ex-HV 4) Taiyang (Ex-HV 5) Qiuhou (Ex-HV 7) Jinjun (Ex-HV 12) Yuye (Ex-HV 13) Yiming (Ex-HV 14) Jingbailao (Ex-HV 15) Zigong (Ex-CA 1) Dingchuan (Ex-B 1) Jiaji (Ex-B 2) Weiwanxiashu (Ex-B 3) Yaoyan (Ex-B 7) Shiqizhui (Ex-B 8) Yaoqi (Ex-B 9) Erbai (Ex-UE 2) Zhongquan (Ex-UE 3) Zhongkui (Ex-UE 4) Dagukong (Ex-UE 5) Xiaogukong (Ex-UE 6) Baxie (Ex-UE 9) Sifeng (Ex-UE 10) Shixuan (Ex-VE 11) Heding (Ex-LE 2) Baichongwo (Ex-LE 3) Xiyan (Ex-LE 5) Dannang (Ex-LE 6) Lanwei (Ex-LE 7) Bafeng (Ex-LE 10)

腧穴总论

一、腧穴的概念、命名与分类

（一）腧穴的概念

腧穴是脏腑经络之气输注于体表的部位，是针灸防治疾病的刺激部位。在历代文献中，腧穴有"砭灸处"、"节"、"会"、"骨孔"、"气穴"、"穴位"等不同名称。《灵枢·九针十二原》篇在论述腧穴时说："节之交，三百六十五会……所言节者，神气之所游行出入也。"说明腧穴不是孤立于体表的点，而是与经络脏腑之气密切联系的。

（二）腧穴的命名

《千金翼方》指出："凡诸孔穴，名不徒设，皆有深意。"腧穴的名称不仅有其中医学意义，也是古代灿烂文化的一部分。掌握腧穴命名的意义，有助于熟悉腧穴的部位及治疗作用。腧穴的命名，大致分以下三类。

1. 自然类　①以天文命名者，如日月、上星、太白等；②以地貌命名者，腧穴处似山陵丘墟者，如承山、大陵、商丘、丘墟等；似谷溪沟渠者，如合谷、后溪、水沟、经渠等；似海泽池泉者，如小海、尺泽、曲池、涌泉等；似街道市廊者，如气街、水道、风市、步廊等。

2. 物象类　①以动物名称命名者，如鱼际、鱼腰、伏兔、犊鼻等；②以植物名称命名者，如丝竹空、攒竹等；③以建筑物名称命名者，如库房、地仓、气户等。

3. 人体类　①以解剖部位命名者，如大椎、完骨、心俞、肺俞等；②以人体某种功能命名者，如承浆、听会、听宫、血海、气海等；③以腧穴功能作用命名者，如光明、迎香、归来、水分等；④以阴阳属性命名者，如阴陵泉、阳陵泉、三阴交、三阳络等。

（三）腧穴的分类

人体的腧穴很多，概括起来可分为经穴奇穴和阿是穴三类。

1. 经穴　即分布于十二经脉及任、督二脉上并在文献中已归属于十四经中的腧穴。经穴的特点：有一定位置和名称，有一定经属，其主治作用广泛，是腧穴的主要部分。现有经穴361个，绝大部分是晋代以前发现的。

2. 奇穴　又称"经外奇穴"。奇穴是指有一定穴名，又有明确的位置，但文献中尚未列入十四经的腧穴。这些腧穴对某些病证具有较好的疗效，故称奇穴。奇穴与经络系统仍有密切关系，如印堂穴与督脉；太阳穴与手少阳三焦经等。

3. 阿是穴　"阿"有痛的意思，因其按压痛处病人会"阿阿"发声，故名"阿是"。此类穴首载于唐代《千金要方》，书中以痛点取穴、快感取穴为特点。阿是穴没有固定位置，无具体名称，而是以压痛点或其他反应点作为针灸部位。阿是穴多位于病变附近,也可在与其距离较远的部位。

二、腧穴的主治作用

腧穴的主治作用,又称腧穴的主治规律。腧穴的作用,与经络脏腑有密切关系,即"经络所通,主治所及"。

(一)近治作用

腧穴的近治作用,即人体腧穴均能治疗所在部位及邻近脏腑及体表的局部病证。包括对体表和内脏的主治,这是人体所有腧穴的主治共性。如头面部腧穴,大多能治疗局部疾患。睛明、四白位于眼区,均能治疗眼疾;听宫、听会、翳风位于耳区,均能治疗耳病等。

(二)远治作用

腧穴的远治作用,是十四经腧穴主治作用的基本规律。在十四经腧穴中,尤其是十二经脉在四肢肘膝关节以下的腧穴,不仅能治疗局部病证,而且还可以治疗本经循行所及的远隔部位的脏腑、五官九窍等的病证,有的腧穴甚至具有影响全身的作用。例如合谷穴,不仅能治疗手腕部病证,而且能治疗颈部和头面五官病证,同时,还能治疗外感病的发热,足三里穴不仅能治疗下肢病证,而且对调整消化系统的功能,甚至对人体防卫、免疫反应方面都具有良好的作用。

(三)特殊作用

1. 双相良性调整作用　针刺某些腧穴,对机体的不同机能状况起着双相性的良性调整作用。例如心动过速时,针刺内关穴有减慢心率,使之恢复正常的作用;反之,当心动过缓时,针刺内关穴,又有增加心率,使之恢复正常的作用。又如天枢穴既有止泻、止痢的作用,又有通便作用等。

2. 相对特异性作用　科学实验证明,某些腧穴具有相对特异性作用,即某腧穴对某脏腑或体表各部病证,具有优于其他腧穴疗效的作用。如内关穴治心脏病、足三里治胃病、天枢穴治泄痢、至阴穴矫正胎位等。

三、腧穴的定位法

在临证中,治疗效果与取穴位置是否正确有着十分重要的关系。为了准确定位,必须掌握腧穴定位方法。目前,腧穴的定位方法有骨度分寸法、体表标志法、手指同身寸法和简便取穴法四种。

(一)骨度分寸法

骨度分寸法,古称"骨度法",此法是以骨节为主要标志来测量人体各部的长短,并以该尺寸按比例折算,作为定穴的标准。不论身材高矮、胖瘦,均可按照此法来测量。全身主要骨度折量寸见表1。

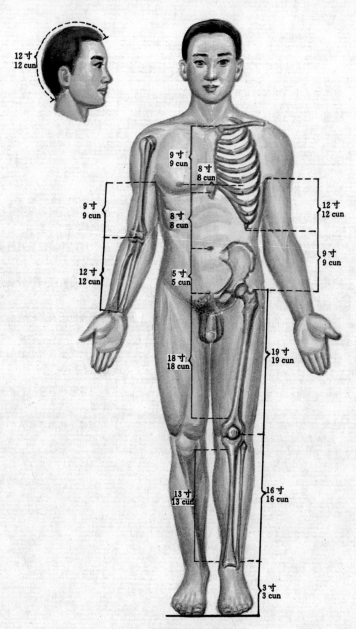

常用骨度分寸示意图

3

表 1 　　　　　　　　常用骨度分寸表

部位	起止点	折量寸	度量法	说　明
头面部	前发际正中→后发际正中	12	直寸	用于确定头部经穴的纵向距离
	眉间(印堂)→前发际正中	3	直寸	
	第 7 颈椎棘突下(大椎)→后发际正中	3	直寸	
	眉间(印堂)→后发际正中→第 7 颈椎棘突下(大椎)	18	直寸	
	前两额发角(头维)之间	9	横寸	用于确定头前部位经穴的横向距离
	耳后两乳突(完骨)之间	9	横寸	用于确定头后部经穴的横向距离
胸腹部	胸骨上窝(天突)→胸剑联合中点(歧骨)	9	直寸	用于确定胸部任脉穴纵向距离
	胸剑联合中点(歧骨)→脐中	8	直寸	用于确定上腹部穴的纵向距离
	脐中→耻骨联合上缘(曲骨)	5	直寸	用于确定下腹部经穴的纵向距离
	两乳头之间	8	横寸	用于确定胸腹部经穴的横向距离
	腋窝顶点→第 11 肋游离端(章门)	12	直寸	用于确定胁肋部经穴的纵向距离

部位	起止点	折量寸	度量法	说　明
背腰部	肩胛骨内缘→后正中线	3	横寸	用于确定背腰部经穴横向距离
	肩峰缘→后正中线	8	横寸	用于确定肩背部经穴的横向距离
上肢部	腋前、后纹头→肘横纹（平肘尖）	9	直寸	用于确定臂部经穴纵向距离
	肘横纹（平肘尖）→腕掌（背）侧横纹	12	直寸	用于确定前臂部经穴的纵向距离
下肢部	耻骨联合上缘→股骨内上髁上缘	18	直寸	用于确定下肢内侧足三阴经穴的纵向距离
	胫骨内侧髁下方→内踝尖	13	直寸	
	股骨大转子→腘横纹	19	直寸	用于确定下肢外后侧足三阳经穴的纵向距离
	腘横纹→外踝尖	16	直寸	

（二）体表标志法

体表标志法，即利用人体的自然标志作为定取穴位的方法。可分为固定标志法和活动标志法两种。

1. 固定标志法　此法是以五官、发际、指（趾）甲、乳头、肚脐、骨节凸起、凹陷及肌肉纹理等作为取穴的标志。这些体表标志固定不移，且便于查寻、记忆等，有利于腧穴定位。如两眉头之间中点取印堂；两乳头之间中点取膻中；肚脐中央旁开2寸取天枢；第7颈椎棘突下取大椎等。另外，利用人体的固定标志作为定位标准，然后再定取某些腧穴，如肩胛冈平第3胸椎棘突；肩胛下角平第7胸椎棘突；髂嵴平第4腰椎棘突；肚脐中央平第2腰椎棘突等。

2. 活动标志法　此法是指在选取穴位时，必须令患者采取相应的姿式或活动相应的部位，才能出现的标志。如取曲池穴，患者要拱手，于肘横纹外方取之；取养老穴时，要患者屈肘，掌心朝胸，当尺骨茎突之桡侧骨缝中取之等。

（三）手指同身寸法

手指同身寸法，是在骨度分寸折量法的基础上，以患者的手指为标准来定取穴位的方法。临床常用有以下三种。

1. 中指同身寸法　亦称"中指寸法"。该法是以患者的中指中节屈曲时,内侧两端纹头之间定为1寸。可用于四肢直寸和背部横寸取穴。

2. 拇指同身寸法　此法是以患者拇指关节的横度定为1寸。可用于四肢直寸取穴。

3. 横指同身寸法　又称"一夫法",该法是将患者食、中、无名和小指四指并拢,以中指中节横纹处为准,四指横量定为3寸。可用于四肢、腹部直寸取穴。

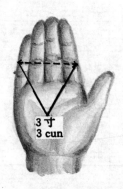

　　中指同身寸法　　　　拇指同身寸法　　　横指同身寸法

（四）简便取穴法

此法是经临床医家长期反复实践总结出的一种简便易行的取穴法。如令患者两手自然下垂,手中指端所到处取风市;令患者两虎口自然交叉,一手食指压在另一手腕后桡骨茎突上,当食指尖端下骨缝处取列缺穴;于两耳尖直上、头顶正中取百会穴等。

四、特定穴

特定穴是指在十四经中具有特殊治疗作用,并予以特定名称的经穴。特定穴在腧穴中占有重要地位。由于这些特定穴主治功能各异,因此各有其特定名称和含义。

（一）五输穴

五输穴是指在十二经中,分布于四肢肘膝部位以下的5个特定穴,即"井、荥、输、经、合"穴,简称"五输"。五输穴的排列次序是依据标本、根结理论,从四肢末端向心性的向肘膝方向排列。古代医家把经气感传,比作自然界水流,以取类比象的方法说明经气的出入和经过部位的深浅及其不同作用。如经气所出,像水的源头,称为"井";经气所溜,像刚出的泉水微流,称为"荥";经气所注,像水流由浅入深,称为"输";经气所行,像水在通畅的河中流过,称为"经";经气最后如百川汇合入海,称为"合"。

(二)原穴、络穴

"原"是本源、原气之意。原气导源于肾间动气,是人体生命活动的原动力。原穴即脏腑原气经过和留止的部位。因此,脏腑的病变,可以反应到十二原穴。在六阳经中,原穴单独存在,排列在"输"穴之后;在六阴经中,是以"输"代原。"络"即联络之意,络脉从经脉分出处各有一个腧穴称"络"穴。络穴具有联络表里两经的作用。

(三)俞穴、募穴

俞穴,是脏腑经气输注于背部的腧穴。募穴是脏腑经气汇集于胸腹部的腧穴。俞穴与募穴皆分布在人体的躯干部,并与相应的脏腑前后相对应。

(四)八脉交会穴

八脉交会穴是指奇经八脉与十二经脉之气相交会的 8 个腧穴。这 8 个腧穴有 4 个分布在上肢部,另外 4 个分布在下肢部,主要分布于腕踝关节附近。

(五)八会穴

"会"即聚会之意,八会穴即指脏、腑、气、血、筋、骨、脉、髓的精气聚会之处。分布于躯干部和四肢部。

(六)郄　穴

"郄"有孔隙之意,是指各经经气深集的部位。郄穴大多分布于四肢肘膝关节附近及其以下。十二经脉及阴阳跷、阴阳维各有一个郄穴,共 16 郄穴。

(七)下合穴

下合穴是指六腑之气下合于足三阳经的 6 个腧穴。大肠、小肠下合于足阳明经,三焦下合于足太阳经。此外,胃、胆、膀胱三腑的下合穴与五输穴中的"合"相同。这 6 个下合穴主要分布于下肢膝关节附近。

(八)交会穴

交会穴是两条以上经脉相交或相会于某一腧穴,这个穴位即为交会穴。如三阴交穴,即为足太阴、足厥阴、足少阴三条阴经交会穴;迎香穴为手阳明经与足阳明经交会穴。交会穴大多分布于头面与躯干部。

General Introduction To Acupoints

1. Concept, nomenclature and classifications of acupoints

(1) Concepts of acupoints

Acupoints are where Qi of zang-fu organs and meridians is transported to the surface of the body and where the acupuncture and moxibustion are applied to prevent and treat diseases. In the medical literatures throughout the history of China, they are also named "site of puncturing with sharp stone and moxibustion", "segment", "confluencial sites", "hole of bone", "hole of Qi" or just "points". They are not the sites located at the surface without any connections with the interior of the body, instead, they are closely related to Qi of meridians and zang-fu organs. Just as the chapter of Jiu Zhen Shi Er Yuan (Nine Kinds of Needles And 12 Kinds of Primary Points) of the book Ling Shu (The Miraculous Pivate) said: "The connecting points of segments of the body, 365 in all, are where vital Qi exits and enters."

(2) Nomenclature of acupoints

It is pointed out in the book Qian Jin Yi Fang (A Supplementary to the Essential Prescriptions Worth A Thousand Gold) that "All the names of the acupoints have special meanings rather than only the sympols of different acupoints." The names of acupoints not only have specific meanings in traditional Chinese medicine, but also serve as reflection of the brilliant Chinese ancient culture. So, knowing about the meanings of the names can facilitate mastering of the sites and therapeutic effects of the acupoints. Usually, acupoints are named in the following three ways:

① Named after natural things: Some points are named after the planets such as Riyue (GB 24), Shangxing (DU 23), and Taibai (SP 3). Some are named after the geographical features. For example, Chengshan (BL 57), Daling (PC 7), Shangqiu (SP 5) and Qiuxu (GB 40) are so named because they are located in the sites which take a shape of moutains, hills or basin; Hegu (LI 4), Houxi (SI 3), Shuigou (DU 26) and Jingqu (LU 8) are so named because they are located in the sites like valley, river, irrigation cannel and ditch; Xiaohai (SI 8), Chize (LU 5), Quchi (LI 11) and Yongquan (KI 1) are so named because they are located in the sites like sea, pools and spring; and Qijie (), Shuidao (ST 38), Fengshi (GB 31) and Bulang (KI 22) are so named because they are located in the sites like street, market and corridor.

② Named after animals, plants or buidings: For example, Yuji (LU 10), Yuyao 9 (Ex-HV 4), Futu (LI 18) and Dubi (ST 35) are named after the animals; Sizhukong (SJ 29) and Zanzhu (BL 2) are named after the plants, and Kufang (ST 14), Dicang (ST 4) and Qihu (ST 13) are named after buildings.

③ Named after the human body: For example, Dazhui (DU 14), Wangu (GB 12), Xinshu (BL 15) and Feishu (BL 13) are named after the anatomical positions; Chengjiang (RN 24), Tinghui (GB 2), Tinggong (SI 19), Xuehai (SP 10) and Qihai (RN 6) are named after some functions of the human body; Guangming (GB 37), Yingxiang (LI 20), Guilai (ST 29) and Shuifen (RN 9) are named after the actions of the acupoints; and Yinlinquan (SP 9), Yanglinquan (GB 34), Sanyinjiao (SP 6) and Sanyangluo (SJ 8) are named after the properties of Yin or Yang.

(3) Classifications of acupoints

There is a great number of acupoints in the human body, which can be generalised as three groups: the acupoints of meridians, the extra acupoints and the A Shi points.

① The acupoints of meridians: This refers to the acupoints located in the Twelve Regular Meridians, the Du Meridian and the Ren Meridian, which have been attributed to these fourteen meridians in the literature. They have relatively fixed locations and names, pertain to certain meridians and have a wide indication, thus they constitute the majority of the acupoints. At present, there are 361 acupoints of meridian, which were mostly found prior to Jin Dynasty.

② Extra acupoints: Also named acupoints out of meridians. They are the acupoints that have certain names and exact locations but haven't been attributed to the fourteen meridians in the literature. They are called extra acupoints because they often bring about better therapeutic effects for some diseases. Besides, extra acupoints have close relationships with meridians, for example, Yintang (Ex- HV 3) is closely related to the Du Meridian, and Taiyang (Ex-HV 5) is closely related to the Sanjiao Meridian of Hand-Shaoyang.

③ A Shi Points: "A" means pain. These points are so named because patients would pronounce "A" when their painful sites are pressed. They are firstly recorded in the book of Qian Jin Yao Fang (Prescriptions Worth A Thousand Gold) written in the Tang Dynasty, in which the A Shi points were said to be the points on the painful sites or the sites which brought about happiness to patient when pressed. A Shi points are the acupuncture and moxibustion locations marked by pain when pressed or the locations reflecting disease, without definate locations and names. They are mostly located nearby the diseased positions, but they may also be located in the remote sites of the diseased positions.

2. Therapeutic effects of the acupoints

This is also called the therapeutic rules of the acupoints, which is closely related to the meridians and zang-fu organs. So, there is the saying that where the meridians is distributed, where the disease of the distributed area of the meridians can be treated with the acupoints of the meridians.

(1) The local and adjacent therapeutic effect

This means that all the acupoints of human body can be used to treat the diseases where the acupoints are located, adjacent to the acupoints and the diseases of the surface of the human body, including both the diseases of the surface of the human body and those of the internal organs, which serves as the common property of the therapeutic effects of all the acupoints of human body. For instance, most of the acupoints on the head or face can treat local diseases on the head and face. Both Jingming (BL 1) and Sibai (ST 2), located in the eye region, can treat eye disorders, and Tinggong (SI 19), Tinghui (GB 2) and Yifeng (SJ 17), located in the ear region, can treat ear diseases.

(2) The remote therapeutic effect

This is the basic law of the therapeutic effects of the acupoints of the fourteen meridians. These acupoints, especially those located below the elbow and knee joints of the Twelve Regular Meridians, have the therapeutic effects not only on the diseases of the local regions, but also on the diseases of the remote regions, such as diseases of the zang-fu organs, the five sense organs and the nine orifices where the meridians pass through. Some acupoints can exert its influence on the whole body. For example, Hegu (LI 4) can be used to treat disorders of the hand and wrist, diseases of the neck, head and the five sense organs, as well as fever in exogenous diseases. Take Susanli (ST 36) for another example, it can treat disorders of the legs, regulate the functions of the digestive system, and have better effects of enhancing the defensive function and the immunological reactions of the human body.

(3) Special therapeutic effect

12

① Favorable two-way regulatory effects: Puncturing of cetain acupoints may have a favorable two-way regulatory effects on the different functional states of the human body. For example, puncturing Neiguan (PC 6) can slow the heart rate and restore it to normal when there is cardiac tachycardia, while it can accelerate the heart rate to restore it to normal when there is cardiac bradycardia; Tianshu (ST 25) can be used to treat both diarrhea or dysentery and constipation, etc.

② Relative specific effects: Related scientific experiments proved that some acupoints have specific effects relatively. That is, the effect of an acupoint on the diseases of one zang-fu organ or the diseases of the different parts of the surface of the body is superior to the effect of other acupoints. For example, Neiguan (PC 6) has specific therapeutic effect on the heart disease, Zusanli (ST 36) on the stomach diseases, Tianshu (ST 25) on diarrhea or dysentery, and Zhiyin (BL 67) on deposition of the fetus.

3. Method of locating acupoint

In clinical work, the therapeutic effects are closely related to the locating of acupoints. In order to locate an acupoint correctly, one must master the method of locating acupoints. Concurrently, there are four kinds of commonly used methods of locating acupoints: proportional measurements, anatomical landmarks, finger measurements and the simple and convenient methods.

(1) Proportional measurement

Proportional measurements is also named "Bone Measurement" in ancient times. It is a method using the main bones or joints of the human body to measure the length and width of various portions of the human body by dividing the length and width of the bones and joints into definite numbers of equal units as standards for locating the acupoints. This method can be applied to patients with various physiques, tall or short, fat or thin. The units of the main bones and joints divided in accordance with the proportional measurement are listed as follows:

Table 1. Standards for Proportional Measurement

Body Parts	Distance	Proportional Measurement	Method	Explanation
Head	From the midpoint of the anterior hairline to that of the posterior hairline	12 cun	Vertical measurement	Used to measure the vertical distance of the acupoints on the head
	From the midpoint of the two eyebrows to the midpoint of the anterior hairline	3 cun	Vertical measurement	
	From the place below the spinous process of the 7th cervical vertebrae to the midpoint of the posterior line	3 cun	Vertical measurement	
	From the midpoint of the two eyebrows to the area below the 7th cervical vertebrae througy the midpoint of the posterior hairline	18 cun	Vertical measurement	
	Between the two corners of the hairline	9 cun	Horizontal measurement	Used to measure the distance of the acupoints on the anterior part of the head
	Between the two mastoid process	9 cun	Horizontal measurement	Used to measure the distance of the acupoints on the posterior part of the head
chest and abdomen	From the suprasternal fossa to the midpoint of sternoxphoid junction	9 cun	vertical measurement	Used to measure the vertical distance of the acupoints of Ren Channel in the chest
	From the midpoint of sternoxphoid junction to the centre of umbilicus	8 cun	vertical measurement	Used to measure the vertical distance of the acupoints in the upper abdomen
	From centre of the umbilicus to the upper border of the pubic symphysis	5 cun	vertical measurement	Used to measure the vertical distance of the acupoints in the lower abdomen
	Between the two nipples	8 cun	horizontal measurement	Used to measure the horizontal distance of the acupoints in the chest and abdomen
	From the top point of the axillary fossa to the free end of the 11th rib	12 cun	vertical measurement	Used to measure the horizontal distance of the acupoints in the costal and hypochondriac region

15

Body Parts	Distance	Proportional Measurement	Method	Explanation
back and lumbar region	From the medial border of scapula to the posterior midline	3 cun	horizontal measurement	Used to measure the horizontal distance of the acupoints on the back and lumbar region
	From border of acromion to the posterior midline	8 cun	horizontal measurement	Used to measure the horizontal distance of the acupoints on the shoulder and the back
upper limbs	From the ends of the anterior and posterior creases of armpit to the cubital crease at the level of the Zhoujian	9 cun	vertical measurement	Used to measure the vertical distance of the acupoints in the arms
	From the cubital crease at the level of Zhoujian to dorsal crease of the wrist	12 cun	vertical measurement	Used to measure the vertical distance of the acupoints in the forearm
lower limbs	From the upper border of the pubic symphysis to the upper border of the internal epicondyle of femur	18 cun	vertical measurement	Used to measure the vertical distance of the acupoints of the three foot meridians on the medial aspects of the lower limbs
	From the lower border of the internal condyle of femur to the tip of medial malleolus	13 cun	vertical measurement	
	rom the trochanter to the popliteal crease	19 cun.	vertical measurement	Used to measure the vertical distance of the acupoints of the three yang foot meridians on the latero-posterior aspect of the lower limbs
	From the popliteal crease to the tip of the extenal malleolus	16 cun	vertical measurement	

(2) Anatomical landmarks

This is a method to locate acupoints by the aid of the natural landmarks of the human body. It falls into two groups, the fixed landmarks and the moving landmarks.

① Fixed landmarks: This is a method to locate the acupoints by the aid of the five sense organs, hairline, nails, nipples, umbilicus, prominence of bones and joints and muscular striae. As these landmarks would not change and are easy to be found and remembered, they are very helpful in locating acupoints. For example, one can locate Yintang (Ex-HV 3) between the two eyebrows, Danzhong (RN 17) between the two nipples, Tianshu (ST 25) 2 cun distal to the umbilicus, and Dazhui (DU 14) below the spinous process of the 7th cervical vertebra. Besides, some acupoints can be located by means of more than one kind of landmarks that have special relations. For example, the spine of scapula is at the level with the spinous process of the third thoracic vertebra, the inferior angle of the scapula is at the level of the spinous processe of the 7th cervical vertebra, the illiac crest is at the level of the spinous process of the 4th lumbar vertebra, and the centre of the umbilicus is at the level of the spinous process of the 2nd lumbar vertebra, etc.

② Moving landmarks: Moving landmarks are those that will appear only when patient takes a specific position or does specific movements. For instances, Quchi (LI 11) can be found in the lateral end of the cubital crease only when patient flexes his arm; Yanglao (SI 6) can be located in the bony cleft on the radial side of the styloid process of the ulna only when patient flexes his arm with the palm facing the chest, etc.

(3) Finger measurements: This is a method of locating acupoints by using the length and width of the patient's finger(s) as a standard on the basis of the proportional measurements. Clinically, the following three kinds are commonly adopted.

① Middle finger measurement: When the patient's middle finger is flexed, the distance between the two medial ends of the creases of the interphalangeal joints is taken as one cun. It is often used to measure the vertical distance to locate the acupoints on the four limbs, or to measure the horizontal distance to locate the acupoints on the back. (See Fig)

② Thumb measurement: This method takes the width of the interphalangeal joint of the patient's thumb as one cun. It is mainly employed to measure the vertical distance to locate the acupoints on the four limbs. (See Fig)

③ Four-fingers measurement: The width of the four fingers (index, middle, ring and little) close together at the level of the dorsal skin crease of the proximal interphalangeal joint of the middle finger is taken as three cun. It is applied to measure the vertical distance to locate the acupoints on the limbs and in the abdomen. (See Fig)

(4) Simple and convenient measurement: This is a method to locate the acupoints summarized based on long-standing clinical practice of physicians. For example, Fengshi (GB 31) can be located where the tip of the middle finger touches when the patient's hand drops naturally; Lieque (LU 7) can be located in the depression right under the tip of the index finger when patient's index fingers and thumbs of both hands are crossed with the index finger of one hand placed on the styloid process of the radius of the other; and Baihui (DU 20) can be located in the centre of the vertex directly above the apexes of the ears.

4. Specific acupoints

The specific acupoints refer to those of the fourteen meridians having specific therapeutic effects and having been given special names. They occupy very important positions among acupoints, and because they have different indications, they have different names and connotations.

(1) The Five-Shu Points

The Five-Shu points refer to five special points distributed below the elbows and knees on each of the twelve regular meridians, namely, Jing-Well, Ying-Spring, Shu-Stream, Jing-River and He-Sea. They are situated in the above order from the distal extremities to the elbow or knee in the light of the theory superficial and fundamental, the root and the knot. The ancient doctors described the transmission of the meridian Qi as flow of the river, to elaborate the emerging and entering of meridian Qi, the depth of the portions the meridian passes through and the different therapeutic effects of these acupoints. The place where the meridian Qi emerges, assembling the source of river, is called Jing (well); the Ying-Spring point is so called because it is where the meridian Qi starts to gush, like small water stream; the Shu-Stream point is so called because it is where the meridian Qi starts to enter the depth; the Jing-River point is where the meridian Qi is pouring abundantly assembling water flowing in an unobstructed river; and the He-Sea point is where the meridian Qi collects, assembling confluence of rivers in the sea.

(2) The Yuan-Primary points and the Luo-Connecting points

Yuan means source or the premordial Qi which is originated from the moving Qi between the kidneys and serves as the primary motive force for the life activities. The Yuan-Source points are where the premordial Qi of zang-fu organs passes through and is retained, therefore, diseases of the zang-fu organs can be reflected on the Yuan-Source points. Each of the six Yang meridians has its Yuan-Source point other than the Shu-Stream point, while in the six Yin meridians, the Yuan-Source points overlap with the Shu-Stream points. Luo means connection. Luo-connecting points are located in the places where the collaterals branch off from the meridians, and function to connect the two meridians exterior-interiorly related.

(3) The Shu-Stream points and the Front-Mu points

Shu-Stream points are the points through which Qi of the zang-fu organs is transported to the back. The Front-Mu points are where Qi of the zang-fu organs is infused and converged in the chest and abdomen. Both the Shu-Stream points and the Front-Mu points are located in the back or front of the trunk of the body, corresponding to the locations of their corresponding zang-fu organs.

(4) The confluent points of the eight extraordinary meridians

These refer to the eight points where the Qi of the extraordinary meridians communicates with that of the twelve regular meridians. Of the eight points, four are situated in the upper limbs, and four in the lower limbs, and they mainly exist near the wrists and ankles.

(5) The eight confluent points

The eight confluent points indicate the eight points where the essence-Qi of the zang organ, fu organ, Qi, blood, tendon, bone, vessel and marrow converges respectively. They are mainly located in the trunk and the limbs of the body.

(6) The Xi-Cleft points

The Xi-Cleft points are where the Qi of each of the meridians collects in the depth of the body. Most of them are located around or below the elbows and knees of the four limbs. Each of the twelve regular meridians and the Yinqiao Meridian, the Yangqiao Meridian, the Yinwei Meridian and the Yangwei Meridian has a Xi-Cleft point, so there are sixteen Xi-Cleft points in all.

(7) The lower He-Sea points

The lower He-Sea points refer to the six points through which Qi of the six fu communicates with the three foot Yang meridians in the lower part of the body. The large intestine and the small intestine communicate with the foot Yangming meridian, and the Sanjiao communicates with the foot Taiyang meridian. In addition, the lower He-Sea points of the stomach, the gallbladder and the bladder overlap with the He-Sea points of the Five-Shu Points of their meridians. These points are mainly located around the knees.

(8) Crossing points

Crossing points are those at the intersections of two or more meridians. For instances, Sanyinjiao (SP 6) is a crossing point of the foot Taiyin meridian, the foot Jueyin meridian and the foot Shaoyin meridian; Yingxiang (LI 20) is the crossing point of the hand Yangming meridian and the foot Yangming meridian. Most of the crossing points are distributed on the head and trunk.

经络腧穴各论

一、手太阴肺经

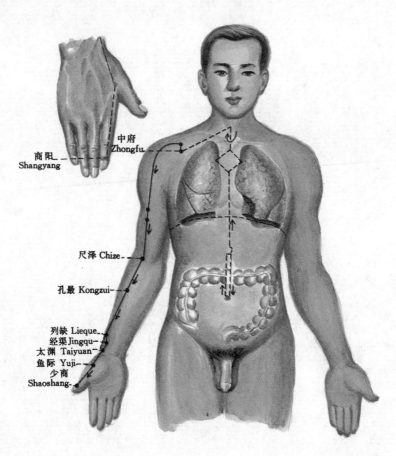

商阳
Shangyang

中府
Zhongfu

尺泽 Chize

孔最 Kongzui

列缺 Lieque
经渠 Jingqu
太渊 Taiyuan
鱼际 Yuji
少商
Shaoshang

起于中焦,向下联络大肠,回绕过来沿着胃的上口,通过横膈,属于肺脏,从"肺系"(肺与喉咙相联系部位)横行出来(中府),向下沿上臂内侧,行于手少阴经和手厥阴经的前面,下行到肘窝中,沿着前臂内侧前缘,进入寸口,经过鱼际,沿着鱼际的边缘,出拇指内侧端(少商)。手腕后方的支脉:从列缺处分出,一直走向食指内侧端(商阳),与手阳明大肠经相接。

Acupoints of Meridians

1. The Lung Meridian of Hand-Taiyin

The Lung Meridian of Hand-Taiyin originates from the middle jiao, then it goes downwards to connect with the large intestine. Winding back, it goes along the upper orifice of the stomach, passes through the diaphragm and reaches the lung, its pertaining organ. From the lung system, the portion of the lung communicating with the throat, it runs transversely and emerges, at Zhongfu (LU 1). Then it descends along the medial aspect of the upper arm, travelling in front of the Heart Meridian of Hand-Shaoyin and the Pericardium Meridian of Hand-Jueyin and reaching the cubital fossa. It then goes continuously downwards along the anterior border of the forearm and enters Cunkou (the radial artery at the wrist for pulse taking). Passing the thenar eminence along its border, it goes to and ends of the radial side of the tip of the thumb (Shaoshang, LI 11). The branch proximal to the wrist emerges from Lieque (LU 7) and runs directly to the radial side of the tip of the index finger (Shangyang, LI 1), where it links with the Large Intestine Meridian of Hand-Yangming.

中府 Zhōngfù(LU 1)

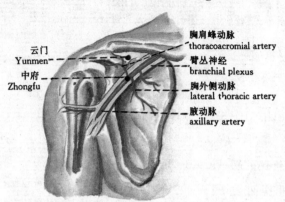

云门
Yunmen

中府
Zhongfu

胸肩峰动脉
thoracoacromial artery

臂丛神经
branchial plexus

胸外侧动脉
lateral thoracic artery

腋动脉
axillary artery

〔取穴法〕(1)在胸部的上外方,任脉旁开6寸,平第1肋间隙处。

(2)正坐位,以手叉腰,先取锁骨外端(肩峰端)下方凹陷处的云门穴,当云门穴直下约1寸,第1肋间隙平齐处是穴。

(3)仰卧位,当乳头(指男子)向外2寸,再直线向上当第1肋间隙处。

〔功效与主治〕调理肺气,养阴清热。咳嗽,哮喘,胸痛。

〔操作〕向外斜刺或平刺0.5～0.8寸,不可深刺,以免伤及肺脏。

〔备注〕肺的募穴;手足太阴之会。

Method of locating the point:

(1) This point is in the laterosuperior part of the chest, 6 cun lateral to the Ren Meridian, at the level with the first intercostal space.

(2) Ask patient to take a sitting position with his or her arms akimbo, locate Yunmen (LU 2) in the depression below the end of the clavicle distal to the acromion, then locate Zhongfu (LU 1) point 1 cun below Yumen (LU 2) at the level with the first intercostal space.

(3) Ask patient to lie on his or her back, locate the point in the first intercostal space directly above the point 2 cun lateral to the nipple in male.

Actions and indications: Regulate flow of the lung Qi, nourish Yin and clear away heat, used to treat cough, asthma and chest pain.

Manipulations: Puncture laterally and obliquely 0.5－0.8 cun. Deep needling is not employed to avoid injury to the lung.

Notes: Zhongfu (LU 1) is the Front-Mu point of the Lung Meridian of Hand-Taiyin and the crossing point of the Lung Meridian of Hand-Taiyin and the Spleen Meridian of Foot-Taiyin.

尺泽 Chǐzé（LU 5）

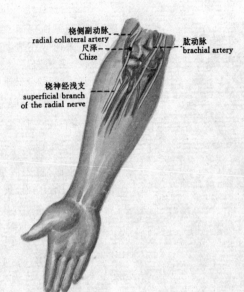

桡侧副动脉
radial collateral artery

尺泽
Chize

肱动脉
brachial artery

桡神经浅支
superficial branch
of the radial nerve

〔取穴法〕（1）在肘横纹上，当肱二头肌腱的桡侧缘。

（2）仰掌，肘关节微屈，在肘横纹中，肱二头肌腱的桡侧缘。

〔功效与主治〕调理肺气，清热和中。咳嗽，哮喘，咯血，肘臂挛痛，腹痛吐泻。

〔操作〕直刺 0.5～0.8 寸，或点刺出血。

〔备注〕手太阴肺经"合"穴。

Method of locating the point：

(1) This point is on the cubital crease, on the radial side of the tendon of m. biceps brachii.

(2) When the palm faces upwards with the elbow slightly flexed, it is found on the radial side of the tendon of m. biceps brachii.

Actions and indications：Regulate flow of the lung Qi, clear away heat and normalize the function of the middle jiao, used to treat cough, asthma, hemoptysis, spasmodic pain of the elbow and arm, abdominal pain accompanied with vomiting and diarrhea.

Manipulation：Puncture perpendicularly 0.5—0.8 cun, or prick with a three-edged needle to cause bleeding.

Notes：This point is the He-Sea point of the Lung Meridian of Hand-Taiyin.

孔最 Kǒngzuì （LU 6）

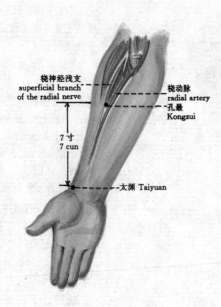

桡神经浅支
superficial branch
of the radial nerve

桡动脉
radial artery

孔最
Kongzui

7寸
7 cun

太渊 Taiyuan

〔取穴法〕（1）在前臂掌侧面桡侧,当尺泽与太渊穴连线上,腕横纹上7寸处。

（2）伸臂仰掌,于尺泽与太渊连线的中点上1寸,当桡骨内缘处是穴。

〔功效与主治〕润肺止血,解表清热。咳嗽,气喘,咯血,失音,痔疮。

〔操作〕直刺0.5～0.8寸。

〔备注〕手太阴肺经"郄"穴。

Method of locating the point:

(1) This point is located on the radial side of the palmar aspect of the forearm, on the line connecting Chize (LU 5) with Taiyuan (LU 9), 7 cun above the transverse crease of the wrist.

(2) Locate the point 1 cun above the midpoint of the line connecting Chize (LU 5) and Taiyuan (LU 9) on the medial border of the radius when the arm is stretched with the palm facing upwards.

Actions and indications: Moisten the lung, stop bleeding, relieve exterior syndrome and clear away heat, used to treat cough, asthma, hymoptysis, hoarseness and hemorrhoid.

Manipulation: Puncture perpendicularly 0.5—0.8 cun.

Notes: This point is the Xi-Cleft point of the Lung Meridian of Hand-Taiyin.

列缺 Lièquē（LU 7）

〔取穴法〕(1)在前臂桡侧缘，桡骨茎突上方，腕横纹上1.5寸，侧掌取之。

(2)两虎口自然交叉，一手食指压在另一手的桡骨茎突上，当食指尖端到达的凹陷中是穴。

(3)握拳，拳眼向上，拇指向外上方翘起，先取两筋之间的阳溪穴，在阳溪穴上1.5寸的桡骨茎突中部有一凹陷处是穴。

〔功效与主治〕宣肺疏风，通调任脉。头痛，项强，咳嗽，气喘，牙痛，阴中痛，尿血，小便热。

〔操作〕向肘部斜刺0.3～0.5寸。

〔备注〕手太阴肺经"络"穴；八脉交会穴之一，通于任脉。

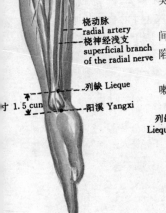

桡动脉 radial artery
桡神经浅支 superficial branch of the radial nerve
列缺 Lieque
阳溪 Yangxi
1.5 cun 寸
列缺 Lieque

Method of locating the point:

(1) When the palm is placed upwards, this point is on the radial aspect of the forearm, superior to the styloid process of the radius, 1.5 cun above the transverse crease of the wrist.

(2) Locate the point in the depression right under the tip of the index finger when patient's index fingers and thumbs of both hands are crossed with the index finger of one hand placed on the styloid process of the radius of the other.

(3) When patient clenches his fist with the thumb side in the upper and the thumb projecting towards the latero-superior side, find out Yangxi (LI 5) point bwteen the two tendons, then locate the point 1.5 cun above Yangxi (LI 5) in the depression of the middle part of the styloid process of the radius.

Actions and indications: Disperse the lung Qi, expel wind, regualte the Ren Meridian and promotes flow of Qi and blood in the Ren Meridian, used to treat headache, stiff neck, cough, asthma, toothache, pain in the external genitalia, uremia, and a feeling of hotness in the penis during urination.

Manipulation: Puncture obliquely towards the elbow 0.3－0.5 cun.

Notes: This point is the Luo-Connecting point of the Lung Meridian of Hand-Taiyin. It is also one of the confluence points of the eight meridians, communicating with the Ren Meridian.

经渠 Jīngqù (LU 8)

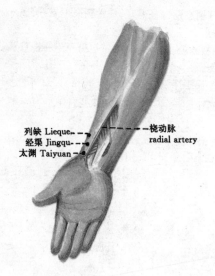

列缺 Lieque
经渠 Jingqu
太渊 Taiyuan

桡动脉
radial artery

〔取穴法〕(1)在前臂掌面桡侧下段,腕横纹上1寸,当桡骨茎突内缘与桡动脉之间凹陷处。

(2)手侧伸,拇指与掌心向上,距腕横纹1寸的桡动脉搏动处,亦即中医诊脉时中指所着之处。

〔功效与主治〕宣肺平喘,清热止痛。咳嗽,气喘,咽喉肿痛,胸部胀满。

〔操作〕避开动脉,直刺0.2~0.3寸。

〔备注〕手太阴肺经"经"穴。禁灸。

Method of locating the point:

(1) This point is on radial side of the palmar aspect of the lower part of the forearm, 1 cun above the transverse crease of the wrist, in the depression between the medial border of the styloid process of the radius and the radial artery.

(2) When the arm is stretched out with the thumb and the palm facing upwards, it is found 1 cun lateral to the transverse crease of the wrist where the radial artery is felt, or the point under the middle finger when taking a pulse.

Actions and indications: Facilitate flow of the lung Qi, relieve asthma, clear away heat and relieve pain, used to treat cough, asthma, sore throat, and fullness of the chest.

Manipulation: Puncture perpendicularly 0.2—0.3 cun. Avoid puncturing the radial artery.

Notes: This point is the Jing-River point of the Lung Meridian of Hand-Taiyin. Moxibustion is not recommended.

太渊 Tàiyuān（LU 9）

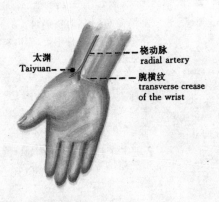

太渊
Taiyuan

桡动脉
radial artery

腕横纹
transverse crease
of the wrist

〔取穴法〕（1）仰掌，在腕横纹上，于桡动脉桡侧陷中取穴。当拇长展肌腱与桡侧腕屈肌腱连线之中点。

（2）仰掌，当掌后第1横纹上，用手摸有脉搏跳动处是穴。

〔功效与主治〕调肺止咳，通脉理血。咳嗽，气喘，胸痛，无脉症。

〔操作〕避开动脉，直刺 0.2～0.3 寸。

〔备注〕手太阴肺经"输"穴、"原"穴，八会穴之一，脉会太渊。

Method of locating the point:

(1) When the palm is placed upwards, it is on the transverse crease of the wrist, in the depression on the radial side of the radial artery, at the midpoint of line connecting the tendon of the long extensor muscle of thumb and the tendon of the radial flexor muscle of the wrist.

(2) Ask patient to place his palm upwards, locate the point on the first transverse crease of the wrist distal to the palm where the pulsation can be felt.

Actions and indications: Regulate the function of the lung, relieve cough, promote flow of Qi and blood in the meridians and normalize blood, used to treat cough, asthma, chest pain and pulseless disease.

Manipulation: Puncture perpendicularly 0.2 — 0.3 cun. Avoid puncturing the radial artery.

Notes: This point is the Shu-Stream point and the Yuan-Primary point of the Lung Meridian of Hand-Taiyin. It is also one of the eight confluence points, the confluential point of vessels.

鱼际 Yújì（LU 10）

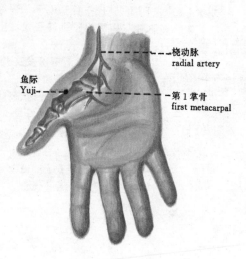

鱼际
Yuji

桡动脉
radial artery

第1掌骨
first metacarpal

〔取穴法〕（1）仰掌，在手掌侧面鱼际部的桡侧缘，第1掌指关节后，掌骨中点，赤白肉际处取之。

（2）侧掌，微握拳，腕关节稍向下屈，于第1掌骨中点之掌侧赤白肉际处取穴。

〔功效与主治〕清肺解热，开音利咽。咳嗽，气喘，咯血，咽喉肿痛，失音，发热，乳痈，掌心热。

〔操作〕直刺 0.5～0.8寸。

〔备注〕手太阴肺经"荥"穴。

Method of locating the point:

（1）When the palm is placed upwards, it is located on the radial side of the lateral border of the thenar eminence of the palm, posterior to the first metaphalangeal joint, at the midpoint of the metacarpal bone, at the junction of the red and white skin.

（2）When the palm is placed erect with a loose fist clenched and the wrist flexed downwards slightly, locate the point in the midpoint of the first metacarpal bone, at the junction of the red and white skin.

Actions and indications: Clear away heat from the lung, relieve hoarseness and benefit throat, used to treat cough, asthma, hemoptysis, sore throat, hoarseness, fever, acute mastitis, and hotness in the centre of the palm.

Manipulation: Puncture perpendicularly 0.5—0.8 cun.

Notes: This point is the Ying-Spring point of the Lung Meridian of Hand-Taiyin.

少商 Shàoshāng (LU 11)

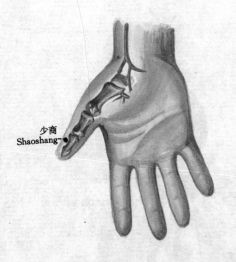

少商
Shaoshang

〔取穴法〕(1)在手拇指末节桡侧,当平齐桡侧指甲角与指腹桡侧缘连线之中点处,距指甲角0.1寸。

(2)侧掌,微握拳,拇指上翘,手拇指爪甲桡侧缘和基底部各作一线,相交处取穴。

〔功效与主治〕清肺利咽,泄热醒神。咽喉肿痛,重舌,鼻衄,昏迷,热病,小儿惊风。

〔操作〕向腕平刺0.2~0.3寸,或三棱针点刺出血。

〔备注〕手太阴肺经"井"穴。

Method of locating the point:

(1) This point is located on the radial side of the thumb, at the level with the midpoint of the line connecting the radial corner of the nail and the radial border of the belly, 0.1 cun lateral to the corner of the nail.

(2) When the palm is placed erect with a loose fist clenched and the thumb projecting upwards, locate the point at the intersection of the line drawn along the radial side of the nail of the thumb and that drawn along the base of the nail.

Actions and indications: Clear away heat from the lung, benefit the throat, purge heat and restore consciousness, used to treat sore throat, stiff tongue, hymoptysis, coma, febrile diseases and infantile convulsion.

Manipulation: Puncture subcutaneously towards the wrist 0.2—0.3 cun, or prick with a three edged needle to cause bleeding.

Notes: This point is the Jing-Well point of the Lung Meridian of Hand-Taiyin.

31

二、手阳明大肠经

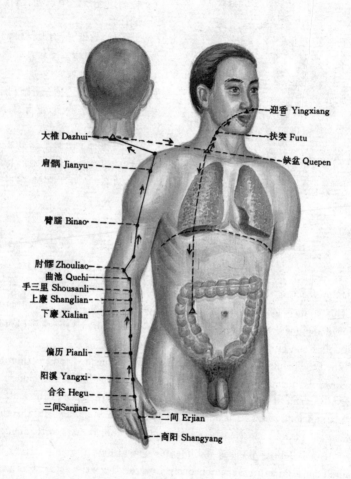

大椎 Dazhui

肩髃 Jianyu

臂臑 Binao

肘髎 Zhouliao
曲池 Quchi
手三里 Shousanli
上廉 Shanglian
下廉 Xialian

偏历 Pianli

阳溪 Yangxi
合谷 Hegu
三间 Sanjian

二间 Erjian
商阳 Shangyang

迎香 Yingxiang
扶突 Futu
缺盆 Quepen

起于食指末端(商阳),沿着食指桡侧向上,通过一二掌骨之间(合谷),向上进入拇长伸肌腱与拇短伸肌腱之间的凹陷处,沿前臂前方,至肘部外侧,再沿上臂外侧前缘,上走肩端,沿肩峰前缘,向上出于颈椎"大椎"穴(督脉),再向下进入缺盆(锁骨上窝)部,联络肺脏,通过横膈,属于大肠。缺盆部支脉:上走颈部,通过面颊,进入下齿龈,回绕至上唇,交叉于人中,左脉向右,右脉向左,分布在鼻孔两侧(迎香),与足阳明胃经相接。

2. The Large Intestine
Meridian of Hand-Yangming

The Large Intestine Meridian of Hand-Yangming originates from the tip of the index finger (Shangyang, LI 1). Running upwards along the radial side of the index finger and passing through the interspace of the 1st and the 2nd metacarpal bones (Hegu, LI 4), it enters the depression between the tendons of m. extensor pollicis longus and brevis. Then, along the lateroanterior aspect of the forearm, it reaches the lateral side of the elbow. From there, it goes upwards along the anterior border of the lateral side of the upper arm to the highest point of the shoulder and further to the Dazhui point (DU 14) along the anterior border of the acromion. Then, it runs downwards and enters the supraclavicular fossa to connect with the lung. Passing through the diaphragm, it enters the large intestine. The branch from the supraclavicular fossa runs upwards to the neck. Passing through the cheek, it enters the gums of the lower teeth. Then it curves around the upper lips and crosses the opposite meridian at the philtrum, where the left meridian goes to the right and the right goes to the left, ending at the both sides of the nose (Yingxiang, LI 20), in which it links with the Stomach Meridian of Foot-Yangming.

商阳 Shāngyáng（LI 1）

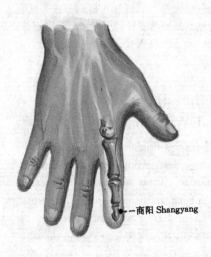

——商阳 Shangyang

〔取穴法〕（1）在食指末节桡侧，当平齐桡侧指甲角与指腹桡侧缘间连线之中点处。距指甲角 0.1 寸。

（2）微握拳，食指前伸，手食指爪甲桡侧缘与基底部各作一线，相交处是穴。

〔功效与主治〕泄热消肿，开窍醒神。中风，昏迷，齿痛，颈肿，痄腮，手指麻木，咽喉肿痛。

〔操作〕浅刺 0.1 寸，或三棱针点刺出血。

〔备注〕手阳明大肠经"井"穴。

Method of locating the point:

(1) This point is located on the radial side of the index finger, at the level with the midpoint of the line connecting the radial corner of the nail and the radial border of the belly, 0.1 cun lateral to the corner of the nail.

(2) Ask patient to make a loose fist with his index finger entended forwards, locate the point at the intersection of the line drawn along the radial side of the nail of the index finger and that drawn along the base of the nail.

Actions and indications: Purge heat, subdue swelling, induce resuscitation and restore consciousness, used to treat apoplexy, coma, toothache, swellon neck, mumps, numbness of fingers, and sore throat.

Manipulation: Puncture superficially 0.1 cun, or prick with a three-edged needle to cause bleeding.

Notes: This point is the Jing-Well point of the Large Intestine Meridian of Hand-Yangming.

二间 Erjiān (LI 2)

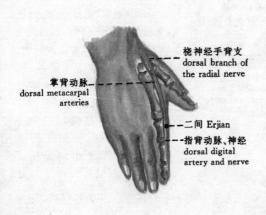

桡神经手背支
dorsal branch of
the radial nerve

掌背动脉
dorsal metacarpal
arteries

二间 Erjian

指背动脉、神经
dorsal digital
artery and nerve

〔取穴法〕(1)在手食指根部桡侧,握拳时在第2掌指关节前下方之凹陷处,即当食指的掌指纹桡侧端上之凹陷处。

(2)侧掌,微握拳,在食指掌指关节前方桡侧,正当食指第1节指骨小头的前方,赤白肉际处。

〔功效与主治〕清热散风,消肿止痛。鼻衄,齿痛,咽喉肿痛。

〔操作〕直刺 0.2～0.3寸。

〔备注〕手阳明大肠经"荥"穴。

Method of locating the point:

(1) This point is located on the radial side of the index finger, distal to the metacarpal-phalangeal joint. When a fist is clenched, it is found in the depression inferoanterior to the 2nd metaphalangeal joint, or in the depression above the radial end of the palmar crease of the index finger.

(2) When a loose fist is made, the point is located in front of the metacarpalphlangeal joint of index finger, at the junction of the red and white skin just in front of the first phalangeal bone of the index finger.

Actions and indications: Clear away heat, disperse wind, subdue swelling and relieve pain, used to treat hemoptysis, toothache and sore throat.

Manipulation: Puncture perpendicularly 0.2－0.3 cun.

Notes: This point is the Ying-Spring point of the Large Intestine Meridian of Hand-Yangming.

三间 Sānjiān (LI 3)

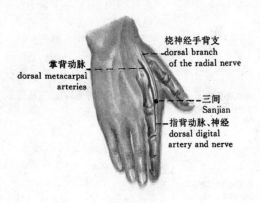

掌背动脉
dorsal metacarpal
arteries

桡神经手背支
dorsal branch
of the radial nerve

三间
Sanjian

指背动脉、神经
dorsal digital
artery and nerve

〔取穴法〕(1)在手背部,当第2掌指关节后,桡侧凹陷处。

(2)侧掌,微握拳,在食指掌指关节后方桡侧,正当第2掌骨小头的后方,赤白肉际处。

〔功效与主治〕清热,散风,行气。齿痛,目痛,咽喉肿痛,面痛。

〔操作〕直刺 0.5～0.8寸。

〔备注〕手阳明大肠经"输"穴。

Method of locating the point:

(1) This point is located on the dorsum of the hand, in the radial depression posterior to the second metacarpal bone.

(2) When the palm is in an erecting position with a loose fist made, locate the point on the radial side of the metacarpal-phalangeal joints of the index finger, just behind the head of the second metacarpal bone, at the junction of the red and white skin.

Actions and indications: Clear away heat, disperse wind, and promote flow of Qi, used to treat toothache, pain of eyes, sore throat, and pain in the face.

Manipulation: Puncture perpendicularly 0.5－0.8 cun.

Notes: This point is the Shu-Stream point of the Large Intestine Meridian of Hand-Yangming.

合谷 Hégǔ (LI 4)

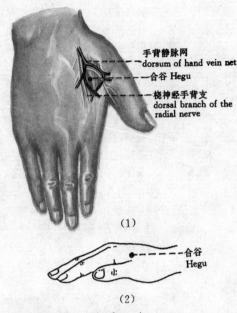

手背静脉网
dorsum of hand vein net

合谷 Hegu

桡神经手背支
dorsal branch of the
radial nerve

(1)

合谷
Hegu

(2)

〔取穴法〕(1)在手背,当第1掌骨间隙之中点处。

(2)第2掌指关节与阳溪穴之间的中点处,稍靠近食指侧。

(3)拇、食两指张开,以另一手的拇指关节横纹放在虎口上,当拇指尖到达之处是穴。

(4)拇、食两指并拢,在肌肉的最高处取穴。

〔功效与主治〕疏风解表,镇痛通络。头痛,目赤肿痛,齿痛,口眼㖞斜,牙关紧闭,腹痛,肠痈,经闭,风疹。

〔操作〕直刺 0.5~1 寸。

〔备注〕手阳明大肠经"原"穴。孕妇不宜针。

Method of locating the point:

(1) This point is on the dorsum of the hand, at the midpoint of the first and the second metacarpal bones.

(2) Locate the point at the midpoint of the line joining the second metacarpal-phalangeal joint and Yangxi point (LI 5), slightly proximal to the radial side.

(3) The point is located just below the tip of the thumb when the thumb and index finger of one hand is kept at a distance and then the crease of the first phalangeal joint of the thumb of the other hand is placed on the web connecting the index finger and the thumb.

(4) Ask patient to close his thumb and index finger, locate the point at the highest point of the muscle between the two fingers.

Actions and indications: Expel wind, relieve exterior syndrome, alleviate pain and promote flow of Qi and blood in the vessels, used to treat headache, redness, swelling and pain of eye, toothache, deviation of mouth and eye, trismus, abdominal pain, carbuncle of intestine, amenorrrhea, and rubella.

Manipulation: Puncture perpendicularly 0.5—1 cun.

Notes: This point is the Yuan-Primary point of the Large Intestine Meridian of Hand-Yangming. Moxibustion is not applicable in pregnant woman.

阳溪 Yángxī (LI 5)

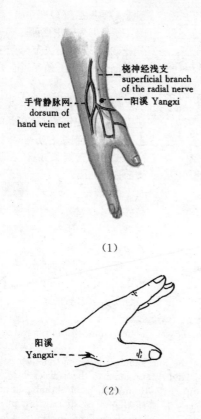

桡神经浅支
superficial branch
of the radial nerve

阳溪 Yangxi

手背静脉网
dorsum of
hand vein net

(1)

阳溪
Yangxi- - - -

(2)

〔取穴法〕（1）在腕背侧横纹桡侧，手拇指向上翘起时，当拇长伸肌腱、拇短伸肌腱与拇长伸肌腱和桡骨下端所构成的凹陷处。

（2）在腕上桡侧，当拇短伸肌腱与拇长伸肌腱之间凹陷处。

〔功效与主治〕清热散风，疏筋活络。头痛，目赤，耳聋，齿痛，腕痛。

〔操作〕直刺 0.3～0.5 寸。

〔备注〕手阳明大肠经"经"穴。

Method of locating the point:

(1) This point is on the radial side of the dorsal aspect of the transverse crease of the wrist, in the depression between the tendons of m. extensor pollicis longus and brevis, or between the tendon of m. extensor pollicis longus and the lower end of the radius when the thumb is tilted upwards.

(2) Locate the point on the radial side of the transverse crease of the wrist, in the depression between the tendones of m. pollicis longus and brevis.

Actions and indications: Clear away heat, disperse wind, relax tendons and promote flow of Qi and blood in the vessels, used to treat headache, red eyes, deafness, toothache and pain in the wrist.

Manipulation: Puncture perpendicularly 0.3—5 cun.

Notes: This point is the Jing-River point of the Large Intestine Meridian of Hand-Yangming.

偏历 Piānlì（LI 6）

〔取穴法〕（1）在前臂背面桡侧的下段,在阳溪穴上 3 寸处。

（2）屈肘,当阳溪穴与曲池穴连线之下 1/2 的中点处。

〔功效与主治〕清热疏肺,通调水道。目赤,耳鸣,鼻衄,喉痛,水肿。

〔操作〕直刺 0.3～0.5 寸。

〔备注〕手阳明大肠经"络"穴。

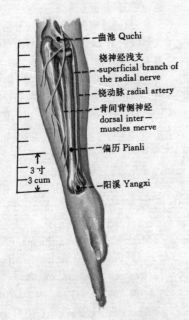

曲池 Quchi

桡神经浅支
superficial branch of
the radial nerve

桡动脉 radial artery

骨间背侧神经
dorsal inter—
muscles merve

一偏历 Pianli

3 寸
3 cum

—阳溪 Yangxi

Method of locating the point:

(1) This point is lcoated in the lower part of the forearm, on the proximal side of the dorsal aspect, 3 cun above Yangxi (LI 5).

(2) When the elbow is flexed, it is located at the midpoint of the lower 1/2 of the line joining Yangxi (LI 5) and Quchi (LI 11).

Actions and indications: Clear away heat, disperse the Lung Qi, and regulate water metabolism, used to treat red eyes, tinnitus, hemoptysis, sore throat and edema.

Manipulation: Puncture perpendicularly 0.3—0.5 cun.

Notes: This point is the Luo-Connecting point of the Large Intestine Meridian of Hand-Yangming.

下廉 Xiàlián（LI 8）

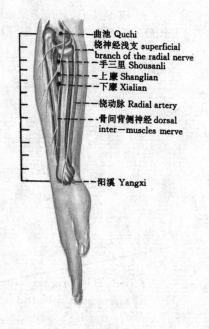

曲池 Quchi
桡神经浅支 superficial branch of the radial nerve
手三里 Shousanli
上廉 Shanglian
下廉 Xialian
桡动脉 Radial artery
骨间背侧神经 dorsal inter—muscles merve
阳溪 Yangxi

〔取穴法〕(1)在前臂背侧面桡侧的上段,当阳溪穴与曲池穴连线上,在阳溪穴上8寸处。

(2)侧腕屈肘,在阳溪穴与曲池穴连线的上 1/3 与下 2/3 的交点处取穴。

〔功效与主治〕通经络,调腑气。头风,眩晕,目痛,腹痛。

〔操作〕直刺 0.5～0.8 寸。

Method of locating the point:

(1) This point is in the upper part of the forearm, on the radial side of the dorsal aspect, on the line connecting Yangxi (LI 5) and Quchi (LI 11), 8 cun above Yangxi (LI 5).

(2) When the elbow is flexed and the radial side of the arm is placed upwards, this point is located at the junction of the upper 1/3 and the lower 2/3 of the line connecting Yangxi (LI 5) and Quchi (LI 11).

Actions and indications: Promote flow of Qi and blood in the channels and collaterals, regualte the function of the fu-organs, used to treat headache due to pathogenic wind, dizziness, pain of eyes, and abdominal pain.

Manipulation: Puncture perpendicularly 0.5—0.8 cun.

上廉 Shànglián （LI 9）

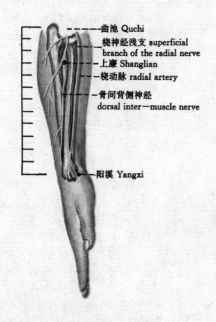

曲池 Quchi

桡神经浅支 superficial
branch of the radial nerve

上廉 Shanglian

桡动脉 radial artery

骨间背侧神经
dorsal inter—muscle nerve

阳溪 Yangxi

〔取穴法〕(1)在前臂背面桡侧的上段，当阳溪穴与曲池穴连线上，曲池穴下3寸处。

(2)侧腕屈肘，于阳溪与曲池连线的上1/4与下3/4的交点处取穴。

〔功效与主治〕通经络，调腑气。肩臂疼痛、麻木，半身不遂，腹痛、肠鸣。

〔操作〕直刺0.3～0.5寸。

Method of locating the point：

(1) This point is lcoated in the upper part of the forearm, on the radial side of the dorsal aspect, on the line joining Yangxi (LI 5) and Quchi (LI 11), 3 cun inferior to Yangxi (LI 5).

(2) When the elbow is flexed and the radial side of the arm is placed upward, locate the point at the junction of the upper 1/4 and the lower 3/4 of the line joining Yangxi (LI 5) and Quchi (LI 11).

Actions and indications: Promote flow of Qi and blood in the channels and collaterals and regulate the function of fu-organs, used to treat pain and numbness of shoulder and arm, hemiplegia, abdominal pain, borborygmus.

Manipulation: Puncture perpendicularly 0.3—0.5 cun.

手三里 Shǒusānlǐ (LI 10)

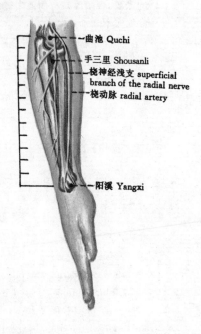

曲池 Quchi
手三里 Shousanli
桡神经浅支 superficial branch of the radial nerve
桡动脉 radial artery

阳溪 Yangxi

〔取穴法〕(1)屈肘,在阳溪穴与曲池穴的连线上,曲池穴下2寸处。

(2)侧腕屈肘,在阳溪与曲池连线的上1/6与下5/6的交点处取穴。

〔功效与主治〕清泄阳明,疏风活络。齿痛,颊肿,上肢不遂,肩臂疼痛。

〔操作〕直刺0.5~1寸。

Method of locating the point:

(1) When the elbow is flexed, the point is located 2 cun inferior to Yangxi (LI 5), on the line connecting Yangxi (LI 5) and Quchi (SI 11).

(2) With the elbow flexed and the radial side of the arm placed upward, locate the point at the junction of the upper 1/6 and the lower 5/6 of the line connecting Yangxi (LI 5) and Quchi (LI 11).

Actions and indications: Clear away and purge heat from Yangming meridian, disperse wind and promote flow of Qi and blood in the channels and collaterals, used to treat toothache, swelling of cheeks, paralysis of the upper limbs and pain of the shoulder and arm.

Manipulation: Puncture perpendicularly 0.5—1 cun.

曲池 Qūchí (LI 11)

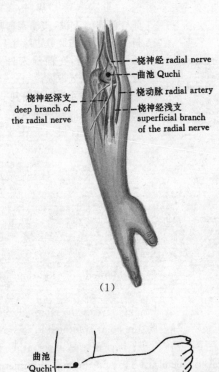

桡神经 radial nerve
曲池 Quchi
桡动脉 radial artery
桡神经深支 deep branch of the radial nerve
桡神经浅支 superficial branch of the radial nerve

(1)

曲池 'Quchi'

(2)

〔取穴法〕(1)肘关节屈曲成90度,在肘部的桡侧,当尺泽穴与肱骨外上髁之间的中点处。

(2)屈肘成直角,当肘弯横纹尽头处。

〔功效与主治〕疏风清热,调和营卫。热病,皮肤病,风疹,上肢不遂,腹痛,吐泻,肘臂痛,眩晕。

〔操作〕直刺 0.5~1 寸。

〔备注〕手阳明大肠经"合"穴。

Method of locating the point:

(1) When the elbow is flexed at a degree of 90°, the point is located on the radial side of the elbow, at the midway between Chize (LU 5) and the lateral epicondyle of the humerus.

(2) When the elbow is flexed at a degree of 90°, locate the point at the end of transverse cubital crease.

Actions and indications: Disperse wind, clear away heat, regulate nutritive Qi and defensive Qi, used to treat febrile diseases, skin disorders, rubella, paralysis of the upper arm, abdominal pain, vomiting and diarrhea, pain of the elbow and arm, and dizziness.

Manipulation: Puncture perpendicularly 0.5—1 cun.

Notes: This point is the He-Sea point of the Large Intestine Meridian of Hand-Yangming.

肘髎 Zhǒuliáo（LI 12）

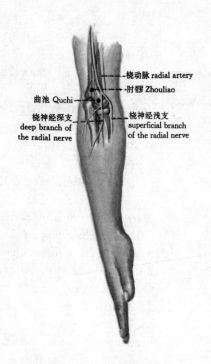

桡动脉 radial artery

肘髎 Zhouliao

曲池 Quchi

桡神经深支
deep branch of
the radial nerve

桡神经浅支
superficial branch
of the radial nerve

〔取穴法〕（1）屈肘,在臂部外侧面的下段,曲池穴向外斜上方1寸,当肱骨边缘处。

（2）屈肘,在曲池穴外上方,肱骨边缘处取穴。

〔功效与主治〕疏筋利节。肩臂肘痛,上肢麻木拘急。

〔操作〕直刺 0.5～1寸。

Method of locating the point:

(1) With the elbow flexed, the point is located in the lower part of the upper arm, on the radial aspect, 1 cun superolateral to Quchi (LI 11), on the medial border of the humerus.

(2) When the elbow is flexed, locate the point superolateral to Quchi (LI 11), on the medial border of the humerus.

Actions and indications: Relax tendons and benefit joints, used to treat pain of the shoulder, arm and elbow, and numbness and convulsion of the upper arm.

Manipulation: Puncture perpendicularly 0.5—1 cun.

臂臑 Bìnào (LI 14)

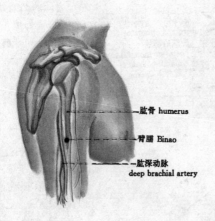

肱骨 humerus

臂臑 Binao

肱深动脉
deep brachial artery

〔取穴法〕(1)垂臂屈肘,在臂部后外侧面的上段,曲池穴与肩髃穴连线上,曲池穴上7寸,三角肌下端处。

(2)垂臂屈肘,在三角肌下端,当肩髃与曲池连线上取穴。

〔功效与主治〕疏筋活络,清热明目。肩臂痛,瘰疬,目疾。

〔操作〕直刺 0.3～0.5寸,如向上斜刺透肩髃可针 1～1.5寸。

Method of locating the point:

(1) When the shoulder is dropped and the elbow flexed, locate the point in the upper part of the upper arm, on the postero-lateral side, on the line connecting Quchi (LI 11) and Jianyu (LI 15), 7 cun above Quchi (LI 11), in the lower part of m. deltoideus.

(2) When the shoulder is dropped and the elbow flexed, locate the point in the lower end of m. deltoideus, on the line connecting Jianyu (LI 15) and Quchi (LI 11).

Actions and indications: Relax tendons, promote flow of Qi and blood in the collaterals, clear away heat and improve eyesight, used to treat pain of the shoulder and arm, scrofula and eye disorders.

Manipulation: Puncture perpendicularly 0.3—0.5 cun, or obliquely upwards towards Jianyu (LI 15) 1—1.5 cun.

肩髃 Jiānyú (LI 15)

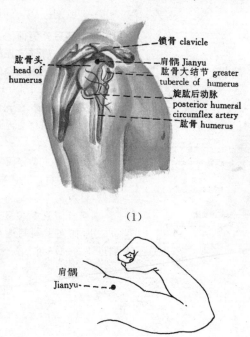

肱骨头 head of humerus

锁骨 clavicle
肩髃 Jianyu
肱骨大结节 greater tubercle of humerus
旋肱后动脉 posterior humeral circumflex artery
肱骨 humerus

(1)

肩髃
Jianyu - - - -

(2)

〔取穴法〕(1)在肩部,肩胛骨肩峰与肱骨大结节之间的凹陷处。

(2)臂外展至水平位时,肩峰下可出现一明显的凹陷处是穴。

(3)垂肩,当锁骨肩峰端前缘直下约2寸,当骨缝之间,手阳明大肠经的循行线上取穴。

〔功效与主治〕祛风热,利关节。肩背、手臂痛,上肢不遂,瘰疬,风热隐疹,眩晕。

〔操作〕针0.5～1寸,沿肱骨长轴向肘部刺入。

Method of locating point:

(1) This point is on the shoulder, in the depression between the acromioclavicular joint and the greater tuberosity of humerus.

(2) When the arm is in full abduction, locate the point in the depression appearing obviously below the acromioclavicular joint.

(3) When the shoulder is dropped, locate the point 2 cun below the anterior border of the acromioclavicular joint, between the two bones, on the route where the Large Intestine Meridian of Hand-Yangming is distributed.

Actions and indications: Expel wind-heat and benefit joints, used to treat pain of the shoulder, back and arm, paralysis of the upper limbs, scrofula, rubella due to wind-heat and dizziness.

Manipulation: Puncture 0.5—1 cun toward the elbow along the long axis of the humerus.

扶突 Fútū (LI 18)

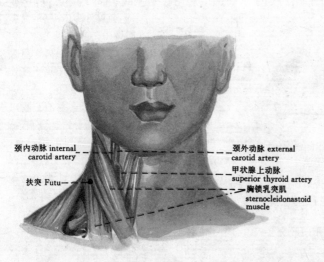

颈内动脉 internal carotid artery

扶突 Futu

颈外动脉 external carotid artery

甲状腺上动脉 superior thyroid artery

胸锁乳突肌 sternocleidonastoid muscle

〔取穴法〕
(1)在颈外侧部，当下颌角直下，结喉旁，当胸锁乳突肌的前、后缘之间。

(2)正坐，头微侧仰，先取甲状软骨与舌骨之间的廉泉穴，再从廉泉向外 3 寸，当胸锁乳突肌的胸骨头与锁骨头之间处取穴。

〔功效与主治〕宣肺利咽。咳喘，咽痛，暴喑气梗，瘰疬，气瘿。

〔操作〕直刺 0.5~0.8 寸。

Method of locating the point:

(1) This point is located on the lateral side of the neck, directly above the angle of jaw, lateral to the Adam's apple, between the anterior and the posterior borders of the sternocleidomastoideus.

(2) Ask patient to sit erect with the head slightly bent backwards, find out the Lianquan point (RN 23) which is located between the thyroid cartilage and the hyroid bone, then locate Futu (LI 18) 3 cun lateral to Lianquan point (RN 23), between the sternal head and the clavicular head of m. sternocleidomastoideus.

Actions and indications: Facilitate flow of the lung Qi and benefit the throat, used to treat cough, asthma, sore throat, sudden hoarseness due to stagnation of Qi, scrofula and goiter due to stagnation of qi.

Manipulation: Puncture perpendicularly 0.5—0.8 cun.

迎香 Yíngxiāng（LI 20）

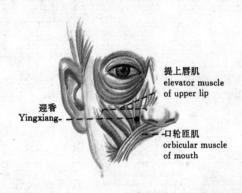

迎香
Yingxiang-

提上唇肌
elevator muscle
of upper lip

口轮匝肌
orbicular muscle
of mouth

〔取穴法〕（1）在面部，鼻翼外缘中点旁，当鼻唇沟中。

（2）正坐仰靠，于鼻唇沟与鼻翼外缘中点平齐处取穴。

〔功效与主治〕散风清热，宣通鼻窍。鼻塞，鼻衄，口喎，鼻渊不闻香臭，面痛。

〔操作〕直刺 0.2～0.3 寸；或向上斜刺 0.5～0.8 寸。

〔备注〕手、足阳明经交会穴。

Method of locating the point:

(1) This point is located on the face, in the nasolabial groove, at the level of the midpoint of the lateral border of ala nasi.

(2) Ask patient to sit erect with the back supported, locate the point at the level of the midpoint of the lateral border of ala nasi.

Actions and indications: Expel wind, disperse heat, and facilitate flow of the lung Qi to relieve nasal obstruction, used to treat nasal obstruction, hemoptysis, deviation of mouth, rhinorrhea with decline of smelling, and facial pain.

Manipulation: Puncture perpendicularly 0.2—0.3 cun, or obliquely upwards 0.5—0.8 cun.

Notes: This point is the crossing point of the Large Intestine Meridian of Hand-Yangming and the Stomach Meridian of Foot Yangming.

三、足阳明胃经

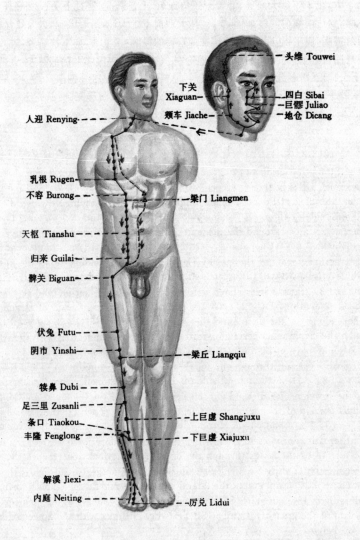

头维 Touwei

下关 Xiaguan

颊车 Jiache

四白 Sibai
巨髎 Juliao
地仓 Dicang

人迎 Renying

乳根 Rugen
不容 Burong

梁门 Liangmen

天枢 Tianshu

归来 Guilai

髀关 Biguan

伏兔 Futu
阴市 Yinshi

梁丘 Liangqiu

犊鼻 Dubi
足三里 Zusanli
条口 Tiaokou
丰隆 Fenglong

上巨虚 Shangjuxu
下巨虚 Xiajuxu

解溪 Jiexi
内庭 Neiting

厉兑 Lidui

起于鼻翼两侧(迎香),上行到鼻根部,与旁侧足太阳经交会,向下沿着鼻的外侧(承泣),进入上齿龈内,回出环绕口唇,向下交会于颏唇沟承浆处,再向后沿着口腮后下方,出于下颌大迎处,沿着下颌角颊车,上行耳前,经过上关(足少阳经),沿着发际,到达前额(神庭)。面部支脉:从大迎前下走人迎,沿着喉咙,进入缺盆部,向下通过横膈,属于胃,联络脾脏。缺盆部直行的经脉:经乳头,向下挟脐旁,进入少腹两侧气冲;胃下口部支脉:沿着腹里向下到气冲会合,再由此下行至髀关,直抵伏兔部,下至膝盖,沿着胫骨外侧前缘,下经足跗,进入第2足趾外侧端(厉兑)。胫部支脉:从膝下3寸(足三里)处分出,进入足中趾外侧。足跗部支脉:从跗上(冲阳)分出,进入足大趾内侧端(隐白),与足太阴脾经相接。

3. The Stomach Meridian of Foot-Yangming.

The Stomach Meridian of Foot-Yangming starts from the lateral side of ala nasi (Yingxiang, LI 20), then it ascends to the bridge of the nose, where it meets the Bladder Meridian of Foot-Taiyang (Jingming, BL 1). Winding downwards along the lateral side of the nose (Chengqi, ST 1), it enters the upper gum. Then, it reemerges and goes around the lips and descends to meet the Ren Meridian at the mentolabial groove (Chengjiang, RN 24). After that, it runs lateroposteriorly across the lower part of the cheek (Daying, ST 5). Winding along the angle of mandible (Jiache, ST 6), it ascends in front of the ear and passes through Shangguan (GB 3) transversely. Then it follows the anterior hairline and reaches the forehead (Shenting, DU 24). The facial branch emerges in front of Daying (ST 5), goes along the throat to enter the supraclavicular fossa. From there, it passes through the diaphragm, pertaining to the stomach and connecting with the spleen. The straight portion of the meridian arising from the supraclavicular fossa runs downwards, passing through the nipple and along the umbilicus. Then it enters Qichong (ST 30) on the lateral side of the lower abdomen. The branch starting from the lower orifice of the stomach descends inside the abdomen and joins the previous portion of the meridain at Qichong (ST 30). Then, it transversely goes to Biguan (ST 31) and passes through Femur-Futu (ST 32), reaching the knee. From there, it continues to go downwards along the anterior border of the lateral aspect of the tibia, passes through the dorsum of the foot and reaches the tip of the second toe (Lidui, ST 45). The tibial branch emerges 3 cun below the knee (Zusanli, ST 36), and enters the lateral side of the middle toe. The branch from the dorsum of the foot starts from Chongyang (ST 42) and ends at the medial side of the tip of the great toe (Yinbai,SP 1), where it links with the Spleen Meridian of Foot-Taiyin.

四白 Sìbái (ST 2)

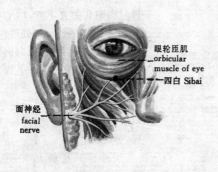

眼轮匝肌 orbicular muscle of eye

四白 Sibai

面神经 facial nerve

〔取穴法〕(1)在下眼睑之下方,直视时当瞳孔的直下方,适对上颌骨的眶下孔凹陷处。

(2)在承泣穴直下 0.3 寸,当眶下孔之凹陷处取穴。

〔功效与主治〕祛风明目。目赤痛痒,头面疼痛,口眼㖞斜,眼睑瞤动。

〔操 作〕直刺 0.2～0.3 寸,横刺可透颧髎、下关针 0.5～1 寸。

Method of lcoating the point：

(1) This point is located inferior to the lower eyelid, directly below the pupil when seeing forwards, just in the depression of the infraorbital foramen of the maxilla.

(2) Locate the point 0.3 cun below Chengqi (ST 1), in the depression of the infraorbital foramen.

Actions and indications: Expel wind and improve eyesight, used to treat redness, itching and pain of eyes, headache, facial pain, deviation of eyes and mouth, and twitching of eyelids.

Manipulation: Puncture perpendicularly 0.2—0.3 cun, or 0.5—1 cun subcutaneously to allow the tip of the needle to reach Quanliao (SI 18) and Xiaguan (ST 7).

巨髎 Jùliáo (ST 3)

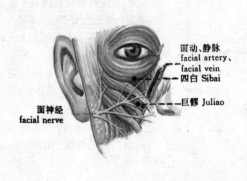

面动、静脉
facial artery、
facial vein

四白 Sibai

巨髎 Juliao

面神经
facial nerve

〔取穴法〕(1)在面部,直视时当瞳孔的直下方,横平鼻翼下缘处,鼻唇沟外侧处取穴。

(2)正坐或仰卧,眼向前平视,于瞳孔垂线与鼻翼下缘平线之交点处取穴。

〔功效与主治〕祛风活络。口眼㖞斜,眼睑瞤动,齿痛,面痛,鼻衄。

〔操作〕直刺 0.3~0.5寸。

〔备注〕足阳明胃经与阳跷脉交会穴。

Method of locating the point:

(1) This point is lcoated on the face, right below the pupil when seeing forwards, at the level of the inferior border of the asa nasi, on the lateral side of the nasolabial groove.

(2) Ask patient to sit erect or takes a suppine position with the eye seeing forwards, locate the point at the junction of the vertical line passing through the centre of the pupil and the transverse line of the inferior border of the ala nasi.

Actions and indications: Expel wind and promote flow of Qi and blood in the channels and collaterals, used to treat twitching of the eyelids, toothache, pain in the face and hemoptysis.

Manipulation: Puncture perpendicularly 0.3—0.5 cun.

Notes: This point is the crossing point of the Stomach Meridian of Foot-Yangming and the Yangqiao Meridian.

地仓 Dìcāng（ST 4）

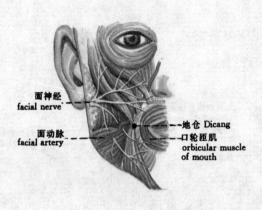

面神经
facial nerve

面动脉
facial artery

地仓 Dicang

口轮匝肌
orbicular muscle
of mouth

〔取穴法〕（1）在面部，口角外侧，上直瞳孔处。

（2）正坐或仰卧，眼向前平视，于瞳孔垂线与口角平线之交点处。

（3）巨髎穴直下，与口角相平，约当口角旁0.4寸处。

〔功效与主治〕祛风，通经活络。口㖞，唇胗，流涎，面痛。

〔操作〕直刺0.2～0.3寸，或向颊车穴方向平刺0.5～1.5寸。

〔备注〕手、足阳明经、阳跷脉交会穴。

Method of locating the point:

(1) This point is located on the face, on the lateral side of the corner of mouth, directly below the pupil.

(2) Ask patient to take a sitting or a supine position with his eyes seeing forwards, locate the point at the junction of the vertical line passing throught he centre of the pupil and the transverse line passing through the corner of mouth.

(3) Locate the point directly below Juliao (ST 3), at the level of the corner of mouth, about 0.4 cun lateral to the corner of the mouth.

Actions and indications: Expel wind and promote flow of Qi and blood in the channels and collaterals, used to treat deviation of mouth, salivation, and twitching of eyelids.

Manipulation: Puncture perpendicularly 0.2－0.3 cun or subcutaneously 0.5－1.5 cun towards Jiache (ST 6).

Notes: This point is the crossing point of the Hand-Yangming Meridian, Foot-Yangming Meridian and the Yangqiao Meridian.

颊车 Jiáchē (ST 6)

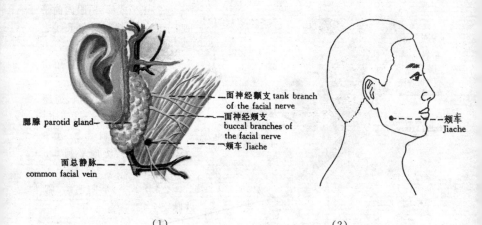

腮腺 parotid gland —
面神经颧支 tank branch of the facial nerve
面神经颊支 buccal branches of the facial nerve
颊车 Jiache
面总静脉 common facial vein

颊车 Jiache

(1)   (2)

〔取穴法〕(1)在面部,下颌角之前上方一横指,当咀嚼时咬肌隆起,按之凹陷处。

(2)正坐或侧伏,于下颌角直上4分,向前一横指处。

〔功效与主治〕开关利机,活络止痛,消肿。口眼㖞斜,颊肿,齿痛,口噤不开,痄腮。

〔操作〕直刺0.3~0.5寸;横刺(透地仓)可针1~1.5寸。

Method of locating the point:

(1) This point is located on the face, about one finger breadth antero-superior to the angle of the jaw. When the teeth are clenched, it is in the depression felt in the prominence of the m. masseter.

(2) Ask patient to sit erect or lie on his back, located the point one finger breadth anterior to the point 4 cun directly above the angle of the jaw.

Actions and indications: Promote movement of joint, activate flow of Qi and blood in the collaterals and relieve pain, used to treat deviation of eye and mouth, swelling of cheeks, toothache, trismus and mumps.

Manipulation: Puncture perpendicularly 0.3—0.5 cun, or 1—1.5 cun obliquely to allow the needle to penetrate Dicang (ST 4).

54

下关 Xiàguān (ST 7)

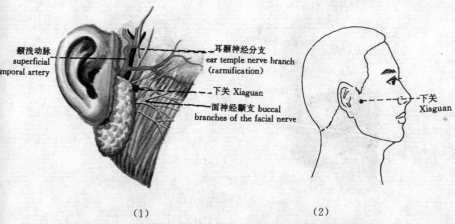

額浅动脉
superficial
mporal artery

耳颞神经分支
ear temple nerve branch
(rarmification)

下关 Xiaguan

面神经颧支 buccal
branches of the facial nerve

下关
Xiaguan

(1)   (2)

〔取穴法〕(1)在面部,耳前方,当颧弓与下颌切迹所围成之凹陷处。

(2)正坐或侧伏,闭口,于耳屏前约一横指处,当颧骨弓下的凹陷处取穴。

〔功效与主治〕疏风清热,通关利窍。齿痛,口噤,耳聋,耳鸣,口眼㖞斜,下颌关节疼痛。

〔操作〕直刺0.3~0.5寸;横刺(透颊车)可针1~1.5寸。

〔备注〕足阳明、足少阳经交会穴。

Method of locating the point:

(1) This point is located on the face, in front of the ear, in the depression between the zygomatic arch and the mandibular notch.

(2) Ask patient to take a sitting or a lateral recumbent position with his mouth shut, locate the point one finger breadth anterior to the tragus, in the depression inferior to the zygomatic arch.

Actions and indications: Disperse wind, clear away heat, and benefit the movement of joint, used to treat toothache, trismus, deafness, tinnitus, deviation of mouth and eyes and pain of the jaw joint.

Manipulation: Puncture perpendicularly 0.3—0.5 cun, or horizontally 1—1.5 cun to allow the needle to penetrate Jiache (ST 5).

Notes: This is a crossing point of the Foot-Yangming Meridian and the Foot-Shaoyang Meridian.

55

头维 Tóuwéi (ST 8)

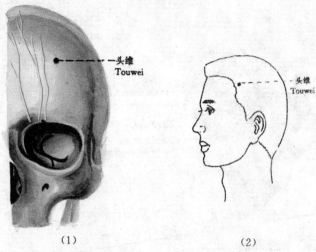

（1）   （2）

〔取穴法〕（1）在头侧部,前发际额曲的上外方,入发际0.5寸,去督脉神庭穴4.5寸处。

（2）正坐,先取头临泣穴,并以此据点,向外量取头临泣至神庭间距离,入前发际0.5寸处。

〔功效与主治〕清头明目。头痛,眩晕,眼痛。

〔操作〕针尖沿皮向上或向下方刺入0.2～0.3寸。

〔备注〕足阳明、足少阳经交会穴。

Method of locating the point:

(1) This point is on the lateral side of the head, laterosuperior to the corner of the anterior hairline, 0.5 cun within the hairline, 4.5 cun lateral to Shenting point (DU 24).

(2) Ask patient to sit erect, locate Toulinqi (GB 15) first, then measure the distance from the point to Shenting (DU 24) laterally, and finally locate Touwei point (ST 8) 0.5 cun within the anterior hairline.

Actions and indications: Clear away heat from the head to improve eyesight, used to treat headache, dizziness and pain of eyes.

Manipulation: Puncture upwards or downwards subcutaneously 0.2—0.3 cun.

Notes: This point is the crossing point of the Stomach Meridian of Foot-Yangming and the Gallbladder Meridian of Foot-Shaoyang.

人迎 Rényíng (ST 9)

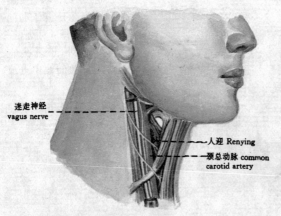

迷走神经
vagus nerve

人迎 Renying

颈总动脉 common
carotid artery

〔取穴法〕(1)结喉旁，当胸锁乳突肌的前缘，适对颈总动脉分出颈内外动脉之部位。

(2)正坐仰靠，于喉结旁开1.5寸，有动脉应手之处，避开动脉取之。

〔功效与主治〕理气，通脉，化瘀。胸闷喘息，咽喉肿痛，头痛，眩晕，发音困难。

〔操作〕直刺0.3～0.4寸，不宜过深，针时宜用手拇指或食指将颈总动脉压向胸锁乳突肌侧，以免刺伤动脉。

〔备注〕足阳明、足少阳经交会穴。

Method of locating the point:

(1) This point is located lateral to the Adam's apple, on the anterior border of m. sterncleidomastoideus, corresponding to the position the external and internal carotid arteries branch off from the common carotid artery.

(2) Ask patient to take a sitting position with his back supported, Locate the point 1.5 cun lateral to the Adam's apple, besides the artery felt.

Actions and indications: Regulate flow of Qi, promote flow of Qi and blood in the channels and collaterals and remove blood stasis, used to treat chest stuffiness, dyspnea, sore throat, headache, dizziness and difficulties in pronounciation.

Manipulation: Puncture perpendicularly 0.3－0.4 cun, deep needling is not advisable. When the point is to be punctured, press the common carotid artery toward m. sternocleidomastoideus with the thumb or index finger to avoid injuring the artery.

Notes: This point is the crossing point of the Stomach Meridian of Foot-Yangming and the Gallbladder Meridian of Foot-Shaoyang.

乳根 Rǔgēn (ST 18)

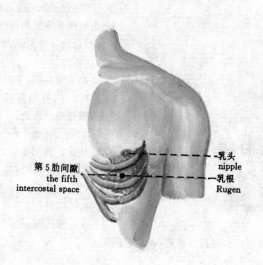

〔取穴法〕（1）在胸部，当乳头直下，第 5 肋间隙，距前正中线 4 寸处。

（2）仰卧，于乳头直下，当第 5 肋间隙中点取穴。

〔功效与主治〕宣肺利气，通乳。胸痛，乳痈，乳少。

〔操作〕斜刺 0.3～0.5 寸。

第 5 肋间隙
the fifth
intercostal space

乳头
nipple

乳根
Rugen

Method of locating the point：

（1）This point is located in the chest, directly below the nipple, level with the 5th intercostal space, 4 cun lateral to the anterior midline.

（2）Ask patient to lie on his back, locate the point directly below the nipple, at the midpoint of the 5th intercostal space.

Actions and indications：Facilitate flow of the lung Qi and promote lactation, used to treat chest pain, acute mastitis and hypogalactia.

Manipulation：Puncture obliquely 0.3—0.5 cun.

不容 Bùróng (ST 19)

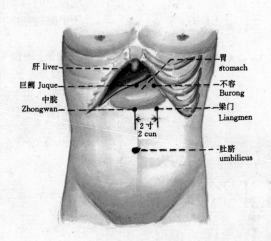

肝 liver
巨阙 Juque
中脘 Zhongwan
胃 stomach
不容 Burong
梁门 Liangmen
2寸 2 cun
肚脐 umbilicus

〔取穴法〕(1)在上腹部,任脉巨阙穴旁开2寸处。

(2)仰卧,当脐上6寸,旁开腹部中线2寸处。

〔功效与主治〕调中和胃,理气。脘腹胀满,呕吐不食,胃痛。

〔操作〕直刺0.5～1寸。

Method of locating the point:

(1) This point is located in the uppwer abdomen, 2 cun lateral to Juque (RN 14).

(2) Ask patient to lie on his back, locate the point 6 cun above the umbilicus, 2 cun lateral to the midline of the abdomen.

Actions and indications: Regulate the function of the stomach and promote flow of Qi, used to treat abdominal fullness and distension, vomiting, anorexia and stomachache.

Manipulation: Puncture perpendicularly 0.5—1 cun.

梁门 Liángmén (ST 21)

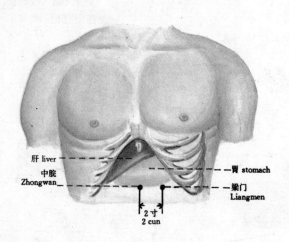

肝 liver
中脘 Zhongwan
胃 stomach
梁门 Liangmen
2 寸
2 cun

〔取穴法〕(1)在上腹部,任脉中脘穴旁开 2 寸处。

(2)仰卧,当脐上 4 寸,前正中线旁开 2 寸处。

〔功效与主治〕消积滞,健脾胃。胃痛,呕吐,纳呆,腹胀。

〔操作〕直刺 0.5～1 寸。

Method of locating the point:

(1) This point is in the upper abdomen, 2 cun lateral to Zhongwan (RN 12).

(2) Ask patient to lie flat, locate the point 4 cun above the umbilicus, 2 cun lateral to the anterior midline.

Actions and indications: Promote discharge of retained food and strengthen the spleen and the stomach, used to treat stomachache, vomiting, anorexia and abdominal distension.

Manipulation: Puncture perpendicularly 0.5－1 cun.

天枢 Tiānshū (ST 25)

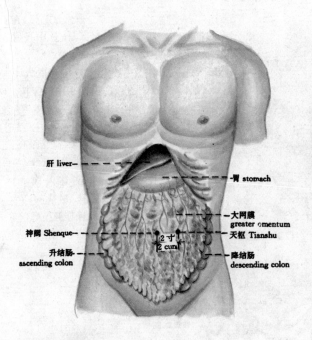

肝 liver
胃 stomach
大网膜 greater omentum
神阙 Shenque
天枢 Tianshu
升结肠 ascending colon
降结肠 descending colon
2 寸 2 cun

〔取穴法〕（1）在中腹部，神阙穴外开2寸处。

（2）仰卧，于脐正中旁开2寸处取穴。

〔功效与主治〕调肠腑，理气滞。绕脐腹痛，腹胀肠鸣，泄泻，便秘，痢疾，月经不调。

〔操作〕直刺0.5～1寸。

〔备注〕大肠的"募"穴。

Method of locating the point:

(1) This point is lcoated in the middle abdomen, 2 cun lateral to Shenque (RN 8).

(2) Ask patient to lie flat, locate the point 2 cun lateral to the centre of the umbilicus.

Actions and indications: Regulate the function of the intestine and relieve stagnation of Qi, used to treat pain around the umbilicus, abdominal distension with borborygmus, diarrhea, constipation, dysentery and irregular menstruation.

Manipulation: Puncture perpendicularly 0.5—1 cun.

Notes: This point is the Front-Mu point of the large intestine.

61

归来 Guīlái (ST 29)

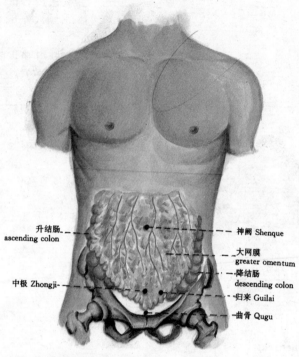

升结肠
ascending colon

中极 Zhongji

神阙 Shenque

大网膜
greater omentum

降结肠
descending colon

归来 Guilai

曲骨 Qugu

〔取穴法〕（1）在下腹部，任脉中极穴外开2寸处。

（2）在天枢穴下4寸，前正中线旁开2寸处。

〔功效与主治〕温经散寒，益气固脱。腹痛，癥瘕，疝气，茎中痛，阴缩入腹，痛经，阳痿，遗精，不孕。

〔操作〕直刺0.5～1寸。

Method of locating the point：

(1) This point is in the lower abdomen, 2 cun lateral to Zhongji (RN 3).

(2) Locate the point 4 cun below Tianshu (ST 25), 2 cun lateral to the anterio midline.

Actions and indications：Warm up channels, disperse cold, supplement Qi and relieve prostration, used to treat abdominal pain, abdominal masses, hernia, pain in the penis, retraction of penis, dysmenorrhea, impotence, emission and sterility.

Manipulation：Puncture perpendicularly 0.5—1 cun.

髀关 Bìguān (ST 31)

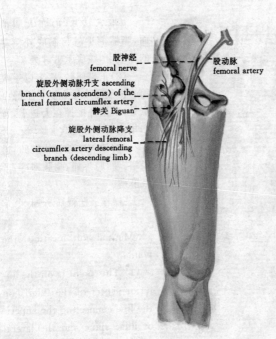

股神经 femoral nerve
旋股外侧动脉升支 ascending branch (ramus ascendens) of the lateral femoral circumflex artery
髀关 Biguan
旋股外侧动脉降支 lateral femoral circumflex artery descending branch (descending limb)
股动脉 femoral artery

〔取穴法〕(1)在大腿前面,当髂前上棘与髌底外侧端的连线上,屈股时,平会阴。居缝匠肌外侧凹陷处,髌底外侧端上12寸处。

(2)在髂前上棘与髌骨外上缘的连线上,平臀横纹,与承扶穴(膀胱经)相对处。

(3)将手掌第一横纹中点按于伏兔穴,手掌平伸向前,当中指尖到处是穴。

(4)仰卧,于髂前上棘至髌骨底外缘连线与臀横纹延伸线之交点处取穴。

〔功效与主治〕健腰膝,通经络。腰腿疼痛,下肢痿软,足麻不仁。

〔操作〕直刺0.6~1寸。

Method of locating the point:

(1) This point is on the anterior aspect of the thigh, on the line connecting the superior illiac spine and the lateral end of the inferior border of the illium, 12 cun above the inferior border of the illium.

(2) Locate the point on the line connecting the superior illiac spine and the latero-superior border of the patella, level with the gluteofemoral crease, opposite to Chengfu point (BL 36).

Actions and indications: Strengthen the loins and knees and promote flow of Qi and blood in the channels and collaterals, used to treat pain of the loins and leg, flaccidity of the lower limb, and numbness of the foot.

Manipulation: Puncture perpendicularly 0.6—1 cun.

伏兔 Fútù (ST 32)

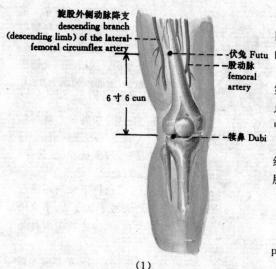

旋股外侧动脉降支
descending branch
(descending limb) of the lateral-
femoral circumflex artery

6寸 6 cun

伏兔 Futu
股动脉
femoral
artery

犊鼻 Dubi

(1)

〔取穴法〕(1)在大腿前面,当髂前上棘与髌底外侧端的连线上,髌底上6寸处。

(2)正坐屈膝,医者以手掌第一横纹正中按在膝盖上缘中点处,手指并拢押在大腿上,当中指尖所止处是穴。

〔功效与主治〕壮腰膝,通经络。腰胯疼痛,腿膝寒冷,下肢麻痹。

〔操作〕直刺0.5~1寸。

Method of locating the point:

(1) This point is on the anterior aspect of the thigh, on the line connecting the superior illiac spine and the lateral end of the lower border of the patella, 6 cun above the lower border of the patella.

(2) Ask patient to sit erect with his knees flexed, press the first transverse crease on the upper border of the kness with the first crease of the

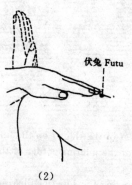

伏兔 Futu

(2)

plam when the fingers are closed and placed on the thigh, locate the point under where the tip of the index finger touches.

Actions and indications: Strengthen the loins and the knees, and promote flow of Qi and blood in the channels and collaterals, used to treat pain in the illiac region, coldness of leg and knees and paralysis of the lower limbs.

Manipulation: Puncture perpendicularly 0.5—1 cun.

64

阴市 Yīnshì (ST 33)

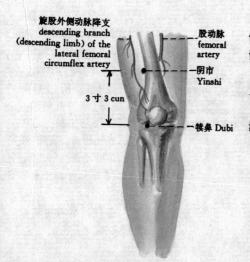

旋股外侧动脉降支
descending branch
(descending limb) of the
lateral femoral
circumflex artery

3 寸 3 cun

股动脉
femoral
artery

阴市
Yinshi

犊鼻 Dubi

〔取穴法〕（1）在大腿前面，当髂前上棘与髌底外侧端的连线上，髌底上 3 寸处。

（2）正坐屈膝，于膝盖外上缘直上四横指（一夫）处是穴。

〔功效与主治〕强腰膝，清热利湿。膝冷疼痛，下肢不遂。

〔操作〕直刺 0.3～0.5 寸。

Method of locating the point：

(1) This point is on the anterior aspect of the thigh, on the line connecting the superior illiac spine and the lateral end of the lower border of the patella, 3 cun above the lower border of the patella.

(2) Ask patient to sit erect with his knees flexed, locate the point four fingers breadth supero-lateral to the knees.

Actions and indications：Strengthen the loins and the knee, clear away heat and remove dampness, used to treat coldness and pain in the lumbar region and paralysis of the lower limbs.

Manipulations：Puncture perpendicularly 0.3—0.5 cun.

梁丘 Liángqiū (ST 34)

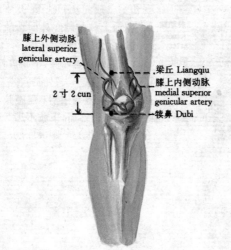

膝上外侧动脉
lateral superior
genicular artery

2寸 2 cun

梁丘 Liangqiu
膝上内侧动脉
medial superior
genicular artery
犊鼻 Dubi

〔取穴法〕(1)屈膝,在大腿前面,当髂前上棘与髌底外侧端的连线上,髌底上2寸处。

(2)正坐屈膝,于膝盖外上缘直上2寸处是穴。

〔功效与主治〕通经活络,理气和胃。胃痛,膝肿痛,下肢不遂。

〔操作〕直刺0.3～0.5寸。

〔备注〕足阳明胃经"郄"穴。

Method of locating the point:

(1) When the knee is flexed, the point is located on the anterior aspect of the thigh, on the line connecting the superior illiac spine and the lateral end of the lower border of the knee, 2 cun above the lower border of the knee.

(2) Ask patient to sit erect with his knee flexed, locate the point 2 cun above the laterosuperior border of the patella.

Actions and indications: Promote flow of Qi and blood in the channels and collaterals, regulate flow of the stomach Qi, used to treat stomachache, swelling and pain of the knee joint and paralysis of the lower limbs.

Manipulation: Puncture perpendicularly 0.3—0.5 cun.

Notes: This point is the Xi-Cleft point of the Stomach Meridian of Foot-Yangming.

犊鼻 Dúbí (ST 35)

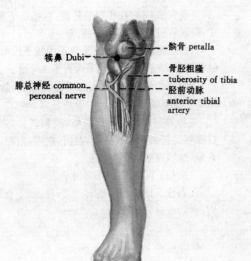

犊鼻 Dubi —
腓总神经 common peroneal nerve
髌骨 petalla
骨胫粗隆 tuberosity of tibia
胫前动脉 anterior tibial artery

〔取穴法〕(1)屈膝,在大腿前面,髌骨与髌韧带外侧凹陷中。

(2)正坐屈膝,于膝盖骨与胫骨之间,髌韧带外侧凹陷中取穴。

〔功效与主治〕通经活络,疏风散寒,消肿止痛。膝关节痛及屈伸不利。

〔操作〕针尖斜向内上方刺入 0.3~0.5 寸。

Method of locating the point:

(1) When the knee is flexed, locate the point on the anterior aspect of the thigh, in the depression lateral to the patella and the patellar ligament.

(2) Ask patient to sit erect with his knee flexed, locate the point in the depression between the patella and the tibia and distal to the petallar ligament.

Actions and indications: Promote flow of Qi and blood in the channels and collaterals, expel wind and disperse cold, subdue swelling and relieve pain, used to treat pain and difficulties in movements of the knee joint.

Manipulation: Puncture 0.3—0.5 cun upwards and inwards obliquely.

足三里 Zúsānlǐ (ST 36)

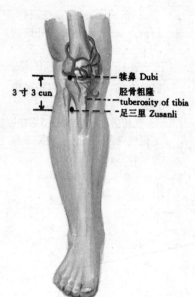

牍鼻 Dubi
胫骨粗隆
tuberosity of tibia
足三里 Zusanli

3 寸 3 cun

〔取穴法〕(1)在小腿前外侧,当牍鼻下 3 寸,距胫骨前缘一横指(中指)处。

(2)正坐屈膝,用手从膝盖正中往下摸取胫骨粗隆,在胫骨粗隆外下缘直下 1 寸处。

(3)正坐屈膝,以本人之手按在膝盖,食指抚于膝下胫骨,当中指尖着处是穴。

〔功效与主治〕疏通经络,调和气血,强健脾胃。胃痛,呕吐,腹胀,泄泻,痢疾,疳积,头晕,腰膝疼痛,虚劳羸瘦。

〔操作〕直刺 0.5~1.5 寸。

〔备注〕足阳明胃经"合"穴;胃的"下合"穴;强壮保健穴。

Method of locating the point:

(1) This point is on the lateral side of the anterior aspect of the lower leg, 3 cun below Dubi (ST 35), one finger (the middle finger) breadth from the anterior crest of the tibia.

(2) Ask patient to sit erect with the knee flexed, press from the centre of the patella downwards until the tuberosity of the tibia is felt, then locate the point 1 cun directly below the latero-inferior border of the tuberosity of tibia.

(3) Ask patient to sit erect with his knee flexed, locate the point in the place where the tip of the middle finger touches when patient places his hand over the petalla and his index fingers touches the tibia below the knee.

Actions and indications: Dredge channels and collaterals, regulate Qi and blood, and strengthen the spleen and the stomach, used to treat stomachache, vomiting, abdominal distension, diarrhea, dysentery, malaria, dizziness, pain of the loins and knees, emaciation due to excessive sexual activities.

Manipulation: Puncture perpendicularly 0.5—1.5 cun.

Notes: This point is the He-Sea point of the Stomach Meridian of Foot-Yangming, the Lower-He point of the stomach and an important point for health preservation and constitution improvement.

上巨虚 Shàngjùxū (ST 37)

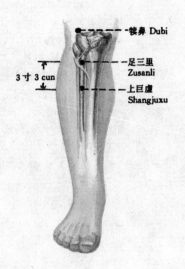

牍鼻 Dubi

足三里
Zusanli

3 寸 3 cun

上巨虚
Shangjuxu

〔取穴法〕(1)在小腿前外侧,当牍鼻下 6 寸,距胫骨前缘一横指(中指)处。

(2)正坐屈膝,于外膝眼(牍鼻)直下二夫(6 寸),即足三里穴直下 3 寸处取之。

〔功效与主治〕清热利湿,调理胃肠。腹痛,腹胀,肠鸣,痢疾,泄泻,便秘,肠痈。

〔操作〕直刺 0.5～1.5寸。

〔备注〕大肠的"下合"穴。

Method of locating the point:

(1) This point is on the antero-lateral side of the lower leg, 6 cun below Dubi (ST 35), one finger breadth from the anterior crest of the tibia.

(2) Ask patient to sit erect with his leg flexed, locate the point 6 cun below Dubi (ST 35) or 3 cun below Zusanli (ST 36).

Actions and indications: Clear away heat, remove dampness, and regulate the function of the gastrointestinal tract, used to treat abdominal pain, abdominal distension, borborygmus, dysentery, diarrhea, constipation and intestinal carbuncles.

Manipulations: Puncture perpendicularly 0.5—1.5 cun.

Notes: This point is the Lower-He point of the large intestine.

条口 Tiáokǒu (ST 38)

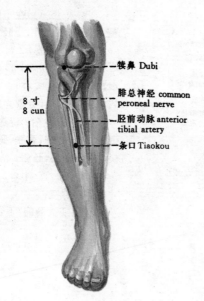

牍鼻 Dubi

腓总神经 common
peroneal nerve

胫前动脉 anterior
tibial artery

条口 Tiaokou

8 寸
8 cun

〔取穴法〕(1)在小腿前外侧,当牍鼻下 8 寸,距胫骨前缘一横指(中指)处。

(2)正坐屈膝,足三里穴直下,于外膝眼与外踝尖连线之中点同高处取穴。

〔功效与主治〕理气,疏筋。下肢痿痹冷痛,转筋,足缓不收,肩背痛。

〔操作〕直刺 0.5～1.5寸。

Method of locating the point:

(1) This point is on the latero-anterior side of the lower leg, 8 cun below Dubi (ST 35), one finger breadth from the anterior crest of the tibia.

(2) Ask patient to sit erect with the knee flexed, locate the point directly below Zusanli (ST 36), at the level of the midpoint of the line connecting the Dubi point (ST 35) and the tip of the external malleolus.

Actions and indications: Regulate flow of Qi and relax tendons, used to treat atrophy, coldness and pain of the lower limbs, systremma, motor impairment of the lower leg, pain of shoulder and back.

Manipulation: Puncture perpendicularly 0.5—1.5 cun.

下巨虚 Xiàjùxù (ST 39)

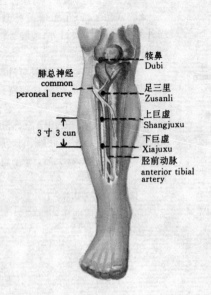

腓总神经
common
peroneal nerve

犊鼻
Dubi

足三里
Zusanli

上巨虚
Shangjuxu

下巨虚
Xiajuxu

胫前动脉
anterior tibial
artery

3 寸 3 cun

〔取穴法〕(1)在小腿前外侧,当犊鼻下9寸,距胫骨前缘一横指(中指)处。

(2)正坐屈膝,足三里直下二夫(6寸)处取之。

〔功效与主治〕调肠腑,理气滞。小腹痛,泻痢脓血,腰脊痛引睾。

〔操作〕直刺 0.3～0.7寸。

〔备注〕小肠的"下合"穴。

Method of locating the point:

(1) This point is on the latero-anterior side of the lower leg, 9 cun below Dubi (ST 35), one finger breadth from the anterior crest of the tibia.

(2) Ask patient to sit erect with the knee flexed, locate the point 6 cun directly below Zusanli (ST 36).

Actions and indications: Regulate function of intestines and relieve stagnation of Qi, used to treat pain in the lower abdomen, diarrhea, dysentery marked by loose stools with pus and blood, pain of the spine radiating to the testis.

Manipulation: Puncture perpendicularly 0.3—0.7 cun.

Notes: This point is the Lower-He point of the small intestine.

丰隆 Fēnglóng (ST 40)

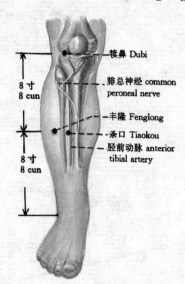

- 犊鼻 Dubi
- 腓总神经 common peroneal nerve
- 丰隆 Fenglong
- 条口 Tiaokou
- 胫前动脉 anterior tibial artery

8 寸 8 cun

8 寸 8 cun

〔取穴法〕(1)在小腿前外侧，当外踝尖上8寸，条口外，距胫骨前缘二横指(中指)处。

(2)正坐屈膝，于外膝眼与外踝尖连线之中点同高，距胫骨前嵴约二横指处取穴。

〔功效与主治〕安神宁志，清热化湿，降逆通便。痰多、咳喘、咽喉肿痛，下肢痿、痹，头晕头痛，癫狂痫，便秘。

〔操作〕直刺0.5～1寸。

〔备注〕足阳明胃经"络"穴。

Method of locating the point:

(1) This point is located on the latero-anterior aspect of the lower leg, 8 cun above the tip of the external malleolus, lateral to Tiaokou (ST 38), two fingers breadth from the anterior border of the crest of tibia.

(2) Ask patient to sit erect with his knee flexed, locate the point at the level with the midpoint of the line connecting Dubi (ST 35) and the tip of the external malleolus, two finger breath lateral to the anterior crest of the tibia.

Actions and indications: Tranquilize the mind, clear away heat, remove dampness, and lower down the upward adverse flow of Qi, used to treat expectoration of profuse sputum, cough, asthma, sore throat, atrophy of muscles and arthralgia in the lower leg, dizziness, headache, depressive schizophrenia, mania, epilepsy and constipation.

Manipulation: Puncture perpendicularly 0.5—1 cun.

Notes: This point is the Luo-Connecting point of the Stomach Meridian of Foot-Yangming.

解溪 Jiěxī（ST 41）

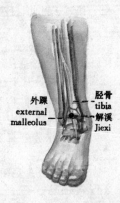

外踝
external
malleolus

胫骨
tibia

解溪
Jiexi

〔取穴法〕(1)在足背与小腿交界处的横纹中央凹陷中,当跗长伸肌腱与趾长伸肌腱之间取穴。

(2)仰卧或正坐,从第2趾直上至踝关节前面横纹,于两筋(跗长伸肌腱与趾长伸肌腱)之间取穴。

〔功效与主治〕清胃降逆,健脾化湿。头痛,眩晕,面浮肿,踝关节肿痛。

〔操作〕直刺0.3～0.5寸。

〔备注〕足阳明胃经"经"穴。

Method of locating the point:

(1) This point is at the midpoint of the transverse crease of the ankle joint where the dorsum of foot is linked with the lower leg, in the depression between the tendons of m. extensor digitorium longus and hallucis longus.

(2) When the patient takes a supine or a sitting position, locate the point directly above the second toe, in the crease anterior to the ankle joint between the tendons of m. extensor digitorium longus and hallucis longus.

Actions and indications: Clear away stomach heat, lower down adverse flow of the stomach Qi, strengthen the spleen and remove dampness, used to treat headache, dizziness, edema on the face and swelling and pain of the ankle joint.

Manipulation: Puncture perpendicularly 0.3—0.5 cun.

Notes: This point is the Jing-River point of the Stomach Meridian of Foot-Yangming.

内庭 Nèitíng (ST 44)

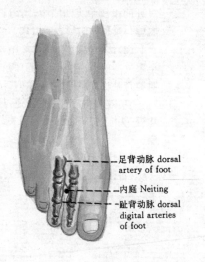

足背动脉 dorsal artery of foot

内庭 Neiting

趾背动脉 dorsal digital arteries of foot

〔取穴法〕(1)在足背,当第二三趾间,趾蹼缘后方赤白肉际处。

(2)仰卧或正坐,于第二三跖趾缝间的缝纹端取穴。

〔功效与主治〕清胃肠湿热,理气镇痛。齿痛,口喝,咽喉肿痛,鼻衄,痢疾,足背肿痛。

〔操作〕直刺 0.2～0.4寸。

〔备注〕足阳明胃经"荥"穴。

Method of locating the point:

(1) This point is on the dorsum of the foot, posterior to the web between the second and third toes, at the junction of the red and white skin.

(2) When patient takes a supine or a sitting position, locate the point between the second and the third toes at the end of their web.

Actions and indications: Clear away heat from the stomach and the intestine, regulate flow of Qi and relieve pain, used to treat toothache, deviation of mouth, sore throat, hemoptysis, dysentery, swelling and pain of the dorsum of foot.

Manipulation: Puncture perpendicularly 0.2—0.4 cun.

Notes: This point is the Ying-Spring point of the Stomach Meridian of Foot-Yangming.

厉兑 Lìduì (ST 45)

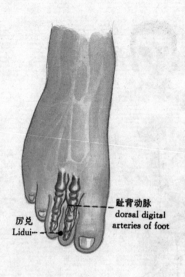

厉兑
Lidui

趾背动脉
dorsal digital
arteries of foot

〔取穴法〕(1)在足第 2 趾末节外侧,距趾甲角 0.1 寸(指寸)处。

(2)仰卧或正坐,于第 2 趾爪甲外侧缘与基底部各作一线,当二线之交点处是穴。

〔功效与主治〕清胃安神,通调气血。口喝,鼻衄,齿痛,面肿,梦魇不宁,癫狂。

〔操作〕直刺 0.1 寸,或点刺出血。

〔备注〕足阳明胃经"井"穴。

Method of locating the point:

(1) This point is on the lateral side of the second toe, 0.1 cun distal to the corner of the nail (finger measurement).

(2) When patient takes a supine or a sitting position, locate the point at the crossing point of the line drawn along the lateral side of the nail of the second toe and that drawn along the base of the nail.

Actions and indications: Clear away stomach heat, tranquilize mind, promote and regulate flow of Qi and blood, used to treat deviation of mouth, hemoptysis, toothache, swelling of face, dream-disturbed sleep, and schizophrenia.

Manipulation: Puncture perpendicularly 0.1 cun, or prick with a three-edged needle to cause bleeding.

Notes: This point is the Jing-Well point of the Stomach Meridian of Foot-Yang-ming.

四、足太阴脾经

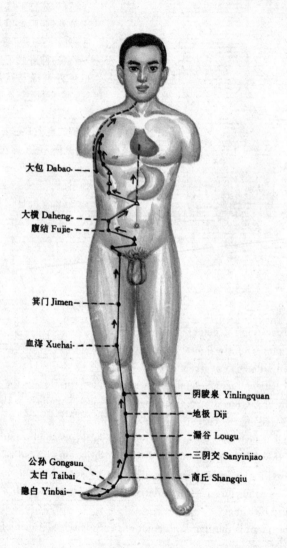

大包 Dabao

大横 Daheng
腹结 Fujie

箕门 Jimen

血海 Xuehai

公孙 Gongsun
太白 Taibai
隐白 Yinbai

阴陵泉 Yinlingquan
地极 Diji
漏谷 Lougu
三阴交 Sanyinjiao
商丘 Shangqiu

起于足大趾末端(隐白),沿着大趾内侧赤白肉际,经过大趾本节后的第1跖趾关节后面,上行至内踝前面,再上腿肚,沿着胫骨后面,交出足厥阴经的前面,经膝股部内侧前缘,进入腹部,属于脾脏,联络胃,通过横膈上行,挟咽部两旁,连系舌根,分散于舌下。胃部支脉:向上通过横膈,流注于心中,与手少阴心经相接。

4. The Spleen Meridian of Foot-Taiyin

The Spleen Meridian of Foot-Taiyin originates from the tip of the big toe (Yinbai, SP 1). It then runs along the medial aspect of the great toe at the junction of the red and white skin. Passing through the region posterior to the first metatarsophalangeal joint, it ascends in front of the medial malleolus up to the posterior aspect of the lower leg. Then, it goes along the posterior aspect of the tibia and crosses and goes in front of the Liver Meridian of Foot-Jueyin. After that, it travels along the anterior medial aspect of the knee and thigh and enters the abdomen, pertaining to the spleen and connects with the stomach. From there, it goes upwards, passing through the diaphragm and alongside the esophagus to connect with the root of the tongue and spread over its lower surface. The branch arising from the stomach goes upward, passes through the diaphragm and flows into the heart, where it links with the Heart Meridian of Hand-Shaoyin.

隐白 Yǐnbái (SP 1)

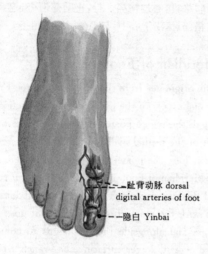

趾背动脉 dorsal digital arteries of foot

隐白 Yinbai

〔取穴法〕(1)在足大趾末节内侧,距趾甲角 0.1 寸(指寸)处。

(2)正坐垂足或仰卧,于足大趾爪甲的侧缘线与基底部线之交点处取穴。

〔功效与主治〕统血,宁神。便血,尿血,月经过多,崩漏,癫狂,梦魇。

〔操作〕浅刺 0.1 寸,或用三棱针点刺出血。

〔备注〕足太阴脾经"井"穴。

Method of locating the point:

(1) This point is on the medial aspect of the phalangette of the great toe, 0.1 cun distal to the corner of the nail.

(2) Ask patient to sit erect with his feet dropped or lie flat, locate the point at the crossing point of the line drawn along the medial side of the nail of the great toe and that drawn along the base of the nail.

Actions and indications: Control blood flow and calm the mind, used to treat hematochezia, hematuria, menorrhagia, metrostaxis and metrorrhagia, mania, epilepsy, and dream-disturbed sleep.

Manipulation: Puncture superficially 0.1 cun, or prick with a three edged needle to cause bleeding.

Notes: This point is the Jing-Well point of the Spleen Meridian of Foot-Taiyin.

太白 Tàibái (SP 3)

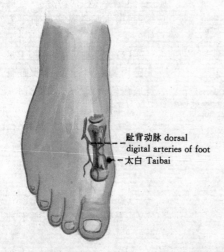

趾背动脉 dorsal digital arteries of foot

太白 Taibai

〔取穴法〕(1)在足内侧缘,当足大趾本节(第1跖趾关节)后下方赤白肉际凹陷处。

(2)正坐或垂足,于足大趾内侧缘,当第1跖趾关节后缘凹陷处取穴。

〔功效与主治〕通经活络,健脾和胃。腹胀,肠鸣,体重节痛。

〔操作〕直刺0.3~0.5寸。

〔备注〕足太阴脾经"输"、"原"穴。

Method of locating the point:

(1) This point is on the medial aspect of the foot, in the depression at the junction of white and red skin posterioinferior to the first metatarsophalangeal joint.

(2) Ask patient to sit erect with his feet dropped, locate the point on the medial border of the great toe, in the depression posterioinferior to the first metatarsophalangeal joint.

Actions and indications: Promote blood flow in channels and collaterals, strengthen the spleen and the stomahc, used to treat abdominal fullness, borborygmus, heaviness of body and arthralgia.

Manipulation: Puncture perpendicularly 0.3—0.5 cun.

Notes: This point is the Shu-Stream and the Yuan-Source point of the Spleen Meridian of Foot-Taiyin.

公孙 Gōngsūn (SP 4)

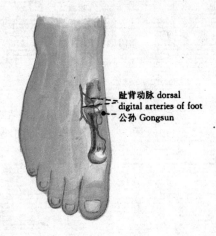

趾背动脉 dorsal digital arteries of foot
公孙 Gongsun

〔取穴法〕(1)在足内侧缘,当第1趾骨基底的前下方处。

(2)正坐垂足或仰卧,于足大趾内侧后方,正当第1趾骨基底内侧的前下方,距太白穴1寸处取之。

〔功效与主治〕理脾和胃,调冲脉。心胸胃痛,呕吐,腹痛。

〔操作〕直刺 0.5～0.8寸。

〔备注〕足太阴脾经"络"穴;八脉交会穴之一,通于冲脉。

Method of locating the point:

(1) This point is on the medial aspect of the foot, antero-inferior to the base of the first metatarsal bone.

(2) Ask patient to sit erect with his feet dropped or lie on his back, locate the point posterior to the medial aspect of the great toe, antero-inferior to the base of the first metatarsal bone, 1 cun distal to Taibai (SP 1).

Actions and indications: Regulate the function of the spleen and the stomach and normalize the Chong Meridian, used to treat cardiac pain, chest pain, stomachache, vomiting and abdominal pain.

Manipulation: Puncture perpendicularly 0.5—0.8 cun.

Notes: This point is the Luo-Connecting point of the Spleen Meridian of Foot-Taiyin. It is also one of the confluence points of the eight meridians, communicating with the Chong Meridian.

商丘 Shānggiū（SP 5）

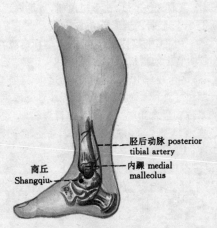

商丘
Shangqiu

胫后动脉 posterior tibial artery

内踝 medial malleolus

〔取穴法〕（1）在足内踝前下方凹陷中，当舟骨结节与内踝尖连线的中点处。

（2）正坐垂足或仰卧，于内踝前缘直线与内踝下缘横线之交点处取穴。

〔功效与主治〕健脾利湿。腹胀，肠鸣，泄泻，黄疸，踝部肿痛。

〔操作〕直刺 0.3～0.5 寸。

〔备注〕足太阴脾经"经"穴。

Method of locating the point：

(1) This point is in the depression antero-inferior to the medial malleolus, at the midpoint of the line connecting the tuberosity of the navicular bone and the tip of the medial malleolus.

(2) When patient sits erect with his foot dropped or takes a supine position, locate the point at the crossing point of the vertical line drawn along the anterior border of the medial malleolus and the horizontal line drawn along the lower border of the medial malleolus.

Actions and indications：Strengthen the spleen to remove dampness, used to treat abdominal distension, borborygmus, diarrhea, jaundice and swelling and pain of the ankle.

Manipulation：Puncture perpendicularly 0.3—0.5 cun.

Notes：This point is the Jing-River point of the Spleen Meridian of Foot-Taiyin.

81

三阴交 Sānyīnjiāo (SP 5)

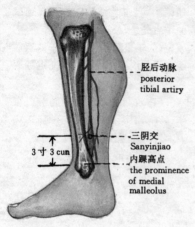

胫后动脉
posterior
tibial artiry

三阴交
Sanyinjiao

3寸 3 cun

内踝高点
the prominence
of medial
malleolus

〔取穴法〕(1)在小腿内侧,当足内踝尖上3寸,胫骨内侧缘后方处。

(2)正坐或仰卧,于胫骨内侧面后缘,内踝尖直上四横指(一夫)处取穴。

〔功效与主治〕补脾胃,助运化,通经络,调和气血。本穴是治疗消化系统和泌尿生殖系统病症常用要穴。主治脾胃虚弱,心腹胀满,妇人癥瘕,崩漏,月经不调,痛经,经闭,遗尿,失眠,眩晕。

〔操作〕直刺1~1.5寸。

〔备注〕足太阴、足少阴与足厥阴经交会穴。孕妇禁针。

Method of locating the point:

(1) This point is on the medial aspect of the lower leg, 3 cun above the tip of the medial malleolus, posterior to the medial border of the tibia.

(2) When patient sits or lies on his back, locate the point on the posterior border of the medial aspect of the tibia, four finger breadth directly above the tip of the medial malleolus.

Actions and indications: Tonify the spleen and the stomach, aid digestion, promote flow of Qi and blood in the channels and collaterals, and regulate Qi and blood. This point is an important commonly used point for diseases of the digestive, the urinary and reproductive systems, it is used to treat deficiency of the spleen and stomach, distension of the abdomen, abdominal masses in females, metrostaxis and metrorrhagia, irregular menstruation, dysmenorrhea, amenorrhea, enuresis, insomnia and dizziness.

Manipulation: Puncture perpendicularly 1—1.5 cun.

Notes: This point is the crossing point of the Spleen Meridian of Foot-Taiyin, the Kidney Meridian of Foot-Shaoyin and the Liver Meridian of Foot-Jueyin. Acupuncture is contraindicated in pregnant women.

漏谷 Lòugǔ (SP 7)

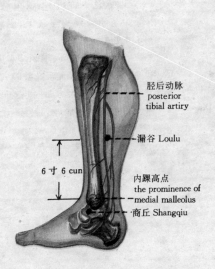

胫后动脉
posterior
tibial artiry

漏谷 Loulu

6 寸 6 cun

内踝高点
the prominence of
medial malleolus

商丘 Shangqiu

〔取穴法〕（1）在小腿内侧，当内踝尖与阴陵泉的连线上，距内踝尖 6 寸，胫骨内侧缘后方取穴。

（2）正坐或仰卧，于三阴交穴直上 3 寸，当胫骨内侧面后缘处取穴。

〔功效与主治〕渗湿利水。小便不利，腹胀，腿膝厥冷。

〔操作〕直刺 0.5～0.8寸。

Method of locating the point:

(1) This point is located on the medial aspect of the lower leg, on the line connecting the tip of the medial malleolus and Yinlingquan (SP 9), 6 cun above the tip of the medial malleolus, on the posterior border of the medial aspect of the tibia.

(2) Ask patient to take a sitting or a supine position, locate the point 3 cun above Sanyinjiao (SP 6), on the posterior border of the medial aspect of the tibia.

Actions and indications: Induce diuresis, used to treat difficulty in urination, abdominal distension and coldness of loins and knees.

Manipulation: Puncture perpendicularly 0.5—0.8 cun.

地机 Dìjī (SP 8)

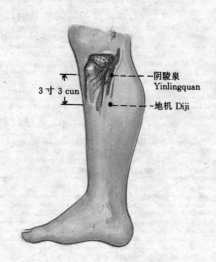

阴陵泉
Yinlingquan

3寸 3 cun

地机 Dìjī

〔取穴法〕(1)在小腿内侧,当内踝尖与阴陵泉的连线上,阴陵泉下3寸处。

(2)正坐或仰卧,于阴陵泉穴直下3寸,胫骨内侧面后缘处取穴。

〔功效与主治〕调和营血,健脾。腹胀,遗精,痛经,月经不调。

〔操作〕直刺0.5~1寸。

〔备注〕足太阴脾经"郄"穴。

Method of locating the point:

(1) This point is on the medial aspect of the lower leg, on the line connecting the tip of the medial malleolus and Yinlingquan (SP 9), 3 cun below Yinlingquan (SP 9).

(2) When patient takes a sitting or a supine position, locate the point 3 cun directly below Yinlingquan (SP 9), on the posterior border of the medial aspect of the tibia.

Actions and indications: Regulate nutritive Qi and blood and strengthen the spleen, used to treat abdominal distension, emission, dysmenorrhea and irregular menstruation.

Manipulation: Puncture perpendicularly 0.5—1 cun.

Notes: This point is the Xi-Cleft point of the Spleen Meridian of Foot-Taiyin.

84

阴陵泉 Yīnlíngquán (SP 9)

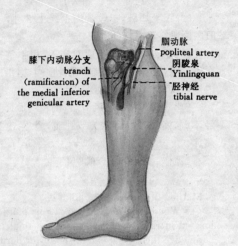

膝下内动脉分支 branch (ramificarion) of the medial inferior genicular artery

腘动脉 popliteal artery

阴陵泉 Yinlingquan

胫神经 tibial nerve

〔取穴法〕（1）在小腿内侧，当胫骨内侧髁后下方凹陷处。

（2）正坐屈膝或仰卧，于膝部内侧，胫骨内侧髁下缘，与胫骨粗隆下缘平齐处取穴。

〔功效与主治〕清化湿热，通利三焦，健脾利水。腹胀，水肿，小便不利，下肢肿痛。

〔操作〕直刺 0.3～0.5寸。

〔备注〕足太阴脾经"合"穴。

Method of locating the point:

(1) This point is on the medial aspect of the lower leg, in the depression posteroinferior to the medial condyle of the tibia.

(2) Ask patient to take a sitting position with his knee flexed or take a supine position, locate the point on the medial side of the knee, on the lower border of the medial condyle of the tibia, at the level of the lower border of the tuberosity of the tibia.

Actions and indications: Clear away heat and remove dampness, promote flow of fluid in the Sanjiao, and strengthen the spleen to induce diuresis, used to treat abdominal distension, edema, dysuria, and swelling and pain of the lower limbs.

Manipulation: Puncture perpendicularly 0.3—0.5 cun.

Notes: This point is the He-Sea point of the Spleen Meridian of Foot-Taiyin.

血海 Xuèhǎi (SP 10)

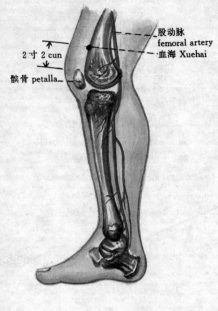

股动脉 femoral artery

血海 Xuehai

2寸 2 cun

髌骨 petalla

(1)

〔取穴法〕(1)屈膝,在大腿内侧,髌底内侧端上2寸,当股四头肌侧头的隆起处。

(2)正坐屈膝,于髌骨内上缘上2寸,当股内侧肌突起中点处取穴。

(3)正坐屈膝,医生面对病人,用手掌按在病人膝盖上,掌心对准膝盖骨顶端,拇指向内侧,当拇指尖所到之处是穴。

〔功效与主治〕祛风清热,调和气血。月经不调,痛经,经闭,膝关节肿痛,瘾疹,全身瘙痒。

〔操作〕直刺0.5～0.8寸。

Method of locating the point:

(1) When the knee is flexed, this point is located in the medial aspect of the thigh, 2 cun above the medial end of the lower border of the patella, on the bulge of the medial portion of m. quadriceps femoris.

(2) Ask patient to sit erect with his knee flexed, locate the point 2 cun above the medial superior border of the petalla, in the centre of the bulges of the medial portion of m. quadriceps femoris.

(3) Ask patient to sit erect with his knees flexed. Facing the patient, the doctor places his palm on the patient's knee with the centre of the plam placed on the upper border of the patella and the thumb placed inward, locate the point where the tip of the thumb touches.

Actions and indications: Expel wind, disperse heat, regulate Qi and blood, used to treat irregular menstruation, dysmenorrhea, amenorrhea, swelling and pain of the knee

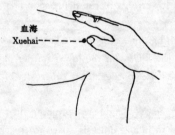

血海
Xuehai

(2)

joint, urticaria, and itching of the whole body.

Manipulation: Puncture perpendicularly 0.5—0.8 cun.

箕门 Jīmén（SP 11）

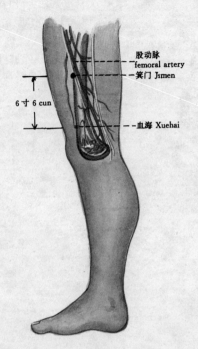

股动脉 femoral artery
箕门 Jīmen
6寸 6 cun
血海 Xuehai

〔取穴法〕（1）在大腿内侧，当血海穴与冲门穴连线上，血海上6寸处。

（2）正坐屈膝，两腿微张开，于缝匠肌内侧缘，距血海穴上6寸处取穴。

〔功效与主治〕利水通淋。小便不利，腹股肿痛，遗尿。

〔操作〕避开动脉，直刺0.3～0.5寸。

Method of locating the point：

(1) This point is located on the medial aspect of the thigh, on the line joining Xuehai (SP 10) and Chongmen (SP 12), 6 cun above Xuehai (SP 10).

(2) Ask patient to take a sitting position with his knee flexed and the two legs slight opened, locate the point on the medial border of the sartorias muscle, 6 cun above Xuehai (SP 10).

Actions and indications：Induce diuresis and relieve stranguria, used to treat dysuria, swelling and pain of the abdomen and buttock, and enuresis.

Manipulation：Puncture perpendicularly 0.3 — 0.5 cun. Avoid injurying the artery.

腹结 Fùjié (SP 14)

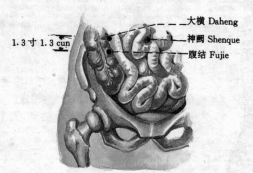

大横 Daheng
神阙 Shenque
腹结 Fujie

1.3寸 1.3 cun

〔取穴法〕(1)在下腹部，大横下1.3寸，距前正中线4寸处取穴。

(2)仰卧，先取气海穴，于其旁开4寸，再略向上0.2寸处取穴。

〔功效与主治〕行气血，调肠腑。绕脐腹痛，疝气，痢疾。

〔操作〕直刺 0.5～0.7寸。

Method of locating the point：

(1) This point is in the lower abdomen，1.3 cun below Daheng (SP 13)，4 cun lateral to the anterior midline.

(2) Ask patient to take a supine position，locate Qihai (RN 6) first，then locate Fujie (SP 14) 0.2 cun above the area 4 cun lateral to Qihai (RN 6).

Actions and indications：Promote flow of Qi and blood，regulate the function of the intestine，used to treat pain around the umbilicus，hernia and dysentery.

Manipulation：Puncture perpendicularly 0.5－0.7 cun.

大横 Dàheng (SP 15)

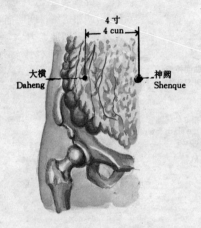

〔取穴法〕(1)在腹中部,脐中旁开 4 寸处。

(2)仰卧,先取肚脐中央的神阙穴,于其旁开 4 寸处是穴。

〔功效与主治〕通调肠腑。痢疾,泄泻,便秘,肠痈,腹痛。

〔操作〕直刺 0.5～1 寸。

〔备注〕足太阴与阴维脉交会穴。

Method of locating the point:

(1) This point is located in the abdomen, 4 cun lateral to the centre of the umbilicus.

(2) When the patient is in a supine position, locate Shenque point (RN 8) in the centre of the umbilicus, then locate Daheng (SP 15) 4 cun lateral to it.

Actions and indications: Promote flow of Qi in the intestine and regulate function of the intestine, used to treat dysentery, diarrhea, constipation, intestinal carbuncle and abdominal pain.

Manipulation: Puncture perpendicularly 0.5 - 1 cun.

Notes: This point is the crossing point of the Spleen Meridian of Foot-Taiyin and the Yinwei Meridian.

大包 Dàbāo (SP 21)

〔取穴法〕在侧胸部，腋中线上，当第 6 肋间隙处取穴。

〔功效与主治〕宽胸利胁，调和诸络。胸胁痛，全身疼痛，四肢无力。

〔操作〕平刺或斜刺 0.5～0.8 寸。

〔备注〕脾的"络"穴。

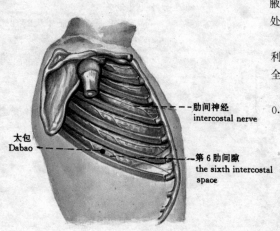

大包
Dabao

肋间神经
intercostal nerve

第 6 肋间隙
the sixth intercostal space

Method of locating the point: This point is located on the side of the chest, on the mid-axillary line, in the sixth intercostal space.

Actions and indications: Relieve stagnation of Qi in the chest and hypochondrium, regulate flow of Qi in all the channels, used to treat pain in the chest and hypochondrium, pain of the whole body and lassitude of the four limbs.

Manipulation: Puncture perpendicularly or obliquely 0.5—0.8 cun.

Notes: This point is the Luo-Connecting point of the spleen.

五、手少阴心经

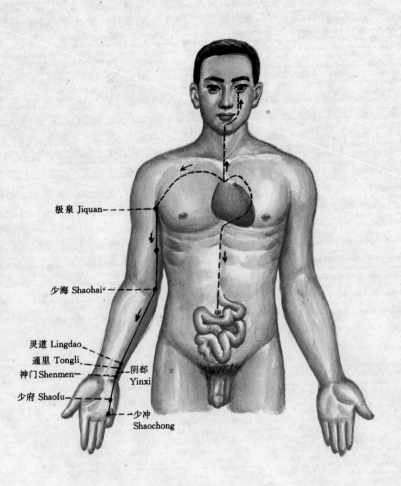

极泉 Jiquan

少海 Shaohai

灵道 Lingdao
通里 Tongli
神门 Shenmen
少府 Shaofu

阴郄
Yinxi

少冲
Shaochong

起于心中,出属"心系"(心与其他脏器相连系的部位),通过横膈,联络小肠。心系向上的脉:挟着咽喉上行,连系"目系"(眼球连系于脑的部位);心系直行的脉:上行于肺部,再向下出于腋窝部(极泉),沿着上臂内侧后缘,行于手太阴经和手厥阴经的后面,到达肘窝,沿前臂内侧后缘,至掌后豌豆骨部,进入掌内,沿小指内侧至末端(少冲),与手太阳小肠经相接。

5. The Heart Meridian of Hand-Shaoyin

The Heart Meridian of Hand-Shaoyin originates from the heart. Emerging, it spreads to the "heart system" (the tissues connecting the heart with the other zang-fu organs). Then, it passes through the diaphragm to connect with the small intestine. The ascending portion of the meridian from the "heart system" runs upwards along the esophagus to connect with the "eye system" (the tissues connecting the eyeball with the brain). The straight portion of the meridian from the "heart system" goes upwards to the lung, then it turns downwards and emergies from the axilla (Jiquan, HT 1). From there, it goes along the posterior border of the medial aspect of the upper arm behind the Lung Meridian of Hand-Taiyin and the Pericardium Meridian of Hand-Jueyin, down to the cubital fossa. Then it runs along the posterior border of the medial aspect of the forearm, passes through the pisiform region paroxysmal to the palm and enters the palm. Then, it follows the medial aspect of the little finger to its tip (Shaochong, HT 9) to link with the Small Intestine of Hand-Taiyang.

极泉 Jíquán (HT 1)

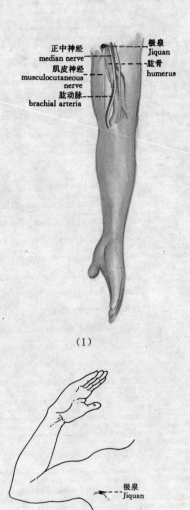

正中神经
median nerve
肌皮神经
musculocutaneous
nerve
肱动脉
brachial arteria

极泉
Jiquan
肱骨
humerus

（1）

极泉
Jiquan

（2）

〔取穴法〕屈肘，手掌按于后枕，于腋窝中部有动脉搏动处取穴。

〔功效与主治〕疏筋活血。心痛，胁痛，腋臭，上肢不遂。

〔操作〕上肢上抬外展，避开动脉向上斜刺0.2～0.3寸。

Method of locating the point: Locate the point at the centre of the axillary fossa where a pulsation is felt when the elbow is flexed and the palm is placed over the occiput.

Actions and indications: Relax muscles and tendons and promote flow of blood, used to treat cardiac pain, hypochondriac pain, bromhidrosis and paralysis of the upper limb.

Manipulation: Puncture upwards obliquely 0.2－0.3 cun when the upper arm is abducted. Avoid puncturing the axillary artery.

93

少海 Shàohǎi (HT 3)

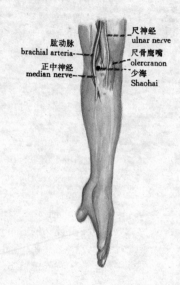

肱动脉 brachial arteria
正中神经 median nerve

尺神经 ulnar nerve
尺骨鹰嘴 olercranon
少海 Shaohai

(1)

〔取穴法〕(1)屈肘,在肘横纹内侧端与肱骨内上髁连线的中点处取穴。

(2)屈肘举臂,以手抱头,在肘内侧横纹尽头处取穴。

〔功效与主治〕清热泄火,安神宁志。心痛,手颤肘挛,两臂顽麻。

〔操作〕直刺 0.5~0.8 寸。

〔备注〕手少阴心经"合"穴。

Method of locating the point:

(1) When the elbow is flexed, locate the point at the midpoint of the line connecting the medial end of the transverse crease of the elbow with the medial epicondyle of the humerus.

(2) Ask patient to flex his elbow and lift his arm with his hands placed on the two sides of the head, locate the point at the end of the medial transverse crease of the elbow.

Actions and indications: Clear away heat and purge fire and tranquilize the mind, used to treat cardiac pain, tremor of hands and convulsion of the elbow, and intractable numbness of the arms.

Manipulations: Puncture perpendicularly 0.5—0.8 cun.

Notes: This point is the He-Sea point of the Heart Meridian of Hand-Shaoyin.

少海 Shaohai

(2)

灵道 Língdào (HT 4)

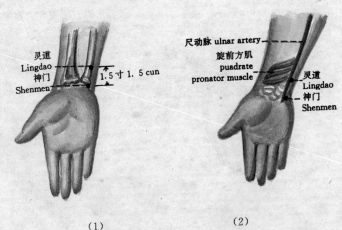

灵道
Lingdao
神门
Shenmen
1.5寸 1.5 cun

尺动脉 ulnar artery
旋前方肌
puadrate
pronator muscle
灵道
Lingdao
神门
Shenmen

(1)   (2)

〔取穴法〕(1)在前臂掌侧,当尺侧腕屈肌腱的桡侧缘,腕横纹上1.5寸处取穴。

(2)在神门穴与少海穴连线上,距神门穴1.5寸处取穴。

〔功效与主治〕疏筋活络,安神宁心。心痛悲恐,暴喑,肘臂挛急疼痛。

〔操作〕直刺0.2～0.3寸。

〔备注〕手少阴心经"经"穴。

Method of locating the point:

(1) This point is on the palmar side of the forearm, in the radial end of the tendon of m. flexor carpi ulnaris, 1.5 cun above the transverse crease of the wrist.

(2) Locate the point on the line connecting Shenmen (HT 7) with Shaohai (HT 3), 1.5 cun distal to Shenmen (HT 7).

Actions and indications: Relax muscles and tendons, promote blood flow in the collaterals and transquilize the mind, used to treat cardiac pain with grief or fright, sudden hoarseness, spasm and pain of the elbow and arm.

Manipulation: Puncture perpendicularly 0.2—0.3 cun.

Notes: This point is the Jing-River point of the Heart Meridian of Hand-Shaoyin.

通里 Tōnglǐ (HT 5)

正中神经 median nerve
旋前方肌 puadrate pronator muscle
通里 Tongli
神门 Shenmen
1 寸 1 cun

〔取穴法〕（1）在前臂掌侧，当尺侧腕屈肌腱的桡侧缘，腕横纹上 1 寸处。

（2）在神门穴与少海穴连线上，距神门穴 1 寸处。

〔功效与主治〕养血安神，熄风开音。暴喑，舌强不语，心悸，怔忡。

〔操作〕直刺 0.3～0.5寸。

〔备注〕手少阴心经"络"穴。

Method of locating the point:

(1) This point is on the palmar side of the forearm, on the radial end of the tendon of m. flexor carpi ulnaris, 1 cun above the transverse crease of the wrist.

(2) Locate the point on the line connecting Shenmen (HT 7) with Shaohai (HT 3), 1 cun distal to Shenmen (HT 7).

Actions and indications: Nourish blood, tranquilize the mind and relieve hoarseness, used to treat sudden hoarseness, aphasia due to stiffness of tongue, palpitation or severe palpitation.

Manipulation: Puncture perpendicularly 0.3—0.5 cun.

Notes: This point is the Luo-Connecting point of the Heart Meridian of Hand-Shaoyin.

阴郄 Yīnxì (HT 6)

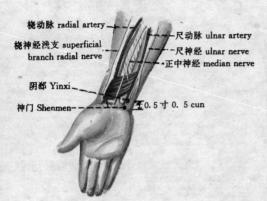

桡动脉 radial artery
桡神经浅支 superficial branch radial nerve
阴郄 Yinxi
神门 Shenmen
尺动脉 ulnar artery
尺神经 ulnar nerve
正中神经 median nerve
0.5 寸 0.5 cun

〔取穴法〕(1)在前臂掌侧,当尺侧腕屈肌腱的桡侧缘,腕横纹上 0.5 寸处。

(2)在神门穴与少海穴连线上,距神门穴 0.5 寸处。

〔功效与主治〕滋养阴血,宁心安神。心痛,心悸,骨蒸盗汗。

〔操作〕直刺 0.3～0.5寸。

〔备注〕手少阴心经"郄"穴。

Method of locating the point:

(1) This point is on the palmar side of the forearm, on the radial end of the tendon of m. flexor carpi ulnaris, 0.5 cun above the transverse crease of the wrist.

(2) Locate the point on the line connecting Shenmen (HT 7) with Shaohai (HT 3), 0.5 cun proximal to Shenmen (HT 7).

Actions and indications: Nourish yin-blood and tranquilize the mind, used to treat cardiac pain, palpitation, night sweating due to bone-heat.

Manipulation: Puncture perpendicularly 0.3—0.5 cun.

Notes: This point is the Xi-Cleft point of the Heart Meridian of Hand-Shaoyin.

神门 Shénmén（HT 7）

〔取穴法〕（1）在腕部，腕掌侧横纹尺侧端，尺侧腕屈肌腱的桡侧凹陷处。

（2）仰掌，于豌豆骨后缘桡侧，当掌后第1横纹上取穴。

〔功效与主治〕镇静，安神，宁心，通络。心痛，心烦，失眠，健忘，惊悸。

〔操作〕直刺 0.2～0.4寸。

〔备注〕手少阴心经"输"、"原"穴。

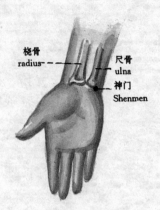

桡骨
radius

尺骨
ulna

神门
Shenmen

Method of locating the point:

(1) This point is located on the wrist, at the ulnar end of the palmar transverse crease of the wrist, in the depression of the radial side of the tendon of m. flexor carpi ulnaris.

(2) When the palm is facing upwards, locate the point on the posterior border of the pisiform bone, on the first transverse crease of the wrist.

Actions and indications: Tranquilize the mind and rest the heart, used to treat cardiac pain, restlessness, insomnia, forgetfulness and palpitation.

Manipulation: Puncture perpendicularly 0.2—0.4 cun.

Notes: This point is the Shu-Stream point and the Yuan-Primary point of the Heart Meridian of Hand-Shaoyin.

少府 Shàofǔ（HT 8）

〔取穴法〕(1)在手掌面，第四五掌骨之间，握拳时，当小指尖处是穴。

(2)在手掌尺侧，第四五掌骨之间，当掌骨头后缘之凹陷处。

〔功效与主治〕清心调神。心悸，掌中热，悲笑，阴痒。

〔操作〕直刺 0.3～0.5 寸。

〔备注〕手少阴心经"荥"穴。

掌心动脉
arteriae metacarpeae
少府 Shaofu

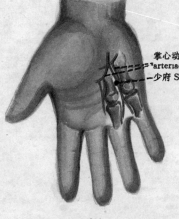

(1)

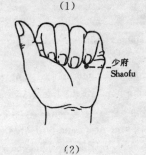

少府
Shaofu

(2)

Method of locating the point:

(1) This point is on the palm, between the 4th and the 5th metacarpal bones. When a fist is made, it is located at the place where the tip of the small finger touches.

(2) Locate the point on the ulnar side of the palm, between the 4th and the 5th metacarpal bones, in the depression posterior to the head of the metacarpal bones.

Actions and indications: Clear away heat from the heart and regulate the mentality, used to treat palpitation, hotness in the palm, liability to get sorrow or excited, pruritis of the external genital.

Manipulation: Puncture perpendicularly 0.3—0.5 cun.

Notes: This point is the Ying-Spring point of the Heart Meridian of Hand-Shaoyin.

少冲 Shàochōng (HT 9)

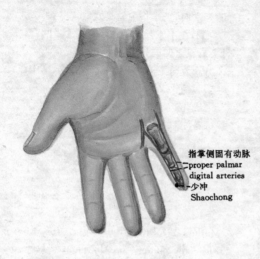

指掌侧固有动脉
proper palmar
digital arteries
少冲
Shaochong

〔取穴法〕(1)在手小指末节桡侧,距指甲角 0.1 寸(指寸)处。

(2)微握拳,掌心向下,小指上翘,于小指爪甲桡侧缘与基底部各作一线,二线相交处取穴。

〔功效与主治〕开窍泄热,宣通气血。中风,热病,烦满。为急救穴之一。

〔操作〕针 0.1 寸,或用三棱针点刺出血。

〔备注〕手少阴心经"井"穴。

Method of locating the point:

(1) This point is on the radial side of the phalangette of the little finger, 0.1 cun lateral to the corner of the nail.

(2) When a loose fist is made with palm facing dowards and the little finger tilted upward slightly, locate the point at the crossing point of the line drawn along the radial side of the nail and that drawn along the base of the nail.

Actions and indications: Restore resuscitation, purge heat, and promote flow of Qi and blood, used to treat apoplexy, febrile diseases, restlessness and chest fullness. It is a point used for emergency case.

Manipulation: Puncture perpendicularly 0.1 cun, or prick with a three edged needle to cause bleeding.

Notes: This point is the Jing-Well point of the Heart Meridian of Hand-Shaoyin.

六、手太阳小肠经

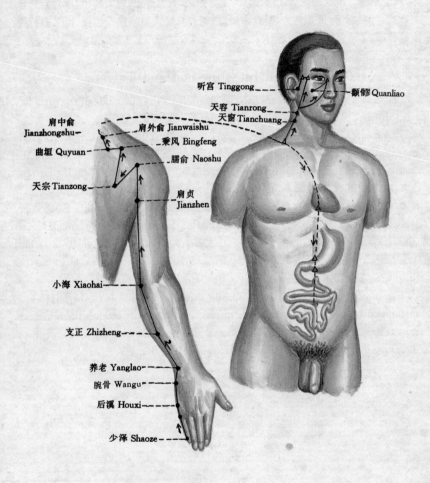

听宫 Tinggong
颧髎 Quanliao
天容 Tianrong
天窗 Tianchuang
肩中俞 Jianzhongshu
肩外俞 Jianwaishu
秉风 Bingfeng
曲垣 Quyuan
臑俞 Naoshu
天宗 Tianzong
肩贞 Jianzhen
小海 Xiaohai
支正 Zhizheng
养老 Yanglao
腕骨 Wangu
后溪 Houxi
少泽 Shaoze

起于手小指外侧端(少泽),沿着手背外侧至腕部,出于尺骨茎突,直上沿着前臂外侧后缘,经尺骨鹰嘴与肱骨内上髁之间,沿上臂外侧后缘,出于肩关节,绕行肩胛部,交会于大椎(督脉),向下进入缺盆部,联络心脏,沿着食管,通过横膈,到达胃部,属于小肠。缺盆部支脉:沿着颈部,上达面颊,至目外眦,转入耳中(听宫);颊部支脉:上行目眶下,抵于鼻旁,至目内眦(睛明),与足太阳膀胱经相接,而又斜行终于颧骨部。

6. The Small Intestine of Hand-Taiyang

The Small Meridian of Hand-Taiyang starts from the ulnar side of the little finger (Shaoze, SI 1). It travels along the ulnar side of the dorsum of hand to the wrist and emerges from the styloid process of the ulna. Running along the posterior border of the lateral side of the forearm, passing between the olecranon of the ulna and the medial epicondyle of the humerus, it runs upwards along the posterior border of the upper arm to the shoulder joint. Then it runs around the scapular region and meets at Dazhui (DU 14). From there it turns downwards to the supraclavicular fossa and further connects with the heart. It then runs through the diaphragm along the esophagus to the stomach, pertaining to the small intestine. The branch starting from the supraclavicular fossa ascends to the neck and further to the cheek. Then it enters the outer canthus and turns to enter the ear (Tinggong, SI 19). The branch from the cheek goes upwards to the infraorbital region and further to the lateral side of the nose. Then, it reaches the inner canthus (Jingming, BL 1), where it links with the Bladder Meridian of Foot-Taiyang. Then it runs obliquely to the zygomatic region.

少泽 Shàozé（SI 1）

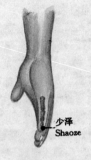

少泽
Shaoze

〔取穴法〕（1）在手小指末节尺侧，距指甲角 0.1 寸（指寸）处。

（2）微握拳，掌心向下，伸小指，于小指爪甲尺侧缘和基底部各作一线，两线相交处取穴。

〔功效与主治〕通经活络，开窍，利乳。乳痈，乳少。

〔操作〕毫针浅刺 0.1 寸，或用三棱针点刺出血。

〔备注〕手太阳小肠经"井"穴。

Method of locating the point:

(1) This point is on the ulnar side of the phalangette of the little finger, 0.1 cun lateral to the nail.

(2) When a loose fist is made with the palm facing downwards and the little finger stretched, locate the point at the crossing point of the line drawn along the ulnar side of the nail of the little finger and that drawn along the base of the nail of the little finger.

Actions and indications: Promote flow of Qi and blood in the channels and collaterals, restore resuscitation and promote discharge of milk, used to treat acute mastitis and hypogalactation.

Manipulation: Puncture 0.1 cun superficially with a filiform needle, or prick with a three edged needle to cause bleeding.

Notes: This point is the Jing-Well point of the Small Intestine Meridian of Hand-Taiyang.

后溪 Hòuxī (SI 3)

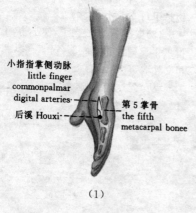

小指指掌侧动脉
little finger
commonpalmar
digital arteries

后溪 Houxi

第5掌骨
the fifth
metacarpal bonee

(1)

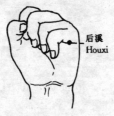

后溪
Houxi

(2)

〔取穴法〕(1)在手掌尺侧,微握拳,当小指末节(第5掌指关节)后的远侧掌横纹头赤白肉际处。

(2)在第5掌指关节后缘尺侧,横纹头赤白肉际处取穴。

〔功效与主治〕宁心安神,清热利湿,通督脉。头项颈肩部疼痛,耳聋,疟疾,手指拘急疼痛,腰扭伤。

〔操作〕直刺0.5~0.8寸。

〔备注〕手太阳小肠经"输"穴;八脉交会穴之一,通于督脉。

Method of locating the point:

(1) This point is on the ulnar side of the palm. When a loose fist is made, the point is at the junction of the red and white skin, at the end of the distal transverse crease of the palm proximal to the fifth metacarpophalangeal joint.

(2) Locate the point on the ulnar side on the posterior border of the fifth metacarpophalangeal joint, at the junction of the red and white skin on the end of the transverse crease.

Actions and indications: Tranquilize the mind, clear away heat, remove dampness and promote flow of Qi and blood in the Du Meridian, used to treat pain in the head, nape, neck and shoulder, deafness, malaria, convulsion and pain of the fingers and lumbar sprain.

Manipulation: Puncture perpendicularly 0.5—0.8 cun.

Notes: This point is the Shu-Stream point of the Small Intestine Meridian of Hand-Taiyang. It is also one of the confluence points of the eight meridians, communicating with the Du Meridian.

腕骨 Wàngǔ (SI 4)

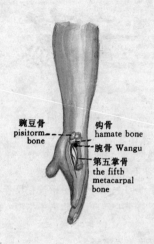

腕豆骨 pisitorm bone
钩骨 hamate bone
腕骨 Wangu
第五掌骨 the fifth metacarpal bone

〔取穴法〕(1)在手掌尺侧,当第 5 掌骨基底与钩骨之间的凹陷处,赤白肉际处。

(2)侧掌,掌心向前,由后溪穴直向上推,当两骨(第 5 掌骨基底与三角骨)结合部的凹陷中取穴。

〔功效与主治〕疏筋活络。头痛项强,肩臂疼痛、麻木,腕痛。

〔操作〕直刺 0.5～1 寸。

〔备注〕手太阳小肠经"原"穴。

Method of locating the point:

(1) This point is on the ulnar side of the palm, in the depression between the base of the fifth metacarpophalangeal joint and the triquetral bone.

(2) When the palm is placed erect with palm facing forwards, press from Houxi (SI 3) forwards until a depression is felt, then locate the point at the junction of the base of the fifth metacarpophalangeal joint and the triquetral bone.

Actions and indications: Relax tendons and promote flow of blood in the collaterals, used to treat headache, stiff nape, pain and numbness of the shoulder and arm, and pain of the wrist.

Manipulation: Puncture perpendicularly 0.5—1 cun.

Notes: This point is the Yuan-Primary point of the Small Intestine Meridian of Hand-Taiyang.

养老 Yánglǎo (SI 6)

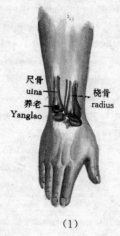

尺骨
ulna
养老
Yanglao
桡骨
radius

(1)

养老 Yanglao

(2)

〔取穴法〕(1)在前臂背面尺侧,当尺骨小头近端桡侧凹陷中。

(2)屈肘,掌心向胸,在尺骨小头高点平齐处的桡侧缘凹陷中。

(3)掌心向下,用另一手指按在尺骨小头的最高点上,然后掌心转向胸部,当手指滑入的骨缝中是穴。

〔功效与主治〕疏筋,明目。目视不明,腕关节疼痛。

〔操作〕斜刺 0.3~0.5 寸。

〔备注〕手太阳小肠经"郄"穴。

Method of locating the point:

(1) This point is on the ulnar side of the dorsal aspect of the forearm, in the depression of the proximal end of the radial aspect of the styloid process of the ulna.

(2) When the elbow is flexed with the palm facing the chest, locate the point in the radial border at the level of the highest point of the styloid process of the ulna.

(3) When the palm is facing downwards, place the other hand over the highest point of the styloid process of the ulna, then turn the palm towards the chest, and locate the point in the space of bones the finger slides into.

Actions and indications: Relax tendons and improve eyesight, used to treat blurred vision and pain of the wrist joint.

Manipulation: Puncture obliquely 0.3—0.5 cun.

Notes: This point is the Xi-Cleft point of the Small Intestine Meridian of Hand-Taiyang.

支正 Zhīzhèng (SI 7)

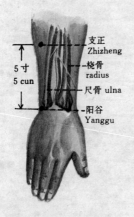

支正 Zhizheng
桡骨 radius
尺骨 ulna
阳谷 Yanggu

5 寸
5 cun

〔取穴法〕（1）在前臂背面尺侧，当阳谷与小海的连线上，腕背横纹上 5 寸处。

（2）手上举，本穴在阳谷穴上 5 寸，当阳谷与小海的连线上，尺骨的里侧面上。

〔功效与主治〕解表清热，宁神。头痛，热病，肘臂挛痛，皮肤赘疣。

〔操作〕直刺 0.3～0.5 寸。

〔备注〕手太阳小肠经"络"穴。

Method of locating the point:

(1) This point is on the ulnar side of the dorsal aspect of the forearm, on the line connecting Yanggu (SI 5) and Xiaohai (SI 8), 5 cun above the transverse crease of the wrist.

(2) When the hand is lifted, this point is 5 cun below Yanggu (SI 5), on the line connecting Yanggu (SI 5) and Xiaohai (SI 8), on the medial aspect of the ulna.

Actions and indications: Relieve exterior syndrome, clear away heat and tranquilize the mind, used to treat headache, febrile diseases, spasmotic pain of the elbow and upper arm, and cutaneous neoplasm.

Manipulation: Puncture perpendicularly 0.3—0.5 cun.

Notes: This point is the Luo-Connecting point of the Small Intestine Meridian of Hand-Taiyang.

小海 Xiǎohǎi (SI 8)

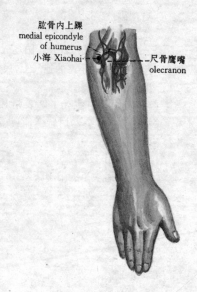

肱骨内上髁
medial epicondyle
of humerus
小海 Xiaohai

尺骨鹰嘴
olecranon

〔取穴法〕(1)在肘内侧,当尺骨鹰嘴与肱骨内上髁之间凹陷处。

(2)微屈肘,与肘窝横纹平齐之尺骨鹰嘴与肱骨内上髁之间;用手指弹敲该部时有触电麻感直达小指。

〔功效与主治〕祛风通经活络。颊肿颈痛,肩臂外后侧痛。

〔操作〕直刺或斜刺 0.3～0.5寸。

〔备注〕手太阳小肠经"合"穴。

Method of locating the point:

(1) This point is on the medial aspect of the elbow, in the depression between the olecranon of the ulna and the medial epicondyle of the humerus.

(2) When the elbow is slightly flexed, locate the point between the olecranon of the ulna of the medial epicondyle of the humerus parallel to the transverse crease of the elbow. When this position is knucked with fingers, a feeling of electric shock transmissing to the little finger can be felt.

Actions and indications: Expel wind, promote flow of Qi and blood in the channels and remove obstruction from the collaterals, used to treat swelling of cheek, pain of the neck, and pain in the lateroposterior aspect of the shoulder and arm.

Manipulation: Puncture perpendicularly or obliquely 0.3—0.5 cun.

Notes: This point is the He-Sea point of the Small Intestine Meridian of Hand-Taiyang.

肩贞 Jiānzhēn (SI 9)

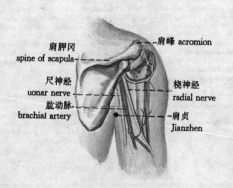

肩胛冈
spine of scapula

尺神经
uonar nerve

肱动脉
brachial artery

肩峰 acromion

桡神经
radial nerve

肩贞
Jianzhen

〔取穴法〕(1)在肩关节后下方,臂内收时,腋后皱襞尽端直上1寸(指寸)处。

(2)正坐垂肩,上臂内收,当腋后纹头直上1寸处是穴。

〔功效与主治〕祛风止痛。肩胛痛,手臂痛麻不举。

〔操作〕直刺0.5～1寸。

Method of locating the point:

(1) This point is postero-inferior to the shoulder joint. When the upper arm is adducted, it is located 1 cun above the posterior end of the axillary fold.

(2) When the patient takes a sitting position with his shoulders dropped and the upper arm adducted, locate the point 1 cun above the posterior end of the axillary fold.

Actions and indications: Expel wind and relieve pain, used to treat pain in the scapular region, pain and numbness of the hand and arm.

Manipulation: Puncture perpendicularly 0.5—1 cun.

臑俞 Nàoshū (SI 10)

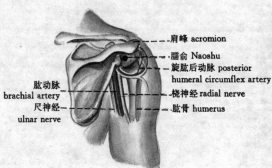

肩峰 acromion
臑俞 Naoshu
旋肱后动脉 posterior humeral circumflex artery
桡神经 radial nerve
肱骨 humerus

肱动脉 brachial artery
尺神经 ulnar nerve

〔取穴法〕（1）在肩部，当腋后纹头直上，肩胛冈下缘凹陷中。

（2）正坐垂肩，上臂内收，用手指从腋后纹端肩贞穴直向上推肩胛冈下缘处是穴。

〔功效与主治〕散风疏筋止痛。肩臂酸痛无力，瘰疬。

〔操作〕直刺 0.5～1 寸。

〔备注〕手、足太阳、阳维脉与阳跷脉交会穴。

Method of locating the point:

(1) This point is on the shoulder, in the depression directly above the posterior end of the axillary crease and the lower border of the scapular spine.

(2) When the patient sits erect with the upper arm adducted, press from Jianzhen (SI 9) which is on the posterior end of the axillary fold upwards to locate the point on the lower border of the scapular spine.

Actions and indications: Expel wind, relax muscles and tendons and relieve pain, used to treat soreness, pain and weaknees of the shoulder and arm, and scrofula.

Manipulation: Puncture perpendicularly 0.5−1 cun.

Notes: This point is the crossing point of the Small Intestine Meridian of Hand-Taiyang, the Bladder Meridian of Foot-Taiyang, the Yangwei Meridian and the Yangqiao Meridian.

天宗 Tiānzōng（SI 11）

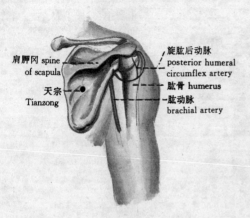

肩胛冈 spine of scapula
天宗 Tianzong

旋肱后动脉 posterior humeral circumflex artery
肱骨 humerus
肱动脉 brachial artery

〔取穴法〕（1）在肩胛部，当冈下窝中央凹陷处，与第4胸椎相平处。

（2）正坐或俯伏，在冈下缘与肩胛骨下角的等分线上，当上、中 1/3 交点处。

（3）正坐或俯伏，肩胛冈下缘与肩胛骨下角连一直线，与第4胸椎棘突下间平齐处，与臑俞、肩贞成三角形处是穴。

〔功效与主治〕疏风活络。肩胛痛，乳痈。

〔操作〕直刺或斜刺 0.5～0.8 寸。

Method of locating the point:

(1) This point is on the scapular region, in the depression of the infrascapular fossa, at the level of the 4th thoracic vertebra.

(2) Ask patient to take a sitting position or a prone position, locate the point at the junction of the upper and middle third of the distance between the lower border of the scapular spine and the inferior angle of the scapula.

(3) Ask patient to take a sitting or a prone position, draw a line from the border of the scapular spine to the inferior angle of the scapula, locate the point parallel to the spinous process of the 4th thoracic vertebra, at the medial angle of the triangle formed by Naoshu (SI 10), Jianzhen (SI 9) and this point.

Actions and indications: Expel wind, activate blood flow in the collaterals, used to treat pain in the scapular region and acute mastitis.

Manipulation: Puncture perpendicularly or obliquely 0.5—0.8 cun.

秉风 Bǐngfēng (SI 12)

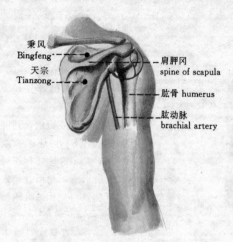

秉风 Bingfeng
天宗 Tianzong
肩胛冈 spine of scapula
肱骨 humerus
肱动脉 brachial artery

〔取穴法〕(1)在肩胛部，冈上窝中央，天宗穴直上，举臂有凹陷处。

(2)正坐俯伏，于肩胛冈上缘中点向上1寸的肩胛冈上窝处取穴，与臑俞、天宗成一三角形处是穴。

〔功效与主治〕疏风活络。肩胛疼痛，肩臂不举。

〔操作〕直刺 0.3～0.5 寸。

Method of locating the point:

(1) This point is on the scapular region, at the centre of the suprascapular fossa, directly above Tianzong (SI 11), where a depression emerges when the arm is lifted.

(2) Ask patient to take a sitting or a prone position, locate the point 1 cun above the midpoint of the upper border of the scapular spine in the suprascapular fossa, at the upper right angle of the triangle formed by this point with Naoshu (SI 10) and Tianzong (SI 11)

Actions and indications: Expel wind and activate blood flow in the collaterals, used to treat pain in the scapular region and motor impairment of the upper arm.

Manipulation: Puncture perpendicularly 0.3—0.5 cun.

曲垣 Qūyuán (SI 13)

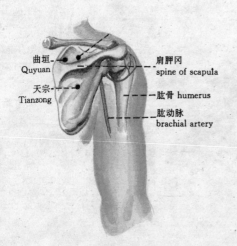

曲垣 Quyuan
天宗 Tianzong
肩胛冈 spine of scapula
肱骨 humerus
肱动脉 brachial artery

〔取穴法〕（1）在肩胛部，冈上窝内侧端凹陷处。

（2）正坐垂肩，约当臑俞与第 2 胸椎棘突连线的中点处是穴。

〔功效与主治〕舒筋散瘀，疏风活络。肩背疼痛，肩臂拘急疼痛。

〔操作〕直刺 0.3 ～ 0.5 寸。

Method of locating the point:

(1) This point is located in the scapular region, in the depression at the medial end of the suprascapular fossa.

(2) Ask patient to sit erect with the shoulder dropped, locate the point at the midpoint of the line connecting the Naoshu (SI 9) and the spinous process of the second thoracic vertebra.

Actions and indications: Relax tendons, dissipate blood stasis, expel wind and activate blood flow in the collaterals, used to treat pain of the shoulder and back, spasm and pain of the shoulder and arm.

Notes: Puncture perpendicularly 0.3—0.5 cun.

肩外俞 Jiānwàishū (SI 14)

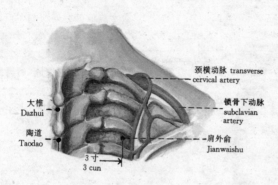

颈横动脉 transverse cervical artery

锁骨下动脉 subclavian artery

大椎 Dazhui

陶道 Taodao

肩外俞 Jianwaishu

3寸
3 cun

〔取穴法〕(1)在背部,当第 1 胸椎棘突下,旁开 3 寸处。

(2)正坐俯伏,于肩胛骨脊柱缘的垂线与陶道穴的水平线相交处是穴。

〔功效与主治〕祛风散寒,疏经活络。肩背酸痛,颈项强急。

〔操作〕斜刺 0.3～0.5 寸。

Method of locating the point:

(1) This point is on the back, 3 cun lateral to the area below the spinous process of the first thoracic vertebra.

(2) Ask patient to take a sitting position with his upper part of the body bent forwards, find out Dazhui (DU 14) which is located below the spinous process of the 7th thoracic vertebra, then locate the point 2 cun lateral to Dazhui (DU 14), about the position where the transverse process of the first thoracic vertebra is.

Actions and indications: Clear away heat, disperse wind, relieve cough and stop asthma, used to treat pain of the shoulder and back, stiff nape and back, and cough.

Manipulation: Puncture obliquely 0.3－0.5 cun.

肩中俞 Jiānzhōngshū (SI 15)

〔取穴法〕(1)在背部,当第 7 颈椎棘突下旁开 2 寸处。

(2)正坐俯伏,先取第 7 颈椎棘突下的大椎穴,再从大椎穴旁开 2 寸,约当第 1 胸椎横突端处是穴。

〔功效与主治〕清热散风,止咳平喘。肩背疼痛,项背拘急咳嗽上气。

〔操作〕斜刺 0.3 ～0.5 寸。

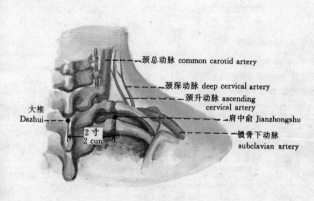

颈总动脉 common carotid artery
颈深动脉 deep cervical artery
颈升动脉 ascending cervical artery
肩中俞 Jianzhongshu
锁骨下动脉 subclavian artery
大椎 Dazhui
2 寸 2 cun

Method of locating the point:

(1) This point is on the back, below the spinous process of the 7th cervical vertebra, 2 cun lateral to the posterior midline.

(2) Ask patient to take a sitting or a recubent position, locate Dazhui (DU 14) first below the spinous process of the 7th cervical vertebra, then locate Jianzhongshu (SI 15) 2 cun lateral to Dazhui (DU 14), about at the end of the transverse process of the first thoracic vertebra.

Actions and indications: Clear away heat, disperse wind, relieve cough and stop asthma, used to treat pain in the back and shoulder, rigidity of back and neck, and cough.

Manipulation: Puncture 0.3 0.5 cun obliquely.

天窗 Tiānchuāng (SI 16)

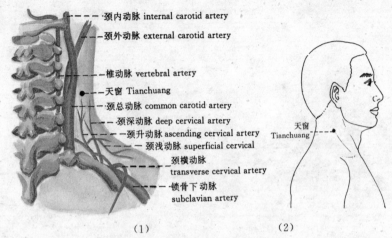

颈内动脉 internal carotid artery
颈外动脉 external carotid artery
椎动脉 vertebral artery
天窗 Tianchuang
颈总动脉 common carotid artery
颈深动脉 deep cervical artery
颈升动脉 ascending cervical artery
颈浅动脉 superficial cervical
颈横动脉 transverse cervical artery
锁骨下动脉 subclavian artery

天窗 Tianchuang

(1)　　　　　(2)

〔取穴法〕（1）在颈外侧部，胸锁乳突肌的后缘，扶突后，与喉结相平处。

（2）在结喉旁开 3.5 寸，胸锁乳突肌的后缘，当扶突穴后 0.5 寸处。

（3）正坐，平甲状软骨与舌骨肌之间的廉泉穴，于胸锁乳突肌后缘处取穴。

〔功效与主治〕清热开窍。颈瘿，中风失语。

〔操作〕直刺 0.3～0.5 寸。

〔备注〕配百会，艾条悬灸，治中风失语。

Method of locating the point：

（1）This point is on the lateral aspect of the neck, on the posterior border of m. sternocleidomastoideus, posterior to Futu (LI 18), at the level of the Adam's apple.

（2）Locate the point 3.5 cun lateral to the Adam's apple, on the posterior border of the sternocleidomastoideus, 0.5 cun posterior to Futu (SI 18).

（3）Ask patient to take a sitting position, locate the point at the level of Lianquan (RN 23) which is located between the thyroid cartilage and the hyroid bone, on the posterior border of the sternocleidomastoideus.

Actions and indications：Clear away heat and restore resuscitation, used to treat goiter and aphasia due to apoplexy.

Manipulation：Puncture perpendicularly 0.3—0.5 cun.

Notes：Suspended moxibustion with moxa roll on this point and Baihui (DU 20) can be used to treat aphasia due to apoplexy.

天容 Tiānróng 9SI 17)

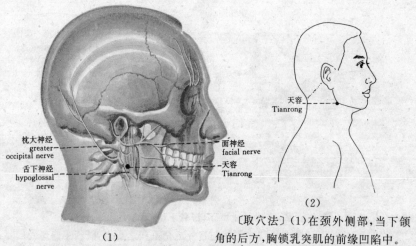

枕大神经
greater
occipital nerve

舌下神经
hypoglossal
nerve

面神经
facial nerve

天容
Tianrong

（1）

天容
Tianrong

（2）

〔取穴法〕（1）在颈外侧部，当下颌角的后方，胸锁乳突肌的前缘凹陷中。

（2）正坐或侧伏，平下颌角，在胸锁乳突肌停止部前缘，二腹肌后腹的下缘处是穴。

〔功效与主治〕聪耳利咽。耳聋，耳鸣，咽痛颊肿。

〔操作〕针尖向舌根方向刺 0.5～0.8 寸。

Method of locating the point:

(1) This point is on the lateral aspect of the neck, posterior to the angle of the mandible, in the depression on the anterior border of m. sternocleidomastoideus.

(2) Ask patient to take a sitting or a recumbent position, locate the point at the level of the angle of the mandible, on the anterior border of the end of m. sternocleidomastoideus, on the lower border of the posterior belly of diagastric muscle.

Actions and indications: Improving hearing and benefit throat, used to treat deafness, tinnitus, sore throat and swelling of the neck.

Manipulation: Puncture 0.5—0.8 cun toward the root of the tongue.

颧髎 Quánliáo (SI 17)

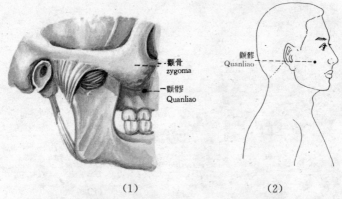

颧骨
zygoma

颧髎
Quanliao

颧髎
Quanliao

(1)　　　　　　(2)

〔取穴法〕(1)在面部,当目外眦直下,颧骨下缘凹陷处。

(2)正坐仰靠,于颧骨下缘水平线与目外眦角垂线之交点处,约于迎香穴同高处。

〔功效与主治〕镇痛止痉,祛风消肿。口眼㖞斜,眼睑瞤动,齿痛,面痛,颊肿。

〔操作〕直刺 0.2～0.3 寸。

〔备注〕手少阳、太阳经交会穴。

Method of locating the point:

(1) This point is on the face, directly below the outer canthus, in the depression of the lower border of zygoma.

(2) Ask patient to sit erect with his back supported, locate the point at the crossing point of the horizontal line drawn along the lower border of the zygoma and the vertical line passing through the outer canthus, at about the level of Yingxiang (LI 20).

Actions and indication: Relieve pain, stop convulsion, expel wind and subdue swelling, used to treat deviation of mouth and eyes, twitching of the eyelids, toothache, pain of the face and swelling of cheek.

Manipulation: Puncture perpendicularly 0.2—0.3 cun.

Notes: This point is the crossing point of the Sanjiao Meridian of Hand-Shaoyang and the Small Intestine Meridian of Hand-Taiyang.

听宫 Tinggōng (SI 19)

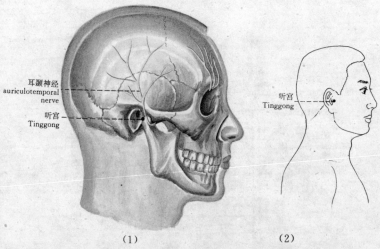

耳颞神经
auriculotemporal
nerve

听宫
Tinggong

听宫
Tinggong

(1)   (2)

〔取穴法〕(1)在面部,耳屏前,下颌骨髁状突的后方,张口时呈凹陷处。

(2)微张口,于耳屏前缘与下颌小头后缘之间凹陷处取穴。

〔功效与主治〕通经络,开耳窍,止痛益聪。耳鸣,耳聋,耳痛,聋哑,下颌关节痛。

〔操作〕微张口,直刺 0.5～1 寸。

〔备注〕手、足少阳与手太阳经交会穴。

Method of locating the point:

(1) This point is on the face, anterior to the tragus and posterior to the condyloid process of the mandible, in the depression formed when the mouth is open.

(2) Ask patient to open his mouth slightly, locate the point in the depression between the anterior border of the tragus and the posterior border of the head of the mandible.

Actions and indications: Promote flow of Qi and blood in the channels and collaterals, promote hearing and relieve pain, used to treat tinnitus, deafness, earache, dumbness due to deafness and pain of the mandible joint.

Manipulation: Puncture 0.5—1 cun when the mouth is open sllightly.

Notes: This point is the crossing point of the Sanjiao Meridian of Hand-Shaoyang, the Gallbladder Meridian of Foot-Shaoyang and the Small Intestine Meridian of Hand-Taiyang.

七、足太阳膀胱经

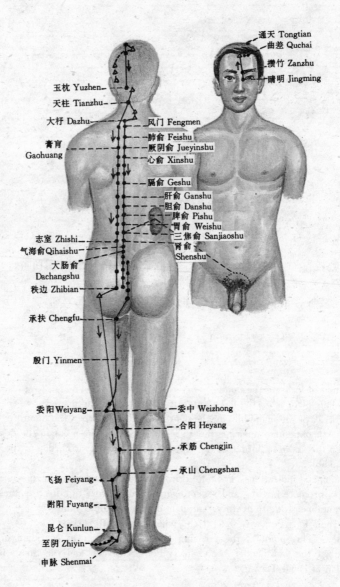

通天 Tongtian
曲差 Quchai
攒竹 Zanzhu
睛明 Jingming

玉枕 Yuzhen
天柱 Tianzhu
大杼 Dazhu
膏肓 Gaohuang
志室 Zhishi
气海俞 Qihaishu
大肠俞 Dachangshu
秩边 Zhibian
承扶 Chengfu
殷门 Yinmen
委阳 Weiyang
飞扬 Feiyang
跗阳 Fuyang
昆仑 Kunlun
至阴 Zhiyin
申脉 Shenmai

风门 Fengmen
肺俞 Feishu
厥阴俞 Jueyinshu
心俞 Xinshu
膈俞 Geshu
肝俞 Ganshu
胆俞 Danshu
脾俞 Pishu
胃俞 Weishu
三焦俞 Sanjiaoshu
肾俞 Shenshu

委中 Weizhong
合阳 Heyang
承筋 Chengjin
承山 Chengshan

起于目内眦（睛明），上额交会于巅顶（百会）。巅顶部支脉：从头顶到颞颥部；巅顶部直行的脉：从头顶入里联络于脑，回出分开下行项后，沿着肩胛部内侧，挟住脊柱，到达腰部，从脊旁肌肉进入体腔，联络肾脏，属于膀胱。腰部的支脉：向下通过臀部，进入腘窝中。后项的支脉：通过肩胛骨内缘直下，经过臀部（环跳）下行，沿着大腿后外侧，与腰部下来的支脉会合于腘窝中，从此向下，通过腓肠肌，出于外踝后面，沿着第 5 跖骨粗隆，至小趾外侧端（至阴），与足少阴经相接。

7. The Bladder Meridian of Foot-Taiyang

The Bladder Meridian of Foot-Taiyang originates from the inner canthus (Jing-ming, BL 1). It runs upwards to the forehead and then meets on the vertex. The branch from the vertex travels from the vertex to the temples. The straight portion of the meridian enters and communicates with the brain from the vertex. It then emerges and bifurcates to descend along the posterior aspect of the neck. Running downward alongside the medial aspect of the scapular region and parallel to the spinal column, it reaches the lumbar region, where it enters the body cavity via the paravertebral muscle to connect with the kidney and pertain to the bladder. The branch arising from the lumbar region runs downwards through the gluteal region and ends in the popliteal fossa. The branch arising from the posterior aspect of the neck runs straight downwards along the medial border of the scapula. Passing through the gluteal region (Huantiao, GL 30), it goes downwards along the lateral aspect of the thigh and meets the preceeding branch descending from the lumbar region in the popliteal fossa. From there, it descends to the gastrocnemius muscle and further to the posterior aspect of the external malleolus. Then, running along the tuberosity of the 5th metatarsal bone, it reaches the lateral side of the tip of the little toe (Zhiyin, GL 67) where it links with the Kidney Meridian of Foot-Shaoyin.

睛明 Jingming (BL 1)

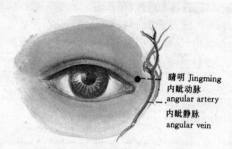

睛明 Jingming
内眦动脉
angular artery
内眦静脉
angular vein

〔取穴法〕(1)在面部,目内眦角稍上方凹陷处。

(2)正坐或仰卧,于目内眦向内0.1寸,再向上0.1寸处,近目眶骨内缘处取穴。

〔功效与主治〕疏风泄热,通络明目。目赤肿痛,夜盲,色弱,近视,视神经萎缩。

〔操作〕嘱患者闭目,医者左手固定眼球,刺手用压入式进针,紧靠眶缘直刺0.5～0.8寸。不捻转、不提插,出针后按压针孔,以防出血。

〔备注〕手足太阳、足阳明、阴阳跷脉五脉交会穴。

Method of locating the point:

(1) This point is on the face, in the depression a bit latero-superior to the inner canthus.

(2) Ask patient to take a sitting or a supine position, locate the point 0.1 cun above the point 0.1 cun proximal to the inner canthus, just below the supraorbital border.

Actions and indications: Expel wind, purge heat and promote flow of Qi and blood in the collaterals to improve eyesight, used to treat redness, swelling and pain of eyes, night blindness, color weaknees, myopia and atrophy of the optic nerve.

Manipulation: Ask patient to close his eye, then, with the left hand, the doctor fixes the patient's eyeball, and with his right hand, the doctor puncture close to the supraorbital border 0.5－0.8 cun taking a pressing-needling method. No rotating, twitching, lifting and thrusting is adopted, and after withdrawal of the needle, press the hole of needling to prevent bleeding.

Notes: This point is the crossing point of the following five meridians: the Small Intestine Meridian of Hand-Taiyang, the Bladder Meridian of Foot-Taiyang, the Stomach Meridian of Foot-Yangming, the Yinqiao Meridian and the Yangqiao Meridian.

攢竹 Cuánzhú (BL 2)

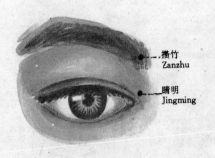

攢竹
Zanzhu

睛明
Jingming

〔取穴法〕(1)在面部,当眉头陷中,眶上切迹处。

(2)正坐或仰卧,于眉头边缘,入眉毛约 0.1 寸处取穴。

〔功效与主治〕宣泄风热,活络明目。头痛,目眩,眉棱骨痛,面痛。

〔操作〕斜刺向下或向外刺 0.1～0.2 寸,或用细三棱针速刺出血。

〔备注〕禁灸。

Method of locating the point:

(1) This point is on the face, in the depression of the medial extremity of the eyebrow, or on the supraorbital notch.

(2) When patient sits erect or takes a supine position, locate the point on the medial extremity of the eyebrow, 0.1 cun within the eyebrow.

Actions and indications: Disperse and purge wind-heat, promote flow of Qi and blood in the collaterals to improve eyesight, used to treat headache, dizziness, pain in the supraorbital region, and pain in the face.

Manipulation: Puncture obliquely downwards or outwards 0.1 − 0.2 cun, or prick with a three edged needle to cause bleeding.

Notes: Moxibustion is contraindicated.

曲差 Qūchā (BL 4)

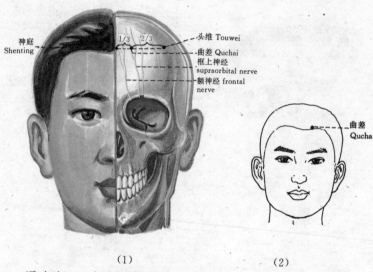

神庭 Shenting
头维 Touwei
曲差 Quchai
框上神经 supraorbital nerve
额神经 frontal nerve
曲差 Qucha

(1)   (2)

〔取穴法〕(1)在头部,当前发际正中直上 0.5 寸,旁开 1.5 寸处。

(2)正坐或仰卧,当神庭与头维连线的内 1/3 与中 1/3 交点处取穴。

〔功效与主治〕泄热开窍,清头明目。头痛,鼻塞,鼻衄。

〔操作〕沿皮刺 0.2～0.3 寸。

Method of locating the point：

(1) This point is on the head, 1.5 cun lateral to a point 0.1 cun directly above the midpoint of the anterior hairline.

(2) Ask patient to take a sitting or a supine position, locate the point at the junction of the medial one third and lateral two-third of the distance from Shenting (DU 24) to Touwei (ST 8).

Actions and indications：Purge heat, restore resuscitation, clear away heat from the head and improve eyesight, used to treat headache, nasal obstruction and hemoptysis.

Manipulation：Puncture subcutaneously 0.2－0.3 cun.

124

通天 Tōngtiān（BL 7）

〔取穴法〕（1）在头部，当前发际正中直上 4 寸，旁开 1.5 寸处。

（2）正坐仰靠，先取曲差，于其后 4 寸处取穴。

（3）先取百会穴，旁开 1.5 寸，再向前 1 寸处定取。

〔功效与主治〕利鼻，止痛。头痛，头重，眩晕，鼻渊。

〔操作〕沿皮刺 0.2～0.3 寸。

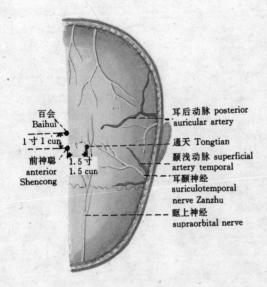

百会 Baihui
1 寸 1 cun
前神聪 anterior Shencong
1.5 寸 1.5 cun
耳后动脉 posterior auricular artery
通天 Tongtian
颞浅动脉 superficial artery temporal
耳颞神经 auriculotemporal nerve Zanzhu
眶上神经 supraorbital nerve

Method of locating the point：

（1）This point is located on the face，1.5 cun lateral to the point 4 cun directly above the midpoint of the anterior hairline.

（2）Ask patient to sit erect with his body supported，locate Quchai（BL 4）first，then，locate Tongtian（BL 7）4 cun posterior to it.

（3）Locate Baihui（DU 20）first，then locate Tongtian（BL 7）1 cun anterior to a point 1.5 cun lateral to Baihui（DU 20）.

Actions and indications：Benefit the nose and relieve pain，used to treat headache，heaviness of the head，dizziness and rhinorrhea.

Manipulation：Puncture subcutaneously 0.2—0.3 cun.

玉枕 Yùzhěn (BL 9)

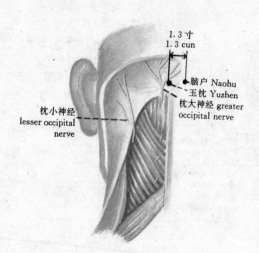

1.3寸
1.3 cun

脑户 Naohu
玉枕 Yuzhen
枕大神经 greater occipital nerve

枕小神经
lesser occipital nerve

〔取穴法〕（1）在后头部，当后发际正中直上 2.5 寸,旁开 1.3 寸,平枕外隆凸上缘的凹陷处。

（2)正坐或俯伏位,先取枕外粗隆上缘凹陷处的脑户穴,当脑户旁开 1.3 寸处取穴。

〔功效与主治〕清头目,开鼻窍。后头痛,恶风,目眩,鼻塞。

〔操作〕沿皮刺 0.2～0.3寸。

Method of locating the point：

(1) This point is on the back of the head，1.3 cun lateral to a point 2.5 cun directly above the midpoint of the posterior hairline，in the depression at the level of the upper border of the external occipital protruberance.

(2) Ask patient to take a sitting or a prone position，locate Naohu (SJ 13, located on the upper border of the external occipital protruberance) first，then locate Yuzhen (BL 9) 1.3 cun lateral to Naohu (SJ 13).

Actions and indications：Clear away heat from the head and eyes and relieve nasal obstruction，used to treat pain on the back head，aversion to wind，dizziness and nasal obstruction.

Manipulation：Puncture subcutaneously 0.2—0.3 cun.

天柱 Tiānzhù (BL 10)

〔取穴法〕(1)在项部,大筋(斜方肌)外缘之后发际凹陷中,约当后发际正中旁开1.3寸处。

(2)正坐,头稍前倾,先取后发际正中点,再旁开1.3寸,当斜方肌外侧处取之。

〔功效与主治〕疏风解表止痛。头痛项强,眩晕,鼻塞。

〔操作〕直刺0.3～0.5寸。

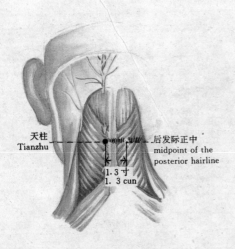

天柱
Tianzhu

后发际正中
midpoint of the posterior hairline

1.3寸
1.3 cun

Method of locating the point:

(1) This point is on the posterior aspect of the neck, in the depression on the lateral side of m. trapezius, about 1.3 cun lateral to the midpoint of the posterior hairline.

(2) Ask patient to take a sitting position with his head slightly bent forwards, locate the midpoint of the posterior hairline first, then, locate the point 1.3 cun lateral to the midpoint on the lateral side of m. trapezius.

Actions and indications: Expel wind, relieve exterior syndrome and alleviate pain, used to treat headache, rigidity of neck, dizziness and nasal obstruction.

Manipulation: Puncture perpendicularly 0.3—0.5 cun.

大杼 Dàzhù (BL 11)

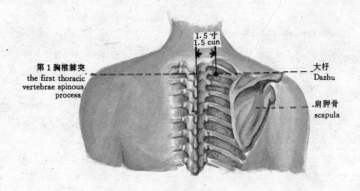

第1胸椎棘突
the first thoracic
vertebrae spinous
process

1.5 寸
1.5 cun

大杼
Dazhu

肩胛骨
scapula

〔取穴法〕(1)在背部,当第1胸椎棘突下,旁开1.5寸处。

(2)俯伏,于第1胸椎棘突下间,陶道穴旁开1.5寸处取穴。

〔功效与主治〕疏风清热,坚筋益骨。咳嗽,发热,项强,脊强。

〔操作〕针尖向脊柱方向斜刺0.5~0.8寸。

〔备注〕八会穴之一,骨会大杼;手足太阳经交会穴。

Method of locating the point:

(1) This point is on the back, 1.5 cun lateral to the point below the spinous process of the 1st thoracic vertebra.

(2) Ask patient to take a prone position, locate the point below the spinous process of the 1st thoracic vertebra, 1.5 cun lateral to Taodao point (DU 13).

Actions and indications: Expel wind, clear away heat, strengthen tendons and benefit bones, used to treat cough, fever, rigidity of neck and back.

Manipulation: Puncture 0.5-0.8 cun obliquely towards the spinal column.

Notes: This point is one of the eight confluence points, communicating with all bones. It is also a crossing point of the Small Intestine Meridian of Hand-Taiyang and the Bladder Meridian of Foot-Taiyang.

风门 Fēngmén（BL 12）

〔取穴法〕（1）在背部，当第2胸椎棘突下，旁开1.5寸处。

（2）俯伏，在第2胸椎棘突下，督脉旁开1.5寸处。

〔功效与主治〕疏散风寒，宣泄热邪，调理肺气。咳嗽，气喘，发热，头痛，恶风寒。

〔操作〕针尖向脊柱方向斜刺0.5～0.8寸。可灸。

〔备注〕足太阳与督脉交会穴。

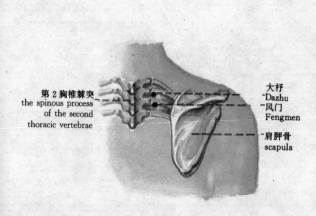

第2胸椎棘突
the spinous process
of the second
thoracic vertebrae

大杼
Dazhu
风门
Fengmen

肩胛骨
scapula

Method of locating the point:

(1) This point is on the back, 1.5 cun lateral to the point below the spinous process of the second thoracic vertebra.

(2) Ask patient to take a prone position, locate the point below the spinous process of the second thoracic vertebra, 1.5 cun lateral to the Du Meridian.

Actions and indications: Expel wind-cold, disperse and purge the lung-heat, regulate the flow of lung-Qi, used to treat cough, asthma, fever, headache, and aversion to wind-cold.

Manipulations: Puncture 0.5—0.8 cun obliquely towards the spinal column.

Notes: This point is a crossing point of the Bladder Meridian of Foot-Taiyang and the Du Meridian.

肺俞 Fèishū (BL 13)

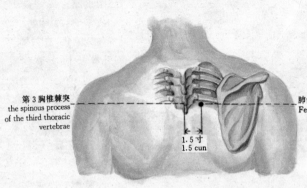

第3胸椎棘突
the spinous process
of the third thoracic
vertebrae

1.5寸
1.5 cun

肺俞
Feishu

〔取穴法〕(1)在背部,当第3胸椎棘突下,旁开1.5寸处。

(2)俯伏,于第3胸椎棘突下的身柱穴(督脉)旁开1.5寸处取穴。

〔功效与主治〕宣散风热,调肺理气。咳嗽,气喘,胸满,盗汗。

〔操作〕向脊柱方向斜刺0.5~0.8寸。

〔备注〕背俞穴之一,肺之背俞。

Method of locating the point:

(1) This point is on the back, 1.5 cun lateral to the point below the spinous process of the third thoracic vertebra.

(2) Ask patient to take a prone position, locate the point 1.5 cun lateral to Shenzhu (DU 12) that is below the spinous process of the third thoracic vertebra.

Actions and indications: Disperse wind-heat and regulate the flow of lung-Qi, used to treat cough, asthma, chest fullness and night sweating.

Manipulation: Puncture 0.5—0.8 cun obliquely towards the spinal column.

Notes: This point is one of the Back-Shu point, related to the lung.

厥阴俞 Júeyīnshū （BL 14）

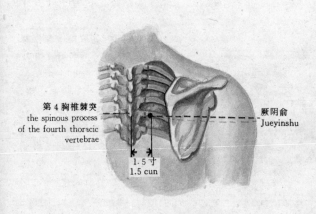

第 4 胸椎棘突
the spinous process
of the fourth thoracic
vertebrae

厥阴俞
Jueyinshu

1.5 寸
1.5 cun

〔取穴法〕（1）在背部，当第 4 胸椎棘突下，旁开 1.5 寸处。

（2）俯伏，于第 4 胸椎棘突下间，再旁开 1.5 寸处。

〔功效与主治〕宁心，止呕。心痛，心悸，胸闷。

〔操作〕向脊柱方向斜刺 0.5～0.8 寸。

〔备注〕背俞穴之一，心包之背俞。

Method of locating the point：

（1）This point is on the back，1.5 cun lateral to the point below the spinous process of the 4th thoracic vertebra.

（2）Ask patient to take a prone position，locate the point 1.5 cun lateral to the point below the spinous process of the 4th thoracic vertebra.

Actions and indications：Tranquilize the heart and stop vomiting，used to treat cardiac pain，palpitation，and chest fullness.

Manipulation：Puncture 0.5—0.8 obliquely towards the spinal column.

Notes：This point is one of the Back-Shu point，related to the liver.

心俞 Xīnshū（BL 15）

〔取穴法〕（1）在背部,当第5胸椎棘突下,旁开1.5寸处。

（2）俯伏,先取第5胸椎棘突下的神道穴,再旁开1.5寸处。

〔功效与主治〕疏通心络,调理气血,安心宁神。心痛,心悸,健忘失眠,癫狂。

〔操作〕向脊柱方向斜刺0.5～0.8寸。

〔备注〕背俞穴之一,心之背俞。

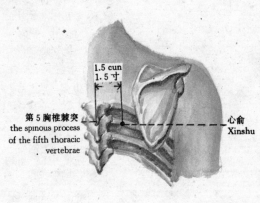

第5胸椎棘突
the spinous process
of the fifth thoracic
vertebrae

1.5 cun
1.5 寸

心俞
Xinshu

Method of locating the point：

（1）This point is on the back，1. 5 cun lateral to the point below the spinous process of the 5th thoracic vertebra.

（2）Ask patient to take a prone position，locate Shendao point (DU 11) below the spinous process of the 5th thoracic vertebra，then，locate the point 1. 5 cun lateral to Shendao (DU 11).

Actions and indications：Dredge and activate flow of Qi and blood in the cardiac vessel，regulate flow of Qi and blood，and tranquilize the mind，used to treat cardiac pain，palpitation，forgetfulness，insomnia，and schizophrenia.

Manipulation：Puncture 0. 5－0. 8 obliquely towards the spinal column.

Notes：This point is one of the Back-Shu point，related to the heart.

132

膈俞 Géshū (BL 17)

〔取穴法〕(1)在背部,当第 7 胸椎棘突下,旁开 1.5 寸处。

(2)俯伏,先取第 7 胸椎棘突下的至阳穴,再旁开 1.5 寸处,约与肩胛下角相平。

〔功效与主治〕理血,宽中,和胃。血虚,吐血,胸满,呃逆,食不下。

〔操作〕向脊柱方向斜刺 0.5～0.8 寸。

〔备注〕八会穴之一,血会膈俞。

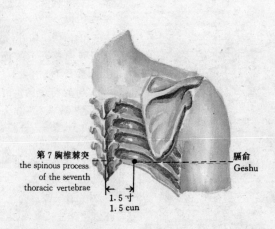

第 7 胸椎棘突
the spinous process
of the seventh
thoracic vertebrae

膈俞
Geshu

1.5 寸
1.5 cun

Method of locating the point:

(1) This point is on the back, 1.5 cun lateral to the point below the spinous process of the 7th thoracic vertebra.

(2) Ask patient to take a prone position, locate the Zhiyang point (DU 9) below the spinous process of the 7th thoracic vertebra, then locate Geshu point (BL 17) 1.5 cun lateral to the point, at the level of the lower angle of the scapula.

Actions and indications: Regulate flow of blood, relieve stagnation of Qi in the chest, and regulate the function of the stomach, used to treat blood deficiency, spitting blood, chest fullness, hiccup, and anorexia.

Manipulation: Puncture 0.5—0.8 obliquely towards the spinal column.

Notes: This point is one of the Back-Shu points, related to the blood.

肝俞 Gānshū（BL 18）

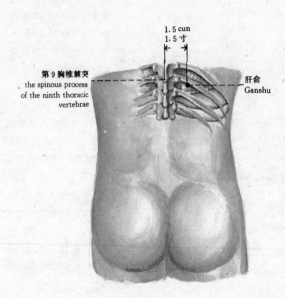

第9胸椎棘突
the spinous process
of the ninth thoracic
vertebrae

1.5 cun
1.5 寸

肝俞
Ganshu

〔取穴法〕（1）在背部，当第9胸椎棘突下，旁开1.5寸处。

（2）俯伏或俯卧，先取第9胸椎棘突下的筋缩穴，再旁开1.5寸处。

〔功效与主治〕舒肝利胆，泄热调气，清头明目。黄疸，胁痛，目眩，夜盲。

〔操作〕向脊柱方向斜刺0.5～0.8寸。

〔备注〕背俞穴之一，肝之背俞。

Method of locating the point:

（1）This point is on the back，1.5 cun lateral to the point below the spinous process of the 9th thoracic vertebra.

（2）Ask patient to take a prone position, locate Jinsuo (DU 8) below the spinous process of the ath thoracic vertebra, then locate Ganshu (BL 18) 1.5 cun lateral to the point.

Actions and indications: Soothe flow of the liver Qi and benefit the gallbladder，purge heat and regulate flow of Qi，clear away heat from the head and improve eyesight，used to treat jaundice，hypochondriac pain，dizziness and night blindness.

Manipulation: Puncture 0.5－0.8 obliquely towards the spinal column.

Notes: This point is one of the Back-Shu point，related to the liver.

胆俞 Dǎnshū (BL 19)

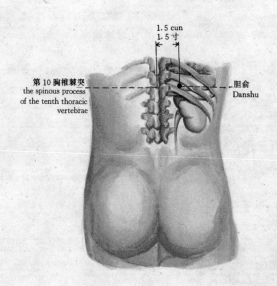

1.5 cun
1.5 寸

第 10 胸椎棘突
the spinous process
of the tenth thoracic
vertebrae

胆俞
Danshu

〔取穴法〕（1）在背部，当第 10 胸椎棘突下，旁开 1.5 寸处。

（2）俯伏或俯卧，先取第 10 胸椎棘突下的中枢穴，再旁开 1.5 寸处。

〔功效与主治〕清泄肝胆邪热，理气宽膈。黄疸，口苦，胸胁痛。

〔操作〕向脊柱方向斜刺 0.5～0.8 寸。

〔备注〕背俞穴之一，胆之背俞。

Method of locating the point:

(1) This point is located on the back, 1.5 cun lateral to the point below the spinous process of the 10th thoracic vertebra.

(2) Ask patient to take a prone position, locate Zhongshu point (DU 7) below the spinous process of the 10th thoracic vertebra, then locate Danshu (BL 19) 1.5 cun lateral to the point.

Actions and indications: Purge heat from the liver and gallbladder, regulate flow of Qi and facilitate flow of Qi in the chest, used to treat jaundice, bitter taste in the mouth and pain in the chest and hypochondrium.

Manipulation: Puncture 0.5—0.8 obliquely towards the spinal column.

Notes: This point is one of the Back-Shu point, related to the gallbladder.

脾俞 Píshū (BL 20)

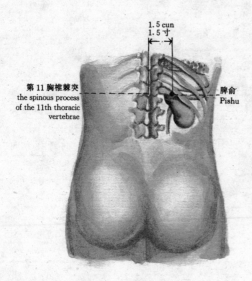

1.5 cun
1.5寸

第11胸椎棘突
the spinous process
of the 11th thoracic
vertebrae

脾俞
Pishu

〔取穴法〕(1)在背部,当第11胸椎棘突下,旁开1.5寸处。

(2)俯伏或俯卧,先取第11胸椎棘突下的脊中穴,再旁开1.5寸处。

〔功效与主治〕除水湿,助运化,补脾阳,益营血。腹胀,泄泻,完谷不化,黄疸。

〔操作〕向脊柱方向斜刺0.5~0.8寸。

〔备注〕背俞穴之一,脾之背俞。

Method of lcoating the point:

(1) This point is on the back, 1.5 cun lateral to the point below the spinous process of the 11th thoracic vertebra.

(2) Ask patient to take a prone position, first locate Jizhong (DU 6) below the spinous process of the 11th thoracic vertebra, then locate Pishu (BL 20) 1.5 cun lateral to the point.

Actions and indications: Remove water-dampness, aid in digestion, supplement the spleen Yang and nourish ying-blood, used to treat abdominal distension, diarrhea with undigested food and jaundice.

Manipulation: Puncture 0.5—0.8 obliquely towards the spinal column.

Notes: This point is one of the Back-Shu points, related to the spleen.

136

胃俞 Wèishū (BL 21)

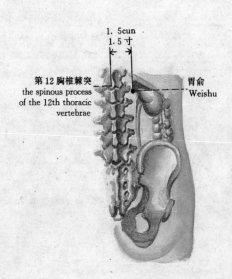

1. 5cun
1.5 寸

第 12 胸椎棘突
the spinous process
of the 12th thoracic
vertebrae

胃俞
Weishu

〔取穴法〕(1)在背部,当
第 12 胸椎棘突下,旁开 1.5 寸
处。

(2)俯伏或俯卧,在第 12
胸椎棘突下,督脉旁开 1.5 寸
处。

〔功效与主治〕振奋胃阳,
健脾和胃,化湿消滞。胃脘痛,
腹胀,呕吐。

〔操作〕向脊柱方向斜刺
0.5～0.8 寸。

〔备注〕背俞穴之一,胃之
背俞。

Method of locating the point:

(1) This point is on the back, 1.5 cun lateral to the point below the spinous process of the 12th thoracic vertebra.

(2) Ask patient to take a prone position, locate the point 1.5 cun lateral to the Du Meridian, below the spinous process of the 12th thoracic vertebra.

Actions and indications: Revive the stomach yang, strengthen the spleen and regulate the function of the stomach, and remove dampness and promote digestion, used to treat epigastric pain, abdominal distension and vomiting.

Manipulation: Puncture 0.5—0.8 obliquely towards the spinal column.

Notes: This point is one of the Back-Shu points, related to the stomach.

三焦俞 Sānjiāoshū（BL 22）

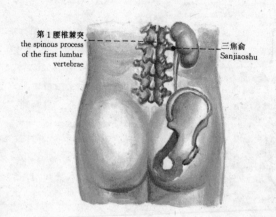

第1腰椎棘突
the spinous process
of the first lumbar
vertebrae

三焦俞
Sanjiaoshu

〔取穴法〕(1)在腰部，当第1腰椎棘突下，旁开1.5寸处。

(2)俯卧，先取第1腰椎棘突下的悬枢穴，再旁开1.5寸处。

〔功效与主治〕调三焦，利水道。腹胀，肠鸣，水谷不化，水肿。

〔操作〕直刺0.5～1寸。

〔备注〕背俞穴之一，三焦之背俞。

Method of locating the point:

(1) This point is located on the lumbar region, 1.5 cun lateral to a point below the spinous process of the first lumbar vertebra.

(2) Ask patient to take a prone position, locate Xuanshu (DU 5, located below the spinous process of the first lumbar vertebra) first, then locate Sanyinjiao (BL 22) 1.5 cun lateral to Xuanshu (DU 5).

Actions and indications: Regulate function of the triple-jiao, promote distribution and discharge of water, used to treat abdominal distension, borborygmus, indigestion and edema.

Manipulation: Puncture perpendicularly 0.5—1 cun.

Notes: This is one of the Back-Shu points, related to the triple-jiao.

肾俞 Shènshū (BL 23)

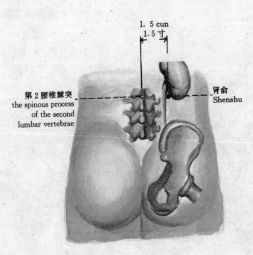

1. 5 cun
1.5 寸

第2腰椎棘突
the spinous process
of the second
lumbar vertebrae

肾俞
Shenshu

〔取穴法〕(1)在腰部,当第2腰椎棘突下,旁开1.5寸处。

(2)俯卧,先取与脐孔基本相对的命门穴,再旁开1.5寸处。

〔功效与主治〕滋补肾阴,强健脑髓,益聪明目,利腰脊。肾虚腰痛,阳痿,遗精,早泄,遗尿,耳聋耳鸣,喘咳少气。

〔操作〕直刺0.5~1寸。

〔备注〕背俞穴之一,肾之背俞。

Method of locating the point:

(1) This point is lcoated in the lumbar region, 1. 5 cun lateral to the point below the spinous process of the second lumbar vertebra.

(2) Ask patient to take a prone position, locate Mingmen (DU 4, located below the spinous process of the second lumbar vertebra) first, then locate Shenshu (BL 23) 1. 5 cun lateral to Mingmen (DU 4).

Actions and indications: Nourish the kidney yin, strengthen the brain marrow, benefit the mind and improve eyesight, and benefit the loins and the spine, used to treat lumbago, impotence, emission, premature ejaculation, enuresis, deafness, tinnitus, asthma and shortness of breath caused by kidney deficiency.

Manipulation: Puncture perpendicularly 0. 5—1 cun.

Notes: This point is one of the Back-Shu points, related to the kidney.

气海俞 Qìhǎishū (BL 24)

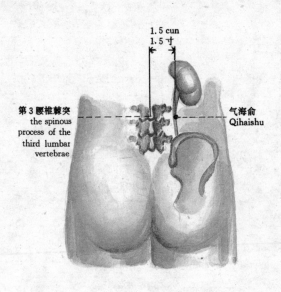

1.5 cun
1.5 寸

第3腰椎棘突
the spinous
process of the
third lumbar
vertebrae

气海俞
Qihaishu

〔取穴法〕（1）在腰部，当第3腰椎棘突下，旁开1.5寸处。

（2）俯卧，先取命门穴，于命门穴下一个棘突，再旁开1.5寸处。

〔功效与主治〕调补气血，强健腰膝。腰背痛，痔疮，痛经，崩漏。

〔操作〕直刺0.5～1寸。

Method of locating the point:

(1) This point is in the lumbar region, 1.5 cun lateral to the point below the spinous process of the third lumbar vertebra.

(2) Ask patient to take a prone position, locate Mingmen point (DU 4, located below the spinous process of the second lumbar vertebra) first, then locate Qihaishu (BL 24) 1.5 cun lateral to the lower border of the spinous process that is one spinous process lower than Mingmen point (DU 4).

Actions and indications: Regulate and nourish Qi and blood, strengthen the loins and the knee, used to treat lumbago, pain in the back, hemorrhoids, dysmenorrhea and metrostaxis and metrorrhagia.

Manipulation: Puncture perpendicularly 0.5—1 cun.

大肠俞 Dàchángshū（BL 25）

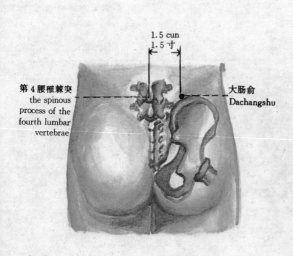

第4腰椎棘突
the spinous process of the fourth lumbar vertebrae

1.5 cun
1.5 寸

大肠俞
Dachangshu

〔取穴法〕（1）在腰部，当第4腰椎棘突下，旁开1.5寸处。

（2）俯卧，先取两髂嵴最高点连线，第4腰椎棘突下的腰阳关穴，再旁开1.5寸处。

〔功效与主治〕调理肠胃，泄热通便，强健腰膝。腰痛，肠鸣，腹胀，泄泻。

〔操作〕直刺0.5～1寸。

〔备注〕背俞穴之一，大肠之背俞。

Method of locating the point:

(1) This point is located in the lumbar region, 1.5 cun lateral to the point below the spinous process of the fourth lumbar vertebra.

(2) Ask patient to take a prone position, locate Yaoyangguan (DU 3, below the spinous process of the 4th lumbar vertebra, at the level of the crista illiaca) first, then, locate Dachangshu (BL 25) 1.5 cun lateral to the point.

Actions and indications: Regulate the function of the gastrointestinal tract, purge heat and relax the bowel, and strengthen the loins and knees, used to treat lumbago, borborygmus, abdominal distension and diarrhea.

Manipulation: Puncture perpendicularly 0.5 1 cun.

Notes: This point is one of the Back-Shu points, related to the large intestine.

关元俞 Guānyuánshū（BL 26）

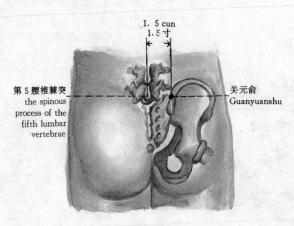

1. 5 cun
1. 5 寸

第 5 腰椎棘突
the spinous
process of the
fifth lumbar
vertebrae

关元俞
Guanyuanshu

〔取穴法〕（1）在腰部，当第 5 腰椎棘突下，旁开 1.5 寸处。

（2）俯卧，先取第 4 腰椎棘突下的腰阳关穴（督脉），并于其下椎棘突之下间旁开 1.5 寸处取穴。

〔功效与主治〕通经活络，疏风散寒，清利湿滞，调理下焦。腰痛，月经不调。

〔操作〕直刺 0.5～1 寸。

Method of locating the point：

（1）This point is in the lumbar region, 1.5 cun lateral to the point below the spinous process of the 5th lumbar vertebra.

（2）Ask patient to take a prone position, locate Yaoyangguan (BL 25, below the spinous process of the 4th lumbar vertebra) first, then, locate Guanyuanshu (BL 26) 1.5 cun lateral to the point located below the next spinous process.

Actions and indications：Promote flow of Qi and blood in the channels and collaterals, expel wind and disperse cold, clear away damp-heat, and regulate function of the lower-jiao, used to treat lumbago and irregular menstruation.

Manipulation：Puncture perpendicularly 0.5－1 cun.

小肠俞 Xiǎochángshū (BL 27)

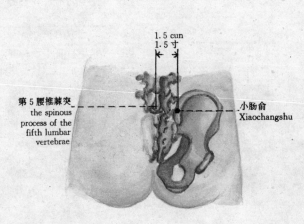

1.5 cun
1.5 寸

第 5 腰椎棘突
the spinous
process of the
fifth lumbar
vertebrae

小肠俞
Xiaochangshu

〔取穴法〕(1)在骶部,当骶正中嵴旁开1.5寸,平第1骶后孔处。

(2)俯卧,于第1骶椎下间后正中线旁开1.5寸处。

〔功效与主治〕培补下元,调膀胱,利水道。小腹胀痛,遗尿,白带,痔疮。

〔操作〕直刺0.5～1寸。

〔备注〕背俞穴之一,小肠之背俞。

Method of locating the point:

(1) This point is in the sacral region, 1.5 cun lateral to the median sacral crest, at the level of the first posterior sacral foramen.

(2) Ask patient to take a prone position, locate the point 1.5 cun lateral to the inferior space of the first sacral vertebra.

Actions and indications: Tonify the premordial Qi, regulate the function of the bladder and promote metabolism of water, used to treat fullness and pain of the lower abdomen, enuresis, leukorrhea and hemorrhoids.

Manipulation: Puncture perpendicularly 0.5—1 cun.

Notes: This point is one of the Back-Shu point, related to the small intestine.

膀胱俞 Pángguāngshū (BL 28)

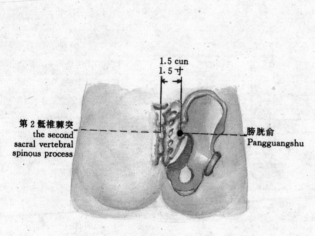

第 2 骶椎棘突
the second
sacral vertebral
spinous process

膀胱俞
Pangguangshu

1.5 cun
1.5 寸

〔取穴法〕(1)在骶部,当骶正中嵴旁开 1.5 寸,平第 2 骶后孔处。

(2)俯卧,于第 2 骶椎下后正中线旁开 1.5 寸处。

〔功效与主治〕培补下元,约束膀胱气机,通利水道。癃闭,遗尿,腰骶痛。

〔操作〕直刺 0.5 ~1 寸。

〔备注〕背俞穴之一,膀胱之背俞。

Method of locating the point:

(1) This point is in the sacral region, 1.5 cun lateral to the median sacral crest, at the level of the second posterior sacral foramen.

(2) Ask patient to take a prone position, locate the point 1.5 cun lateral to the posterior midline at the level of the lower border of the second sacral vertebra.

Actions and indications: Tonify the primordial Qi, consolidate flow of Qi in the bladder and promote water metabolism, used to treat retention of urine, enuresis and pain in the sacral region.

Manipulation: Puncture perpendicularly 0.5—1 cun.

Notes: This point is one of the Back-Shu point, related to the bladder.

144

次髎Ciliáo（BL 32）

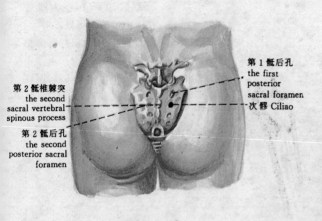

第2骶椎棘突
the second
sacral vertebral
spinous process

第2骶后孔
the second
posterior sacral
foramen

第1骶后孔
the first
posterior
sacral foramen

次髎 Ciliao

〔取穴法〕（1）在骶部，当髂后上棘内下方，适对第2骶后孔处。

（2）俯卧，以食指尖按在小肠俞与脊椎正中的中间，小指按在尾骨上方有小黄豆大的圆骨突起（骶角）的上方，中指与无名指相等距离分开按放，各指尖所到之处是：食指尖为上髎，中指尖为次髎，无名指尖为中髎，小指尖为下髎。

〔功效与主治〕健腰膝，调下焦。腰骶痛，下肢痿、痹，二便不利，痛经。

〔操作〕直刺0.5～1.2寸。

Method of locating the point:

(1) This point is in the sacral region, medial and inferior to the posterior superior illiac spine, in the second posterior sacral foramen.

(2) When the patient takes a prone position, press the region between Xiaochangshu (BL 27) and the midpoint of the sacral vertebrae with the index finger while the little finger is placed superior to the sacral horn which is in the upper part of the sacral vertebra and is soyae-bean-like in size, and the middle and the ring fingers are placed at equal distances between the index and the little fingers, then locate Shangliao (BL 31) where the tip of the index finger touches, locate Ciliao (BL 32) where the tip of the middle finger touches, locate Zhongliao (BL 33) where the the tip of the ring finger touches and locate Xialiao (BL 34) where the tip of the little finger touches.

Actions and indications: Strengthen the loin and the knee and regulate function of the lower-jiao, used to treat pain in the sacrococcygeal region, paralysis of arthralgia of the lower limb, difficulty in urination and defecation, and dysmenorrhea.

Manipulation: Puncture perpendicularly 0.5—1.2 cun.

承扶 Chéngfú (BL 36)

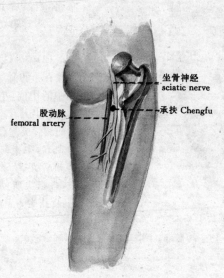

坐骨神经
sciatic nerve

股动脉
femoral artery

承扶 Chengfu

〔取穴法〕(1)在大腿后面,臀下横纹的中点处。

(2)俯卧,于大腿与臀部交界之臀沟中点取穴。

〔功效与主治〕舒筋,调肛肠。腰脊臀股疼痛,痔疾,下肢痿、痹。

〔操作〕直刺1~1.5寸。

Method of locating the point:

(1) This point is lcoated on the posterior aspect of the thigh, at the midpoint of the transverse gluteal fold.

(2) Ask patient to take a prone position, locate the point at the midpoint of the transverse gluteal fold.

Actions adn indications: Relax tendons and regulate the function of the intestine and anus, used to treat pain of the loin, spine, buttock and thigh, hemorrhoids, paralysis or arthralgia of the lower limbs.

Manipulation: Puncture perpendicularly 1—1.5 cun.

殷门 Yīnmén (BL 37)

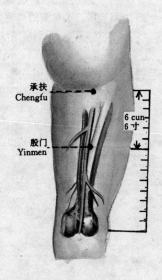

承扶
Chengfu

殷门
Yinmen

6 cun
6 寸

〔取穴法〕（1）在大腿后面，当承扶与委中的连线上，承扶下 6 寸处。

（2）俯卧，先取承扶、委中，于两穴连线的上 3/7 与下 4/7 的交点处取穴。

〔功效与主治〕舒筋，健腰膝。腰腿痛，下肢痿、痹。

〔操作〕直刺 0.5～1 寸。

Method of locating the point:

(1) This point is on the posterior aspect of the thigh, on the line joining Chengfu (BL 36) and Weizhong (BL 40), 6 cun below Chengfu (BL 36).

(2) Ask patient to take a prone position, find out Chengfu (BL 36) and Weizhong (BL 40), then locate the point at the junction of the upper three seventh and the lower four seventh of the line connecting Chengfu (BL 36) and Weizhong (BL 40).

Actions and indications: Relax tendons and strengthen the loin and the knee, used to treat lumbago, pain of the leg, and paralysis or arthralgia of the lower limb.

Manipulation: Puncture perpendicularly 0.5—1 cun.

委阳 Wěiyáng（BL 39）

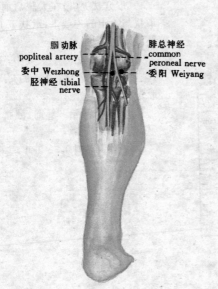

腘动脉
popliteal artery

委中 Weizhong
胫神经 tibial
nerve

腓总神经
common
peroneal nerve

委阳 Weiyang

〔取穴法〕（1）在腘横纹外侧端，当股二头肌腱的内侧处。

（2）俯卧，于腘窝横纹正中委中穴外开1寸处取穴。

〔功效与主治〕通三焦，利水道。腰脊强痛，小腹胀，小便不利。

〔操作〕直刺0.3～0.8寸。

〔备注〕三焦的"下合"穴。

Method of locating the point:

(1) This point is on the lateral end of the transverse popliteal crease, on the medial border of the tendon of m. biceps femoris.

(2) Ask patient to take a prone position, locate the point 1 cun lateral to Weizhong (BL 40) which is at the midpoint of the transverse crease of the popliteal fossa.

Actions and indications: Promote flow of Qi in the triple-jiao and water metabolism, used to treat lumbar rigidity and pain, distension in the lower abdomen and dysuria.

Manipulation: Puncture perpendicularly 0.3—0.8 cun.

Notes: This point is the Lower He-Sea point of the triple-jiao.

委中 Wěizhōng（BL 40）

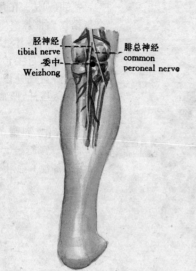

胫神经
tibial nerve
委中
Weizhong

腓总神经
common
peroneal nerve

〔取穴法〕在腘横纹中点，当股二头肌腱与半腱肌肌腱的中间处。

〔功效与主治〕舒筋活络，强健腰膝，泄暑热，止吐泻。腰背膝痛，腘筋拘急，下肢痿、痹，腹痛吐泻。

〔操作〕避开动脉，直刺 0.6～1寸，或于浅静脉速刺出血。

〔备注〕足太阳膀胱经"合"穴；膀胱之"下合"穴。

Method of locating the point: This point is in the midpoint of the transverse crease of the popliteal fossa, between tendons of m. biceps femoris and m. semitendinosus.

Actions and indications: Relax muscles and tendons, promote flow of blood in the collaterals, strengthen the loins and knees, purge the summer-heat and relieve vomiting, used to treat pain in the lumbar region, back and knee, contraction of the tendons in the popliteal fossa, paralysis or arthralgia in the lower limbs, abdominal pain with vomiting and diarrhea.

Manipulation: Puncture perpendicularly 0.6 — 1 cun, or prick the superficial vein quickly with a three-edged needle to cause bleeding. Avoid injuring the artery.

Notes: This point is the He-Sea point of the Bladder Meridian of Foot Taiyang, it is also the lower He-Sea point of the bladder.

149

膏肓 Gāohuāng（BL 43）

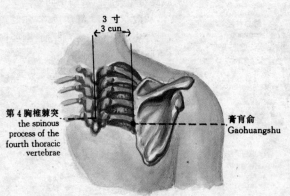

3 寸
3 cun

第4胸椎棘突
the spinous
process of the
fourth thoracic
vertebrae

膏肓俞
Gaohuangshu

〔取穴法〕在背部，当第4胸椎棘突下，后正中线旁开3寸处。

〔功效与主治〕通宣理肺，益气补虚。肺痨，骨蒸盗汗，咳血，哮喘，遗精。

〔操作〕斜刺0.3～0.5寸。宜灸。

〔备注〕强壮保健要穴。

Method of locating the point: This point is located on the back, below the spinous process of the 4th thoracic vertebra, 3 cun lateral to the posterior midline.

Actions and indications: Facilitate flow of the lung Qi, supplement Qi and tonify deficiency, used to treat lung tuberculosis, bone-heat, night sweating, spitting of blood, asthma and emission.

Manipulation: Puncture obliquely 0.3—0.5 cun. Moxibustion is advisable.

Notes: This is an important point for strengthening the body and keeping health.

神堂 Shéntáng（BL 44）

〔取穴法〕在背部，当第 5 胸椎棘突下，后正中线旁开 3 寸处。

〔功效与主治〕宽胸理气，宁心。咳嗽，气喘，胸闷，心痛。

〔操作〕斜刺 0.3～0.5 寸。

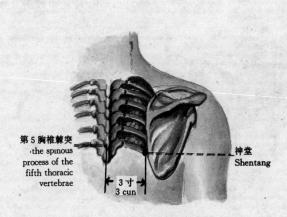

第 5 胸椎棘突
the spinous
process of the
fifth thoracic
vertebrae

3 寸
3 cun

神堂
Shentang

Method of locating the point: This point is on the back, below the spinous process of the 5th thoracic vertebra, 3 cun lateral to the posterior midline.

Actions and indications: Soothe flow of Qi in the chest, regulate flow of Qi and rest the heart, used to treat cough, asthma, chest stuffiness and cardiac pain.

Manipulation: Puncture obliquely 0.3—0.5 cun.

谚谙 Yìxǐ (BL 45)

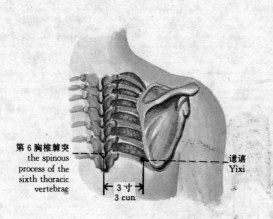

第 6 胸椎棘突
the spinous
process of the
sixth thoracic
vertebrae

3 寸
3 cun

谚谙
Yixi

〔取穴法〕在背部，当第 6 胸椎棘突下，后正中线旁开 3 寸处。

〔功效与主治〕清热，止咳平喘。咳喘，肩背痛。

〔操作〕斜刺 0.3 ～0.5 寸。

Method of locating the point: This point is on the back, below the spinous process of the 6th thoracic vertebra, 3 cun lateral to the posterior midline.

Actions and indications: Clear away heat, relieve cough and stop asthma, used to treat cough, asthma, and pain of the shoulder and back.

Manipulation: Puncture obliquely 0.3—0.5 cun.

膈关 Géguān (BL 46)

〔取穴法〕在背部,当第 7 胸椎棘突下,后正中线旁开 3 寸处。

〔功效与主治〕宽胸,利气,降逆。呕吐,饮食不下,呃逆。

〔操作〕针刺 0.3～0.5 寸。

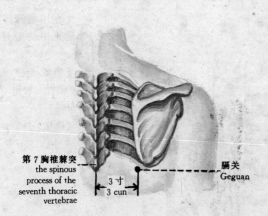

第 7 胸椎棘突
the spinous
process of the
seventh thoracic
vertebrae

3 寸
3 cun

膈关
Geguan

Method of locating the point: This point is on the back, below the spinous process of the 7th thoracic vertebra, 3 cun lateral to the posterior midline.

Actions and indications: Soothe flow of Qi in the chest, promote flow of Qi and lower adverse flow of Qi, used to treat vomiting, anorexia and hiccup.

Manipulation: Puncture obliquely 0.3—0.5 cun.

胃仓 Wèicāng (BL 50)

〔取穴法〕在背部,当第12胸椎棘突下,后正中线旁开3寸处。

〔功效与主治〕理气和胃。腹胀,胃痛,痞疾。

〔操作〕斜刺0.3~0.5寸。

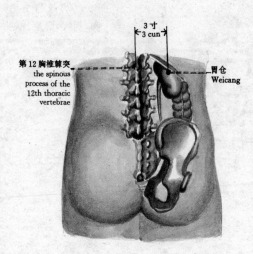

第12胸椎棘突
the spinous
process of the
12th thoracic
vertebrae

3 寸
3 cun

胃仓
Weicang

Method of locating the point: This point is on the back, below the spinous process of the 12th thoracic vertebra, 3 cun lateral to the posterior midline.

Actions and indications: Regulate flow of Qi, normalize the function of the stomach, used to treat abdominal distension, stomachache and malnutrition.

Manipulation: Puncture obliquely 0.3—0.5 cun.

志室 Zhishi（BL 51）

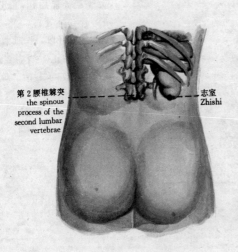

第 2 腰椎棘突
the spinous
process of the
second lumbar
vertebrae

志室
Zhishi

〔取穴法〕（1）在腰部，当第 2 腰椎棘突下，后正中线旁开 3 寸处。

（2）俯卧，先取命门穴（与脐相对），再旁开 3 寸处。

〔功效与主治〕滋补肾阴，清利下焦湿热。腰酸痛，遗精，阳痿，早泄。

〔操作〕直刺 0.3～0.5 寸。

Method of locating the point：

（1）This point is on the back，below the spinous process of the 2th lumbar vertebra，3 cun lateral to the posterior midline.

（2）Ask patient to take a prone position，locate Mingmen (LU 4，located on the back opposite to the umbilicus) first，then locate the point 3 cun lateral to Mingmen (DU 4).

Actions and indications：Nourish the kidney yin，clear away damp-heat from the lower-jiao，used to treat soreness and pain in the lumbar region，emission. impotence and premature ejaculation.

Manipulation：Puncture perpendicularly 0.3—0.5 cun.

秩边 Zhìbiān（BL 54）

〔取穴法〕（1）在臀部，平第4骶后孔，骶正中嵴旁开3寸处。

（2）俯卧，平骶管裂孔，旁开后正中线3寸处。

〔功效与主治〕疏通经络，强健腰膝。下肢痿、痹，二便不利，痔疾。

〔操作〕直刺1.5～2寸。

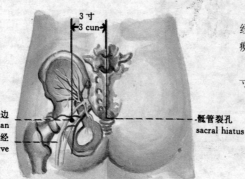

Method of locating the point:

（1）This point is on the buttock, at the level of the 4th posterior sacral foramen, 3 cun lateral to median sacral crest.

（2）Ask patient to take a prone posititon, locate the point at the level of the sacral hiatus, 3 cun lateral to the posterior midline.

Actions and indications: Dredge channels and collaterals, strengthen the loins and knees, used to treat paralysis and arthralgia of the lower limbs, difficulty in defecation and urination and hemorrhoids.

Manipulation: Puncture perpendicularly 1.5－2 cun.

合阳 Héyáng（BL 55）

〔取穴法〕在小腿后面,当委中与承山的连线上,委中下2寸处。

〔功效与主治〕调下焦,健腰膝。腰脊痛,下肢酸痛,下肢痿、痹。

〔操 作〕直刺 0.3～0.5寸。

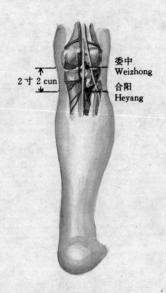

2寸 2 cun

委中 Weizhong

合阳 Heyang

Method of locating the point: This point is on the posterior aspect of the leg, on the line connecting Weizhong (BL 40) and Chengshan (BL 57), 2 cun below Weizhong (BL 40).

Actions and indications: Regulate function of the lower-jiao, strengthen the loins and knees, used to treat pain of the loins and spinal column, soreness in the lower leg, and paralysis and arthralgia of the lower leg.

Manipulation: Puncture perpendicularly 0. 3—0. 5 cun.

承筋 Chéngjīn (BL 56)

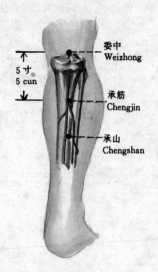

委中
Weizhong

5寸
5 cun

承筋
Chengjin

承山
Chengshan

〔取穴法〕（1）在小腿后面,当委中与承山的连线上,腓肠肌肌腹中央,委中下5寸处。

（2）俯伏或正坐垂足,在合阳穴与承山穴之间,当腓肠肌肌腹中央处。

〔功效与主治〕健腰膝,理肛疾。小腿痛,痔疾,霍乱转筋。

〔操作〕直刺0.5～1寸。

Method of locating the point:

(1) This point is on the posterior aspect of the leg, on the line connecting Weizhong (BL 40) with Chengshan (BL 57), 5 cun below Weizhong (BL 40).

(2) Ask patient to take a prone position or a sitting position with the legs dropped, locate the point between Heyang (BL 55) and Chengshan (BL 57), in the centre of the belly of m. gastrocnemius.

Actions and indications: Strengthen the loins and knees and relieve anal disorders, used to treat pain of the lower legs, hemorrhoids and acute gastroenteritis marked by spasm of the gastrocnemius.

Manipulation: Puncture perpendicularly 0.5—1 cun.

158

承山 Chéngshān （BL 57）

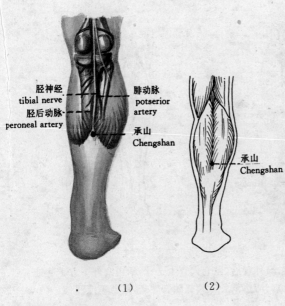

胫神经
tibial nerve
胫后动脉
peroneal artery

腓动脉
potserior
artery

承山
Chengshan

承山
Chengshan

（1）　　　　（2）

〔取穴法〕
(1)在小腿后面正中,委中与昆仑之间,当伸直小腿或足跟上提时腓肠肌肌腹下出现尖角凹陷处。

(2)直立,两手上举按着墙壁,足尖着地,在腓肠肌下部出现人字陷纹,当"人"字尖下取穴。

〔功效与主治〕舒筋活络,调理肠腑。腰背痛,腿痛转筋,痔疾。

〔操作〕直刺0.5～1.5寸。

Method of locating the point：

(1) This point is on the posterior aspect of the lower leg, in the depression of the acute angle formed between Weizhong (BL 40) and Kunlun (BL 69) below the belly of m. gastrocnemius when the lower leg is extended straight or the heel is lifted.

(2) Ask patient to stand erect, raise and place his hands on the wall and touch the ground with his tips of feet, then locate the point below the angle of the Λ shaped depression emerging below m. gastrocnemius.

Actions and indications: Relax muscles and tendons, activate flow of blood in the channels and collaterals, regulate the function of the intestine, used to treat pain of the loins and back, pain of the leg, spasm of m. gastrocnemius, and hemorrhoids.

Manipulation: Puncture perpendicularly 0.5—1.5 cun.

159

飞扬 Fēiyáng (BL 58)

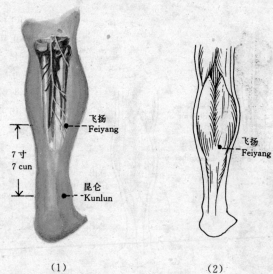

(1)　　　　　　　　(2)

〔取穴法〕在小腿后面,当外踝后,昆仑穴直上 7 寸,承山穴外下方 1 寸处。
〔功效与主治〕疏筋活络,清热消肿。腰腿腨脚肿痛,筋急不能屈伸。
〔操作〕直刺 0.5～1.2 寸。可灸。
〔备注〕足太阳膀胱经"络"穴。

Method of locating the point: This point is on the posterior aspect of the lower leg, behind the external malleolus, 7 cun directly above Kunlun (BL 69), 1 cun lateroinferior to Chengshan (BL 57).

Actions and indications: Relax muscles and tendons, activate flow of Qi and blood in the collaterals, clear away heat and subdue swelling, used to treat swelling and pain of the loins, legs, m. gastrocnemius and foot, failure of the tendons to extend or flex due to spasm.

Manipulation: Puncture perpendicularly 0.5 − 1.2 cun. Moxibustion is advisable.

Notes: This point is the Luo-Connecting point of the Bladder Meridian of Foot Taiyang.

160

跗阳 Fūyáng（BL 59）

〔取穴法〕在小腿后面，外踝后，昆仑穴直上3寸处。

〔功效与主治〕舒筋止痛。头重，头痛，下肢痿、痹。

〔操作〕直刺0.3～0.5寸。

〔备注〕阳跷脉"郄"穴。

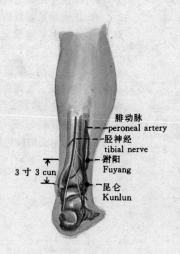

腓动脉
peroneal artery

胫神经
tibial nerve

跗阳
Fuyang

昆仑
Kunlun

3 寸 3 cun

Method of locating the point: This point is on the posterior aspect of the lower leg, behind the external malleolus, 3 cun directly above Kunlun point (BL 69).

Actions and indications: Relax muscles and tendons and relieve pain, used to treat heaviness of head, headache, paralysis and arthralgia of the lower limbs.

Manipulation: Puncture perpendicularly 0.3－0.5 cun.

Notes: This point is the Xi-Cleft point of Yangqiao Meridian.

昆仑 Kūnlún (BL 60)

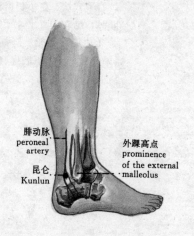

腓动脉
peroneal
artery

昆仑
Kunlun

外踝高点
prominence
of the external
malleolus

〔取穴法〕(1)在足部外踝后方,当外踝尖与跟腱之间的凹陷处。

(2)正坐垂足着地或俯卧,于外踝尖与跟腱水平连线之中点处取穴。

〔功效与主治〕疏通经络,消肿止痛,强健腰腿。头痛连项,腰腿拘急疼痛,足跟痛,难产,目痛如脱。

〔操作〕直刺 0.3～0.5 寸。

〔备注〕足太阳膀胱经"经"穴。

Method of locating the point:

(1) This point is located behind the external malleolus, in the depression between the tip of the external malleolus and the tendo calcaneus.

(2) Ask patient to sit erect with his legs dropped to touch the ground or take a prone position, locate the point at the midpoint of the horizontal line connecting the tip of the external malleolus and the tendo calcaneus.

Actions and indications: Dredge channels and collateral, subdue swelling and relieve pain, strengthen the loins and legs, used to treat headache referring to the posterior aspect of the neck, convulsion and pain of the lumbar region and the leg, heel pain, difficult labour, distension and pain of the eye as if the eyeball is to be exploded.

Manipulation: Puncture perpendicularly 0.3—0.5 cun.

Notes: This point is the Jing-River point of the Bladder Meridian of Foot-Taiyang.

申脉 Shēnmài (BL 62)

〔取穴法〕在足外侧部,外踝直下方凹陷中取穴。

〔功效与主治〕宁神,舒筋。癫狂,痫证,头痛,眩晕,腹泻。

〔操作〕直刺 0.3~0.5 寸。

〔备注〕八脉交会穴之一,通于阳跷脉。

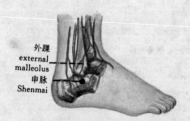

外踝
external
malleolus
申脉
Shenmai

Method of locating the point: This point is on the lateral aspect of the foot, in the depression directly below the external malleolus.

Actions and indications: Rest the heart and relax muscles and tendons, used to treat schizophrenia, epilepsy, mania, headache, dizziness and diarrhea.

Manipulation: Puncture perpendicularly 0.3—0.5 cun.

Notes: This is one of the confluence points of the eight meridians, communicating with the Yangqiao Meridian.

束骨 Shùgǔ（BL 64）

〔取穴法〕在足外侧，足小趾本节（第 5 跖趾关节）的后方，赤白肉际处。

〔功效与主治〕祛风清热。头痛，项强，目眩，腰背及下肢痛。

〔操作〕直刺 0.2～0.3 寸。

〔备注〕足太阳膀胱经"输"穴。

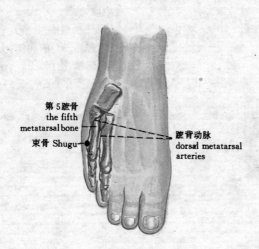

第 5 跖骨
the fifth
metatarsal bone

束骨 Shugu

跖背动脉
dorsal metatarsal
arteries

Method of locating the point: This point is located on the lateral aspect of the foot, posterior to the 5th metatarsal bone, at the junction of the red and the white skin.

Actions and indications: Expel wind and clear away heat, used to treat headache, rigidity of the nape, dizziness, pain of the lumbar region, back and lower leg.

Manipulation: Puncture perpendicularly 0.2－0.3 cun.

Notes: This point is the Shu-Stream point of the Bladder Meridian of Foot-Taiyang.

至阴 Zhiyin （BL 67）

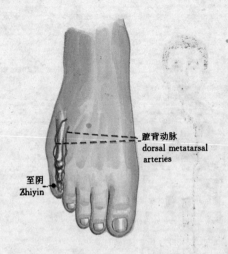

〔取穴法〕（1）在足小趾末节外侧，距趾甲角0.1寸处（指寸）。

（2）正坐垂足着地或仰卧，于足小趾爪甲外侧缘与基底部各作一线，两线交点处即是本穴。

〔功效与主治〕疏通经络，调整阴阳，清头明目，矫正胎位。头痛，头重，内眦痛，胎位不正。

〔操作〕浅刺0.1寸。

〔备注〕足太阳膀胱经"井"穴。

跖背动脉
dorsal metatarsal arteries

至阴
Zhiyin

Method of locating the point：

（1）This point is on the lateral side of the metatarsal bone of the little toe，0.1 cun lateral to the corner of the nail.

（2）Ask patient to sit erect with the foot dropped on the ground or take a supine position，locate the point at the crossing point of the line drawn along the lateral side of the nail of the little toe and the the line drawn along the base of the nail.

Actions and indications：Dredge channels and collaterals，regulate yin and yang，clear away heat from the head to improve eyesight，and correct malposition of fetus，used to treat headache，heaviness of the head，pain in the canthus and improper fetal position.

Manipulation：Puncture superficially 0.1 cun.

Notes：This point is the Jing-Well point of the Bladder Meridian of Foot-Taiyang.

八、足少阴肾经

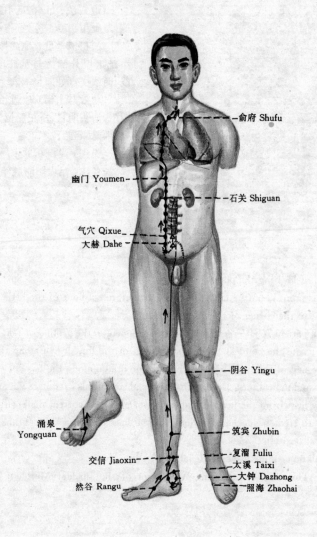

俞府 Shufu

幽门 Youmen

石关 Shiguan

气穴 Qixue

大赫 Dahe

阴谷 Yingu

涌泉 Yongquan

筑宾 Zhubin

交信 Jiaoxin

复溜 Fuliu

太溪 Taixi

大钟 Dazhong

然谷 Rangu

照海 Zhaohai

起于足小趾之下,斜向足心(涌泉),出于舟骨粗隆下,沿内踝后,进入足跟,再向上行于腿肚内侧,出腘窝的内侧,向上行股内后缘,通向脊柱(长强,属督脉),属于肾脏(腧穴通路:还出于前,向上行腹部前正中线旁开 0.5 寸,胸部前正中线旁开 2 寸,终止于锁骨下缘俞府穴),联络膀胱。肾脏部直行的脉:从肾向上通过肝和横膈,进入肺中,沿着喉咙,挟于舌根部。肺部支脉:从肺部出来,联络心脏,流注于胸中,与手厥阴心包经相接。

8. The Kidney Meridian of Foot-Shaoyin

The Kidney Meridian of Foot-Shaoyin originates from the inferior aspect of the small toe. Running obliquely towards the sole (Yongquan, KI 1), it emerges from the lower aspect of the tuberosity of the navicular bone, runs behind the medial malleolus, and enters the heel. Then, it ascends along the medial side of the leg to the medial side of the popliteal fossa and goes further upwards along the medial aspect of the thigh towards the vertebral column (Changqiang, DU 1), where it enters its pertaining organ-the kidney (Pathway of Qi through the acupoints: It winds to the front of the body, goes upwards 0.5 cun lateral to the anterior midline in the abdomen and 2 cun lateral to the anterior midline in the chest, ending at Shufu, KI 27 that is located below the lower border of the clavicular bone), and its connecting organ-the bladder. The straight portion of the meridian from the kidney runs upwards. Passing through the liver and the diaphragm, it enters the lung. Then, alongside the throat, it terminates at the root of the tongue. The branch starting from the chest emerges in the chest to connect with the heart and runs into the chest to link with the Pericardium Meridian of Hand-Jueyin.

涌泉 Yǒngquán (KI 1)

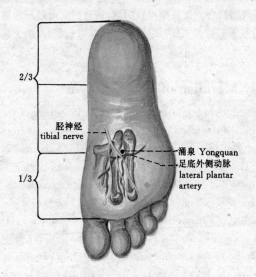

胫神经
tibial nerve

涌泉 Yongquan
足底外侧动脉
lateral plantar
artery

〔取穴法〕(1)在足底部，跷足时前部凹陷处，约当足底二三趾趾缝纹头端与足跟连线的前 1/3 与后 2/3 交点上。

(2)跷足时，在足心前 1/3 的凹陷中取之。

〔功效与主治〕通关，开窍，安神，镇静。晕厥，头痛，目眩，失眠，小儿惊风，下肢瘫，足心热痛。

〔操作〕直刺 0.3～0.8 寸。

〔备注〕足少阴肾经"井"穴。

Method of locating the point:

(1) This point is on the sole of the foot, in the depression of the anterior part of the sole when the foot is in plantar flexion, at the junction of the anterior third and the posterior two thirds of the line connecting the end of the junction of the second and the third toes with the heel.

(2) When the foot is in plantar flexion, locate the point in the depression at the third of the sole.

Actions and indications: Relieve trismus, restore resuscitation, tranquilize the mind and rest the heart, used to treat syncope, headache, dizziness, insomnia, infantile convulsion, paralysis of the lower limb, and feverish sensation in the soles.

Manipulation: Puncture perpendicularly 0.3—0.8 cun.

Notes: This point is the Jing-Well point of the Kidney Meridian of Foot-Shaoyin.

168

然谷 Rángǔ (KI 2)

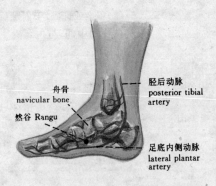

舟骨
navicular bone

然谷 Rangu

胫后动脉
posterior tibial artery

足底内侧动脉
lateral plantar artery

〔取穴法〕（1）在足内侧缘,足舟骨粗隆下方,赤白肉际处。

（2）正坐或仰卧,于内踝前下方,舟骨粗隆前下方凹陷处。

〔功效与主治〕益肾调经,清热利湿。月经不调,阴痒,阳痿,遗精。

〔操作〕直刺 0.3～0.5 寸。

〔备注〕足少阴肾经"荥"穴。

Method of locating the point:

(1) This point is on the medial side of the foot, inferior to the tuberosity of the navicular bone, at the junction of the red and the white skin.

(2) Ask patient to take a sitting or a supine position, locate the point anteroinferior to the medial malleolus, in the depression inferior to the tuberosity of the navicular bone.

Actions and indications: Tonify the kidney, regulate menstruation, clear away heat and remove dampness, used to treat irregular menstruation, pruritus vulvae, impotence and emission.

Manipulation: Puncture perpendicularly 0.3—0.5 cun.

Notes: This point is the Ying-Spring point of the Kidney Meridian of Foot-Shaoyin.

太溪 Tàixī (KI 3)

〔取穴法〕(1)在足内侧,内踝后方,当内踝尖与跟腱之间的凹陷处。

(2)正坐或仰卧,于内踝后缘与跟腱前缘的中间,与内踝尖平齐处取穴。

〔功效与主治〕调补肾气,通利三焦,强健腰膝。头痛,眩晕,咽喉痛,失眠,耳鸣耳聋,遗精,阳痿,内踝痛。

〔操作〕直刺 0.3～0.5 寸。

〔备注〕足少阴肾经"输"、"原"穴。

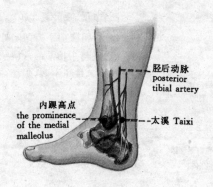

内踝高点
the prominence
of the medial
malleolus

胫后动脉
posterior
tibial artery

太溪 Taixi

Method of locating the point:

(1) This point is on the medial side of the foot, behind the medial malleolus, in the depression between the tip of the medial malleolus and the heel.

(2) Ask patient to take a sitting or a supine position, locate the point between the posterior border of the medial malleolus and the anterior border of the heel, at the level of the tip of the medial malleolus.

Actions and indications: Regulate and tonify the kidney Qi, promote flow of Qi in the triple-jiao, strengthen the loins and the knee, used to treat headache, dizziness, sore throat, insomnia, tinnitus, deafness, emission, impotence and pain in the medial malleolus.

Manipulation: Puncture perpendicularly 0.3—0.5 cun.

Notes: This point is the Shu-Stream and the Yuan-Primary points of the Kidney Meridian of Foot-Shaoyin.

大钟 Dàzhōng（KI 4）

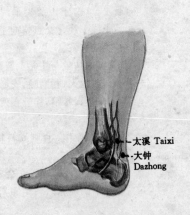

太溪 Taixi
大钟 Dazhong

〔取穴法〕(1)在足内侧，内踝后下方，当跟腱附着部的内侧前方凹陷处。

(2)正坐或仰卧，于内踝下缘平齐而靠跟腱前缘处取穴。

(3)先取太溪、水泉穴，于二穴连线中点平齐而靠跟腱前缘处取穴。

〔功效与主治〕强腰壮肾。腰脊强痛，气喘，痴呆，嗜卧。

〔操作〕直刺 0.2～0.3 寸。

〔备注〕足少阴肾经"络"穴。

Method of locating the point：

(1) This point is on the medial side of the foot, posteroinferior to the medial malleolus, in the depression anterior to the attachment of tendo calcaneus.

(2) Ask patient to take a sitting or a supine position, locate the point on the lower border of the medial malleolus, distal to the anterior border of the tendo calcaneus.

(3) Locate Taixi (KI 3) and Shuiquan (KI 5) first, locate Dazhong point (KI 4) at the level of the midpoint of the line connecting Taixi (KI 3) and Shuiquan (KI 5), proximal to the anterior border of the tendo calcaneus.

Actions and indications：Strengthen the loins and the knees, used to treat rigidity and pain of the lumbar region and the vertebral column, asthma, dementia, and lethargy.

Manipulation：Puncture perpendicularly 0.2—0.3 cun.

Notes：This point is the Luo-Connecting point of the Kidney Meridian of Foot-Shaoyin.

照海 Zhàohǎi (KI 6)

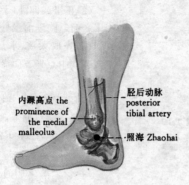

内踝高点 the prominence of the medial malleolus

胫后动脉 posterior tibial artery

照海 Zhaohai

〔取穴法〕（1）在足内侧，内踝尖下方凹陷处。

（2）于内踝尖垂线与内踝下缘平线之交点略向下方之凹陷处取穴。

〔功效与主治〕通经活络，清热泄火，利咽喉，安心神。咽喉干痛，暴喑，痫证夜发，失眠，便秘。

〔操作〕直刺或斜刺 0.3～0.5 寸。

〔备注〕八脉交会穴之一，通于阴跷脉。

Method of locating the point:

(1) This point is on the medial side of the foot, in the depression anteroinferior to the tip of the medial malleolus.

(2) Locate the point in the depression a bit below the junction of the vertical line passing through the tip of the medial malleolus and the horizontal line along the lower border of the medial malleolus.

Actions and indications: Promote flow of Qi and blood in the channels and collaterals, clear away heat and purge fire, benefit the throat, and tranquilize the mind, used to treat dry and sore throat, sudden hoarseness, nocturnal attack of epilepsy, insomnia and constipation.

Manipulation: Puncture perpendicularly or obliquely 0.3—0.5 cun.

Notes: This point is one of the confluence points of the eight meridians, communicating with the Yinqiao Meridian.

复溜 Fùliū (KI 7)

〔取穴法〕在小腿内侧,太溪直上 2 寸,跟腱的前方处。

〔功效与主治〕滋阴,清热,利尿。水肿,泄泻,自汗,盗汗。

〔操作〕直刺 0.3 ～0.5 寸。

〔备注〕足少阴肾经"经"穴。

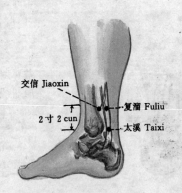

Method of locating the point: This point is on the medial aspect of the lower leg, 2 cun directly above Taixi (KI 3), anteroinferior to the tendo calcaneus.

Actions and indications: Nourish yin, clear away heat and induce diuresis, used to treat edema, diarrhea, spontaneous sweating and night sweating.

Manipulation: Puncture perpendicularly 0.3—0.5 cun.

Notes: This point is the Jing-River point of the Kidney Meridian of Foot-Shaoyin.

交信 Jiāoxìn (KI 8)

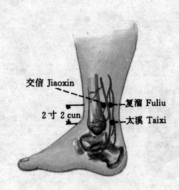

〔取穴法〕在小腿内侧,当太溪直上3寸,复溜穴前0.5寸,胫骨内侧缘的后方。

〔功效与主治〕益肾调经。月经不调,崩漏,睾丸肿痛。

〔操作〕直刺0.3～0.5寸。

〔备注〕足少阴肾经"郄"穴。

Method of locating the point: This point is on the medial aspect of the lower leg, 2 cun directly above Taixi (KI 3), 0.5 cun anterior to Fuliu (KI 7), posterior to the medial border of the tibia.

Actions and indications: Benefit the kidney and regulate menstruation, used to treat irregular menstruation, metrostaxis and metrorrahgia, and swelling and pain of the testis.

Manipulation: Puncture perpendicularly 0.3—0.5 cun.

Notes: This point is the Xi-Cleft point of the Kidney Meridian of Foot-Shaoyin.

筑宾 Zhùbīn (KI 9)

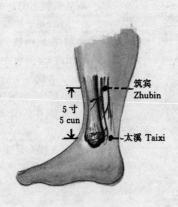

5寸
5 cun

筑宾
Zhubin

太溪 Taixi

〔取穴法〕(1)在小腿内侧,当太溪与阴谷的连线上,太溪上5寸,腓肠肌肌腹的内下方处。

(2)正坐或仰卧,先取太溪穴,于其直上5寸,胫骨内侧面后缘约2寸处。

〔功效与主治〕解痉安神。呕吐涎沫,重舌,疝痛。

〔操作〕直刺0.3～0.5寸。

〔备注〕阴维脉"郄"穴。

Method of locating the point:

(1) This point is on the medial aspect of the lower leg, on the line joining Taixi (KI 3) and Yingu (KI 10), 5 cun above Taixi (KI 3), in the medial portion of the leg inferior to the belly of the m. gastrocnemius.

(2) Ask patient to sit erect or take a supine position, locate Taixi (KI 3) first, then locate the point 5 cun directly above Taixi (KI 3), 2 cun posterior to the border of the medial aspect of the tibia.

Actions and indications: Relieve spasm and tranquilize the mind, used to treat vomiting foamy fluid, swelling of tongue and hernia with pain.

Manipulation: Puncture perpendicularly 0.3—0.5 cun.

Notes: This point is the Xi-Cleft point of the Yinwei Meridian.

阴谷 Yīngǔ (KI 10)

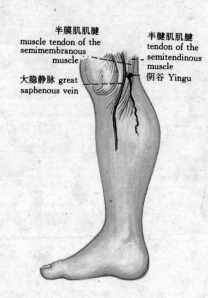

半膜肌肌腱
muscle tendon of the
semimembranous
muscle

半腱肌肌腱
tendon of the
semitendinous
muscle
阴谷 Yingu

大隐静脉 great
saphenous vein

〔取穴法〕(1)在腘窝内侧，屈膝时，当半腱肌肌腱与半膜肌肌腱之间处取穴。

(2)正坐屈膝，从腘横纹内侧端，按取两筋（半膜肌腱和半腱肌腱）之间取穴，平委中穴。

〔功效与主治〕益元壮骨。阳痿，疝痛，崩漏，阴中痛。

〔操作〕直刺 0.3～0.5 寸。

〔备注〕足少阴肾经"合"穴。

Method of locating the point:

(1) This point is on the medial side of the popliteal fossa. Locate the point between the tendons of m. semitendinosus and semimembranosus when the knee is flexed.

(2) Ask patient to sit erect with his leg flexed, find out the two tendons (tendons of m. semitendinosus and semimembranosus), then locate the point between them, at the medial end of the transverse crease of the popliteal fossa, at the level of Weizhong (BL 40).

Actions and indications: Supplement the premordial Qi and strengthen the kidney, used to treat impotence, hernia with pain, metrostaxis and metrorrhagia, and pain of the external genital.

Manipulation: Puncture perpendicularly 0.3—0.5 cun.

Notes: This point is the He-Sea point of the Kidney Meridian of Foot-Shaoyin.

大赫 Dàhè (KI 12)

〔取穴法〕(1)在下腹部,当脐中下4寸,前正中线旁开0.5寸处。

(2)仰卧,先取腹白线上耻骨联合上缘直上1寸的中极穴,再旁开0.5寸处。

〔功效与主治〕调补肾气。遗精,阳痿,阴茎痛,痛经。

〔操作〕直刺0.5~0.8寸。

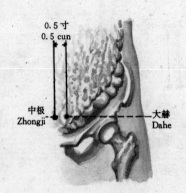

Method of locating the point:

(1) This point is on the lower abdomen, 4 cun below the centre of the umbilicus, 0.5 cun lateral to the anterior midline.

(2) Ask patient to take a supine position, locate Zhongji (RN 3) that is on the linea alba, 1 cun above the upper border of the pubis symphysis, then locate the point 0.5 cun lateral to Zhongji (RN 3).

Actions and indications: Regulate and tonify the kidney Qi, used to treat emission, impotence, pain of the testis and dysmenorrhea.

Manipulation: Puncture perpendicularly 0.5—0.8 cun.

177

气穴 Qìxuè (KI 3)

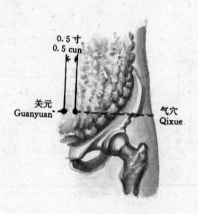

〔取穴法〕(1)在下腹部,当脐下 3 寸,前正中线旁开 0.5 寸处。

(2)关元穴旁开 0.5 寸处。

〔功效与主治〕益气调经。经闭,月经不调,崩漏,白带,不孕,阳痿。

〔操作〕直刺 0.5 ~1 寸。

〔备注〕足少阴经与冲脉交会穴。

Method of locating the point:

(1) This point is in the lower abdomen, 3 cun below the umbilicus, 0.5 cun lateral to the anterior midline.

(2) Locate the point 0.5 cun lateral to Guanyuan point (RN 4).

Actions and indications: Supplement Qi and regulate menstruation, used to treat amenorrhea, irregular menstruation, metrostaxis and metrorrhagia, leukorrhea, sterility and impotence.

Manipulation: Puncture perpendicularly 0.5—1 cun.

Notes: This point is the crossing point of the Kidney Meridian of Foot-Shaoyin and the Chong Meridian.

石关 Shíguān（KI 18）

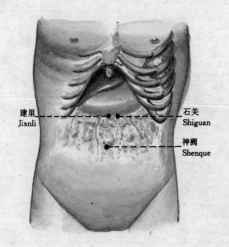

建里
Jianli

石关
Shiguan

神阙
Shenque

〔取穴法〕（1）在上腹部，当脐上 3 寸，前正中线旁开 0.5 寸处。

（2）在商曲穴（当脐中上 2 寸旁开 0.5 寸）上 1 寸处。

〔功效与主治〕调肠胃，理气滞。主治腹痛，胃痛，呕吐，不孕等。

〔操作〕直刺 0.5 ～1 寸。

〔备注〕足少阴经与冲脉交会穴。

Method of locating the point：

(1) This point is in the upper abdomen，3 cun above the umbilicus，0.5 cun lateral to the anterior midline.

(2) Locate the point 0.5 cun lateral to Jianli (RN 11).

Actions and indications：Regulate the function of the gastrointestine，relieve stagnation of Qi，used to treat abdominal pain，stomachache，vomiting and sterility.

Manipulation：Puncture perpendicularly 0.5—1 cun.

Notes：This point is a crossing point of the Kidney Meridian of Foot-Shaoyin and the Chong Meridian.

幽门 Yōumén (KI 21)

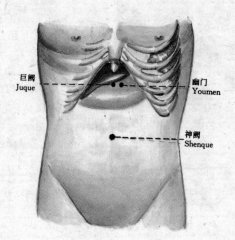

巨阙
Juque

幽门
Youmen

神阙
Shenque

〔取穴法〕仰卧位,在上腹部,当脐中上6寸(任脉巨阙穴)旁开0.5寸处。

〔功效与主治〕疏肝理气,健脾和胃。主治腹痛,腹胀,呕吐。

〔操作〕直刺0.3~0.6寸。

Method of locating the point:

(1) This point is in the upper abdomen, 6 cun above the umbilicus, 0.5 cun lateral to the anterior midline.

(2) Locate the point 0.5 cun lateral to Juque point (RN 14).

Actions and indications: Soothe the flow of the liver Qi, strengthen the spleen and regulate the function of the stomach, used to treat abdominal pain, abdominal distension, vomiting, eructation and anorexia.

Manipulation: Puncture perpendicularly 0.5—1 cun.

俞府 Shūfǔ (KI 27)

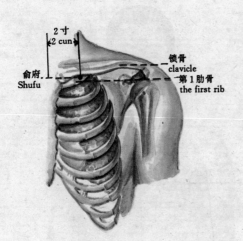

俞府
Shufu

2寸
2 cun

锁骨
clavicle

第1肋骨
the first rib

〔取穴法〕患者取仰卧位或端坐位,在胸上部,锁骨下方,当锁骨与第1肋之间的凹陷处,前正中线旁开2寸处。

〔功效与主治〕止咳,定喘,镇痛。主治咳嗽,气喘,胸痛。

〔操作〕斜刺或平刺0.2~0.3寸。

Method of locating the point:

(1) This point is on the chest, on the lower border of the clavicular bone, 2 cun lateral to the anterior midline.

(2) Ask patient to take a sitting position or a supine position, locate the point at the midway of the mid-sternal line and the mid-clavicular line, on the lower border of the clavicular bone.

Actions and indications: Relieve cough, stop asthma and alleviate pain, used to treat cough, asthma and chest pain.

Manipulation: Puncture obliquely or subcutaneously 0.2—0.3 cun.

九、手厥阴心包经

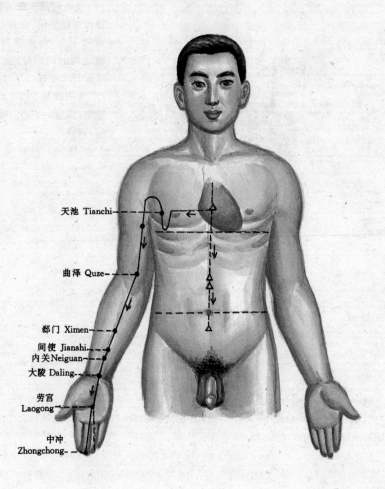

天池 Tianchi

曲泽 Quze

郄门 Ximen
间使 Jianshi
内关 Neiguan
大陵 Daling

劳宫
Laogong

中冲
Zhongchong

起于胸中,出属心包络,向下通过横膈,从胸至腹依次联络上、中、下三焦。胸部支脉:沿着胸中,出于胁部,至腋下 3 寸处(天池),上行到腋窝中,沿上臂内侧,行于手太阴和手少阴之间,进入肘窝中,向下行于前臂两筋(掌长肌腱与桡侧腕屈肌腱)的中间,进入掌中,沿着中指到指端(中冲);掌中支脉:从劳宫分出,沿着无名指到指端(关冲),与手少阳三焦经相接。

9. The Pericardium Meridian of Hand-Jueyin

The Pericardium Meridian of Hand-Jueyin originates from the chest, then it e-merges and pertains to the pericardium. Passing through the diaphragm, it descends from the chest to the abdomen to connect with the upper-, the middle- and the lower-jiao successively. A branch arising from the chest runs inside the chest and emerges in the hypochondriac region at a point 3 cun below the anterior axillary fossa (Tianchi, PC 1). Then it ascends to the axilla. Along the medial aspect of the upper arm, it goes downwards between the Hand-Taiyin Meridian and Hand-Shaoyin Meridian, entering the cubital fossa. Then it goes downwards further between the tendons of m. palmaris longus and m. flexor carpi radialis in the forearm, reaching the centre of the palm. From there, it passes along the middle finger to its tip (Zhongchong, PC 9). The branch arising from the palm starts from Laogong (PC 8), runs along the ring finger to end at its tip (Guanchong, SJ 1),where it links with the Sanjiao Meridian of Hand-Shaoyang.

天池 Tiānchí（PC 1）

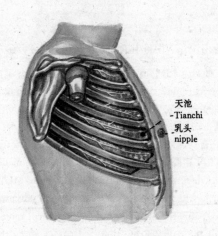

天池
-Tianchi
乳头
nipple

〔取穴法〕（1）在胸部，当第 4 肋间隙，前正中线旁开 5 寸处。

（2）仰卧，当第 4 肋间隙，乳头中点外开 1 寸处。妇女应于第 4 肋间隙，锁骨中线向外 1 寸处取穴。

〔功效与主治〕清热散结，理气宽胸。胸膈烦闷，胁肋痛，乳病。

〔操作〕斜刺 0.2～0.3 寸。

〔备注〕手厥阴、足少阳经交会穴。不可深刺。

Method of Locating the point：

（1）This point is located in the fourth intercostal space，5 cun lateral to the anterior midline.

（2）When patient takes a supine position，the point is found in the fourth intercostal space，1 cun lateral to the nipple. In females，it is found in the fourth intercostal space，1 cun lateral to the midclavicular line.

Actions and indications：Clear away heat，disintegrate nodules，soothe flow of Qi in the chest，used to treat restlessness with suffocating sensation in the chest，pain in the hypochondriac region，diseases of the breast.

Manipulation：Puncture obliquely 0.2—0.3 cun.

Notes：Tianchi（PC 1）is a crossing point of Hand-Jueyin Meridian and the Foot-Shaoyang Meridian. Deep puncture is not advisable.

曲泽 Qūzé (PC 3)

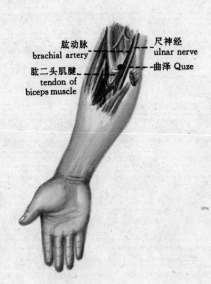

肱动脉
brachial artery

肱二头肌腱
tendon of
biceps muscle

尺神经
ulnar nerve

曲泽 Quze

〔取穴法〕（1）在肘横纹中,当肱二头肌腱的尺侧缘取穴。

（2）仰掌,微屈肘,于肱二头肌腱的尺侧,当肘弯横纹上取穴。

〔功效与主治〕疏通心络,泄湿热,止痛,止泻。热病烦躁,心痛,胃痛,呕吐,肘臂痛。

〔操作〕直刺 0.5~0.8 寸,或三棱针点刺出血。

〔备注〕手厥阴心包经"合"穴。

Method of locating the point：

（1）This point is located on the transverse cubital crease of the wrist, on the ulnar side of the tendon of m. biceps brachii.

（2）When the palm is placed upwards with the elbow slightly flexed, it is found above the transverse cubital crease of the wrist on the ulnar side of the tendon of m. biceps brachii.

Actions and indications：Dredge the cardiac vessels, purge damp-heat, relieve pain and stop diarrhea, used to treat dysphoria in febrile diseases, cardiac pain, stomache, vomiting, pain in the elbow and arm.

Manipulation：Puncture perpendicularly 0.5－0.8 cun, or prick with a three-edged needle to cause bleeding.

Notes：Quze (PC 3) is the He-Sea point of the Pericardium Meridian of Hand-Jueyin.

郄门 Xìmén (PC 4)

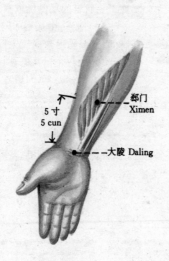

郄门 Ximen

5 寸
5 cun

大陵 Daling

〔取穴法〕(1)在前臂掌侧,当曲泽与大陵的连线上,腕横纹上5寸处。

(2)伸臂仰掌,于掌后第1横纹正中(大陵)直上5寸,当掌长肌腱与桡侧腕屈肌腱之间处取穴。

〔功效与主治〕宁心安神,宽胸理气,通络止痛。心胸部疼痛,呕血,鼻衄。

〔操作〕直刺0.5~1寸。

〔备注〕手厥阴心包经"郄"穴。

Method of locating the point:

(1) This point is located 5 cun above the transverse crease of the wrist, on the line connecting Quze (PC 3) and Daling (PC 7), on the palmar side of the forearm.

(2) When the palm is placed upwards with the arm stretched out, it is found 5 cun above the midpoint of the first transverse crease of the wrist, between the tendons of m. palmaris longus and m. flexor carpi radialis.

Actions and indications: Tranquilize the mind, relieve stagnation of Qi in the chest, promote flow of blood in the collaterals to relieve pain, used to treat pain in the cardiac region and the chest, hematemesis,and epistaxis.

Manipulation: Puncture perpendicularly 0.5—1 cun.

Notes: Ximen (PC 4) is the Xi-Cleft point of the Pericardium Meridian of Hand-Jueyin.

间使 Jiānshǐ (PC 5)

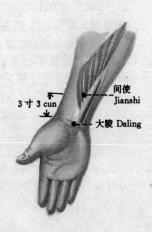

3 寸 3 cun

间使 Jianshi

大陵 Daling

〔取穴法〕(1)在前臂掌侧,当曲泽与大陵的连线上,腕横纹上3寸,当掌长肌腱与桡侧腕屈肌腱之间取穴。

(2)伸臂仰掌,手掌后第1横纹正中(大陵)直上3寸,当掌长肌腱与桡侧腕屈肌腱之间处取穴。

〔功效与主治〕宁心安神,通经活络,和胃祛痰。癫狂,痫证,心痛,心悸,疟疾。

〔操作〕直刺 0.5～0.8 寸。

〔备注〕手厥阴心包经"经"穴。

Method of locating the point:

(1) This point is located 3 cun above the transverse crease of the wrist, on the line connecting Quze (PC 3) and Daling (PC 7), between the tendons of m. palmaris longus and m. flexor carpi radialis.

(2) When the palm is placed upwards with the arm stretched out, it is found 3 cun just above the middle of the transverse crease of the wrist (Daling (PC 7), between the tendons of m. palmaris longus and m. flexor carpi radialis.

Actions and indications: Tranquilize the mind, promote blood flow in the channels and collaterals, regulate function of the stomach and eliminate phlegm, used to treat mania, epilepsy, cardiac pain, palpitation and malaria.

Manipulation: Puncture perpendicularly 0.5—0.8 cun.

Notes: Jianshi (PC 5) is the Jing-Well point of the Pericardium Meridian of Hand-Jueyin.

内关 Nèiguān (PC 6)

〔取穴法〕(1)在前臂掌侧,当曲泽与大陵的连线上,腕横纹上2寸,掌长肌腱与桡侧腕屈肌腱之间。

(2)伸臂仰掌,于尺、桡两骨之间,距腕横纹上2寸处。

〔功效与主治〕宁心安神,镇静镇痛,理气和胃。心痛,心悸,胸胁痛,呕吐,呃逆。

〔操作〕直刺0.5～1寸。

〔备注〕手厥阴心包经"络"穴;八脉交会穴之一,通于阴维脉。

2寸 2 cun

内关
Neiguan

大陵:
Daling

Method of locating the point:

(1) This point is located 2 cun above the transverse crease of the wrist, on the line connecting Quze (PC 3) and Daling (PC 7), between the tendones of m. palmaris longus and m. flexor carpi radialis.

(2) When the palm is placed upwards with the arm stretched out, it is found 2 cun above the transverse crease of the wrist between the ulna and radius.

Actions and indications: Tranquilize the mind, sedate, relieve pain, regulate folw of Qi and function of the stomach, used to treat cardiac pain, palpitation, pain in the chest and hypochondriac region, vomiting and hiccup.

Manipulation: Puncture perpendicularly 0.5—1 cun.

Notes: Neiguan (PC 6) is the Luo-Connecting point of the Pericardium Meridian of Hand-Jueyin and one of the confluence points of the eight meridians, which communicates with Yinwei Meridian.

大陵 Dàlíng（PC 7）

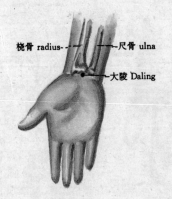

桡骨 radius —— —— 尺骨 ulna

—— 大陵 Daling

〔取穴法〕（1）在腕掌横纹的中点处，当掌长肌腱与桡侧腕屈肌腱之间。

（2）伸臂仰掌，于腕横纹中点处取穴。

〔功效与主治〕宁心安神，宽胸和胃。心痛，心悸，胃痛，呕吐。

〔操作〕直刺 0.3～0.5 寸。

〔备注〕手厥阴心包经"输"、"原"穴。

Method of locating the point:

(1) This point is located in the middle of the transverse crease of the wrist, between the tendons of m. palmaris longus and m. flexor carpi radialis.

(2) When the palm is placed upwards with the arm stretched out, it is found in the midpoint of the transverse crease of the wrist.

Actions and indications: Tranquilize the mind, relieve stagnation of Qi in the chest, regulate function of the stomach, used to treat cardiac pain, palpitation, stomachache and vomiting.

Manipulation: Puncture perpendicularly 0.3 - 0.5 cun

Notes: Daling (PC 7) is the Shu-Stream and Yuan-Primary point of the Pericardium Meridian of Hand-Jueyin.

劳宫 Láogōng (PC 8)

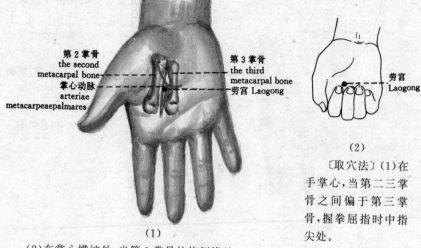

第2掌骨
the second
metacarpal bone
掌心动脉
arteriae
metacarpeaepalmares

第3掌骨
the third
metacarpal bone
劳宫 Laogong

劳宫
Laogong

(1)

(2)

〔取穴法〕(1)在手掌心,当第二三掌骨之间偏于第三掌骨,握拳屈指时中指尖处。

(2)在掌心横纹处,当第3掌骨的桡侧缘处。

〔功效与主治〕开窍回阳,清心醒神,泄热止抽。心痛,中风昏迷,口疮,口臭。

〔操作〕直刺 0.3~0.5 寸。

〔备注〕手厥阴心包经"荥"穴。

Method of locating the point:

(1) This point is located in the centre of the palm, between the second and the third metacarpal bones and is close to the third metacarpal bone. When the fist is clenched, it is just below the tip of the middle finger.

(2) Locate the point on the transverse crease of the palm, in the ulnar side of the third metacarpal bone.

Actions and indications: Induce resuscitation, recuperate depleted yang, clear away heat from the heart, restore consciousness, purge heat to relieve convulsion, used to treat cardiac pain, coma in apoplexy, aphtha, and foul breath.

Manipulation: Puncture perpendicularly 0.3—0.5 cun.

Notes: Laogong (PC 8) is the Ying-Spring point of the Pericardium Meridian of Hand-Jueyin.

190

中冲 Zhōngchōng（PC 9）

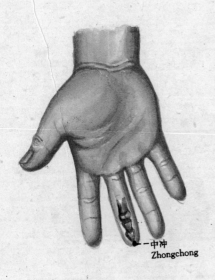

中冲
Zhongchong

〔取穴法〕（1）在手中指末节尖端中央处。

（2）仰掌，于中指尖的中点，距指甲游离缘约 0.1 寸处取穴。

〔功效与主治〕通心络，开神窍。中风，中暑，昏厥，急惊风。

〔操作〕浅刺 0.1 寸，或三棱针点刺出血。

〔备注〕手厥阴心包经"井"穴。

Method of locating the point:

(1) This point is located in the centre of the tip of the middle finger.

(2) When the palm is placed upwards with the arm stretched out, it is found in the centre of the tip of the middle finger, 0.1 cun proximal to the free border of the nail.

Actions and indications: Remove obstructions of the cardiac vessels, restore consciousness, used to treat apoplexy, heat stroke, coma, syncope and acute convulsion.

Manipulation: Puncture superficially 0.1 cun, or prick with a three-edged needle to cause bleeding.

Notes: Zhongchong (PC 9) is the Jing-Well point of the Pericardium Meridian of Hand-Jueyin.

十、手少阳三焦经

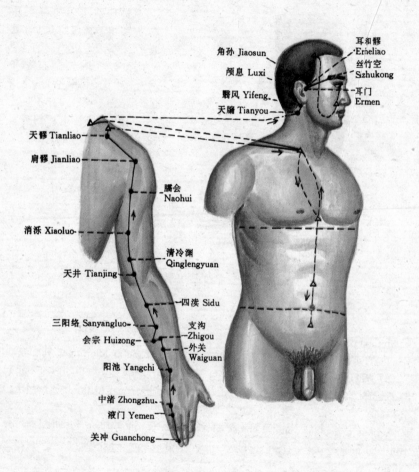

角孙 Jiaosun
颅息 Luxi
翳风 Yifeng
天牖 Tianyou

耳和髎 Erheliao
丝竹空 Szhukong
耳门 Ermen

天髎 Tianliao
肩髎 Jianliao
臑会 Naohui
消泺 Xiaoluo
清冷渊 Qinglengyuan
天井 Tianjing
四渎 Sidu
三阳络 Sanyangluo
支沟 Zhigou
会宗 Huizong
外关 Waiguan
阳池 Yangchi
中渚 Zhongzhu
液门 Yemen
关冲 Guanchong

起于无名指末端(关冲),向上出于第四五掌骨间,沿着腕背,出于前臂外侧桡骨和尺骨之间,向上通过肘尖,沿上臂外侧,上达肩部,交出足少阳经的后面,向前进入缺盆部,分布于胸中,联络心包,向下通过横膈,从胸至腹,属于上、中、下三焦。胸部支脉:从胸向上,出于缺盆部,上走项部,沿耳后直上,出于耳部上行额角,再屈而下行至面颊部,到达眶下部。耳部支脉:从耳后进入耳中,出走耳前,与前脉交叉于面颊部,到达目外眦(丝竹空之下),与足少阳胆经相接。

10. The Sanjiao Meridian of Hand-Shaoyang

The Sanjiao Meridian of Hand-Shaoyang originates from the tip of the ring finger (Guanchong, SJ 1), running upward between the 4th and 5th metacarpal bones and emergng there. Then, it goes between the ulna and radius along the dorsal aspect of the wrist to the lateral aspect of the forearm. Passing through the olecranon, it reaches the shoulder region along the lateral aspect of the upper arm, where it goes across and then behind the Gallbladder Meridian of Foot-Shaoyang, entering the supraclavicular fossa. Then, it spreads in the chest to connect with the pericardium and runs through the diaphragm downwards to the abdomen, where it peratins to the upper-, middle- and lower-jiao. The branch originating from the chest runs upward from the chest and emerges in the supraclavicular fossa. Then, it ascends to the neck and runs along the posterior border of the ear to the corner of the anterior hairline. Turning downwards, it travels to the cheek and terminates in the infraorbital region. The auricular branch starts from the retroauricular region. Entering the ear, it emerges in front of the ear and crosses the previous branch at the cheek, ending in the outer canthus (Sizhukong, SJ 23), where it links with the Gallbladder of Foot-Shaoyang.

关冲 Guānchōng (SJ 1)

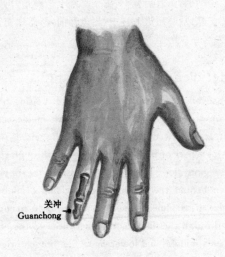

关冲
Guanchong

〔取穴法〕(1)在手环指末节尺侧,距指甲角 0.1 寸(指寸)处。

(2)俯掌,沿无名指尺侧缘和基底部各作一平线,于相交处取穴。

〔功效与主治〕清热开窍,消肿利舌。头痛,目赤,喉痹,舌强。

〔操作〕浅刺 0.1 寸,或用三棱针点刺出血。

〔备注〕手少阳三焦经"井"穴。

Method of locating the point:

(1) This point is located on the lateral side of the ring finger, about 0.1 cun posterior to the corner of the nail.

(2) When the palm is placed downwards, it is found at the junction of the line drawn along the ulnar side of the ring finger and the line drawn along its base.

Actions and indications: Clear away heat, induce resuscitation, subdue swelling and relieve sore throat, used to treat headache, red eyes, sore throat and stiffiness of the tongue.

Manipulation: Puncture superficially 0.1 cun, or prick with a three-edged needle to cause bleeding.

Notes: Guanchong (SJ 1) is the Jing-Well point of the Sanjiao Meridian of Hand-Shaoyang.

194

液门 Yèmén (SJ 2)

〔取穴法〕(1)在手背部,当第四五指间,指蹼缘后方赤白肉际处。

(2)微握拳,掌心向下,于第四五指间缝纹端,当赤白肉际处取穴。

〔功效与主治〕清头明目,消肿止痛.头痛,目赤,耳鸣,耳聋,手指麻木。

〔操作〕直刺 0.2～0.3 寸。

〔备注〕手少阳三焦经 "荥"穴。

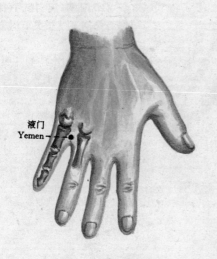

液门
Yemen

Method of locating the point:

(1) This point is located on the dorsal side, just behind the web between the ring and the small fingers.

(2) When the fist is loosely made, it is found at the junction of the white and red skin at the end of the crease between the ring and small fingers.

Actions and indications: Fresh the mind, improve the eyesight, subdue swelling and relieve pain, used to treat headache, red eyes, tinnitus, deafness and numbness of the fingers.

Manipulation: Puncture perpendicularly 0.2—0.3 cun.

Notes: Yemen (SJ 2) is the Ying-Spring point of the Sanjiao Meridian of Hand-Shaoyang.

中渚 Zhōngzhǔ（SJ 3）

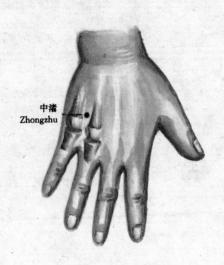

中渚
Zhongzhu

〔取穴法〕（1）在手背部，当环指本节（掌指关节）的后方，第四五掌骨间凹陷处。

（2）俯掌，液门穴直上1寸，当第四五掌指关节后方凹陷中取穴。

〔功效与主治〕聪耳明目，清热止痛。头痛，目赤，耳聋，耳鸣。

〔操作〕直刺 0.3～0.5寸。

〔备注〕手少阳三焦经"输"穴。

Method of locating the point：

（1）This point is located on the dorsum of the hand, in the depression between the 4th and 5th metacarpal bones, posterior to the metacarpophalangeal joint.

（2）When the palm is placed downwards, it is found just 1 cun above Yemen (SJ 2) point, in the depression posterior to the 4th and 5th metacarpal bones.

Actions and indications：Improve hearing and vision, clear away heat to relieve pain, used to treat headache, red eyes, deafness and tinnitus.

Manipulation：Puncture perpendicularly 0.3—0.5 cun.

Notes：Zhongzhu (SJ 3) is the Shu-Stream point of the Sanjiao Meridian of Hand-Shaoyang.

阳池 Yāngchí (SJ 4)

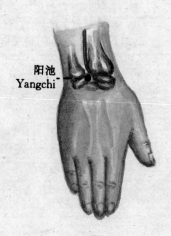

阳池
Yangchi

〔取穴法〕(1)在腕背横纹中,当指伸肌腱的尺侧缘凹陷处。

(2)俯掌,于第三四指掌骨间直上与腕横纹交点处的凹陷中取穴。

〔功效与主治〕清热散风,舒筋活络。腕痛,耳聋,消渴。

〔操作〕直刺 0.3～0.5寸。

〔备注〕手少阳三焦经"原"穴。

Method of locating the point:

(1) This point is located on the transverse crease of the dorsum of wrist, in the depression of the ulnar side of the tendon of m. extensor digitorum communis.

(2) When the palm is placed downwards, it is found in the crossing point of the line passing between the 3rd and 4th metacarpal bones and the tranverse crease of the wrist.

Actions and indications: Clear away heat, dissipate wind, relax muscles and tendons, activate flow of Qi and blood in the channels and collaterals, used to treat pain in the wrist, deafness and diabetes.

Manipulation: Puncture perpendicularly 0.3—0.5 cun.

Notes: Yangchi (SJ 4) is the Yuan-Primary point of the Sanjiao Meridian of Hand-Shaoyang.

外关 Wàiguān (SJ 5)

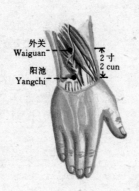

外关
Waiguan

阳池
Yangchi

2 寸
2 cun

〔取穴法〕(1)在前臂背侧,当阳池与肘尖的连线上,腕背横纹上 2 寸,尺骨与桡骨之间。

(2)伸臂俯掌,于腕背横纹中点直上 2 寸,尺、桡骨之间,与内关穴相对处取穴。

〔功效与主治〕疏风解表,通经活络。热病,头痛,耳鸣,耳聋,目赤肿痛,胁痛,手臂麻痛。

〔操作〕直刺 0.5～1 寸。

〔备注〕手少阳三焦经"络"穴;八脉交会穴之一,通于阳维脉。

Method of locating the point:

(1) This point is located in the lateral aspect of the forearm, on the line connecting Yangchi (SJ 4) and the olecranon, 2 cun above the dorsal transverse crease of the wrist, between the ulna and radius.

(2) When the palm is placed downwards with the arm stretched out, it is found 2 cun above the midpoint of the dorsal transverse crease of the wrist between the ulna and radius, in a position opposite to Neiguan (PC 6).

Actions and indications: Expel wind to relieve an exterior syndrome, promote flow of Qi and blood in the channels and collaterals, used to treat febrile diseases, headache, tinnitus, deafness, redness, swelling and pain of eyes, hypochondriac pain, numbness and pain of arm.

Manipulation: Puncture perpendicularly 0.5—1 cun.

Notes: Waiguan (SJ 5) is the Luo-Connecting point of the Sanjiao Meridian of Hand-Shaoyang, and one of the confluence points of the eight meridians, which communicates with Yangwei Meridian.

支沟 Zhīgōu (SJ 6)

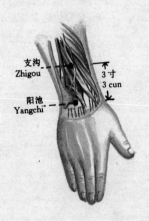

支沟
Zhigou

阳池
Yangchi

下
3寸
3 cun

〔取穴法〕（1）在前臂背侧,当阳池与肘尖的连线上,腕背横纹上3寸,尺、桡骨之间取穴。

（2）伸臂俯掌,于腕背横纹中点直上3寸,尺、桡骨之间,与间使穴相对取穴。

〔功效与主治〕通关开窍,活络散瘀,调理脏腑。便秘,暴喑,胁痛。

〔操作〕直刺0.5～1寸。

〔备注〕手少阳三焦经"经"穴。

Method of locating the point：

(1) This point is located on the dorsal side of the forearm, on the line connecting Yangchi (Sj 4) and the olecranon, 3 cun above the dorsal transverse crease of the wrist, between the ulna and radius.

(2) When the palm is placed downwards with the arm stretched out, it is found 3 cun above the midpoint of the dorsal transverse crease, between the ulna and radius, in a position opposite to Jianshi (PC 5).

Actions and indications：Restore consciousness, induce resuscitation, activate blood flow in the collaterals, dissipate blood stasis and regulate functions of zang-fu organs, used to treat constipation, sudden hoarseness, and hypochondriac pain.

Manipulation：Puncture perpendicularly 0.5—1 cun.

Notes：Zhigou (SJ 6) is the Jing-River point of the Sanjiao Meridian of Hand-Shaoyang.

会宗 Huìzōng (SJ 7)

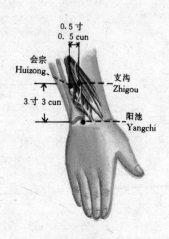

〔取穴法〕(1)在前臂背侧,当腕背横纹上3寸,支沟穴尺侧,尺骨的桡侧缘取穴。

(2)在手腕背侧横纹上3寸,支沟穴尺侧旁开1横指处取穴。

〔功效与主治〕清热解郁,疏通经气。耳聋,痫证,上肢肌肤疼痛。

〔操作〕直刺0.5～0.8寸。

〔备注〕手少阳三焦经"郄"穴。

Method of locating the point:

(1) This point is located in the dorsal side of the forearm, 3 cun above the dorsal transverse crease of the wrist, on the ulnar side of Zhigou (SJ 6) and the radial side of the ulna.

(2) Locate the point 3 cun above the dorsal transverse crease of the wrist, one finger-breadth lateral to Zhigou (Sj 6).

Actions and indications: Clear away heat, relieve stagnation of Qi, dredge channels and collaterals, used to treat deafness, epilepsy, muscular pain of the upper limbs.

Manipulation: Puncture perpendicularly 0.5—0.8 cun.

Notes: Huizong (SJ 7) is the Xi-Cleft point of the Sanjiao Meridian of Hand-Shaoyang.

200

三阳络 Sānyángluò (SJ 8)

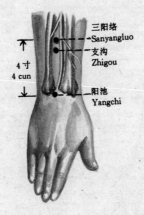

〔取穴法〕在前臂背侧,腕背横纹上4寸,尺、桡骨之间取穴。

〔功效与主治〕通络,开窍,镇痛。暴喑,耳聋,手臂痛。

〔操作〕直刺0.5～1寸。

Method of locating the point:

This point is located on the dorsal aspect of the forearm, 4 cun above the dorsal transverse crease of the wrist between the ulna and radius.

Actions and indications: Remove obstruction from collaterals, induce resuscitation, and relieve pain, used to treat sudden hoarseness, deafness and pain in the arm.

Manipulation: Puncture perpendicularly 0.5—1 cun.

天井 Tiānjǐng (SJ 10)

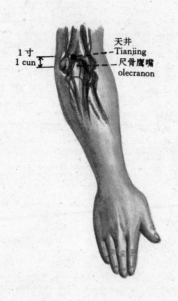

天井
Tianjing
尺骨鹰嘴
olecranon

1 寸
1 cun

〔取穴法〕(1)在臂外侧，屈肘时，当肘尖直上 1 寸凹陷处。

(2)在尺骨鹰嘴后上方，屈肘时呈凹陷处取穴。

(3)以手叉腰，于肘尖(尺骨鹰嘴)后上方 1 寸之凹陷处取穴。

〔功效与主治〕清热散风，祛湿化痰。偏头痛，胁痛，瘰疬。

〔操 作〕直刺 0.3～0.5 寸。

〔备注〕手少阳三焦经"合"穴。

Method of locating the point:

(1) When the elbow is flexed, this point is located in the depression 1 cun above the olecranon, on the medial side of the arm.

(2) When the elbow is flexed, it is found in the depression superio-posterior to the olecranon.

(3) With arms akimbo, it is found in the depression 1 cun superio-posterior to the olecranon.

Actions and indications: Clear away heat, expel wind, remove dampness and dissolve phlegm, used to treat migraine, pain in the hypochondriac region and scrofula.

Manipulation: Puncture perpendularly 0.3—0.5 cun.

Notes: Tianjing (SJ 10) is the He-Sea point of the Sanjiao Meridian of Hand-Shaoyang.

清冷渊 Qīnglěngyuān (SJ 11)

〔取穴法〕(1)在臂外侧,屈肘,当肘尖直上2寸,即天井上1寸处。

(2)以手叉腰,于肘尖(尺骨鹰嘴)后上方2寸,与天井穴相直处取穴。

〔功效与主治〕清热泄火,通经止痛。头痛,目黄,肩背不举。

〔操作〕直刺0.3～0.5寸。

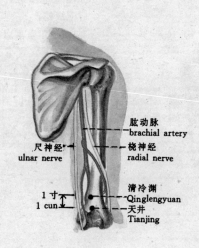

肱动脉
brachial artery

尺神经
ulnar nerve

桡神经
radial nerve

1 寸
1 cun

清冷渊
Qinglengyuan

天井
Tianjing

Method of locating the point:

(1) When the elbow is flexed, the point is located on the medial aspect of the arm, 2 cun above the olecranon, or 1 cun above Tianjing (SJ 10).

(2) With arms akimbo, it is found 2 cun supero-posterior to the olecranon, in a position corresponding to Tianjing point (SJ 10).

Actions and indications: Clear away heat and purge fire, promote flow of Qi and blood in the channels and collaterals to relieve pain, used to treat headache, yellow sclera, failure of the back and shoulder to lift.

Manipulation: Puncture perpendularly 0.3—0.5 cun.

臑会 Nàohuì (SJ 13)

〔取穴法〕(1)在臂外侧,当肘尖与肩髎的连线上,肩髎下3寸,三角肌的后下缘处。

(2)正坐垂肩,于肩头后侧肩髎穴直下3寸,下与天井穴相直处取穴。

〔功效与主治〕疏经活血,消肿散瘀。肩臂痛,肩胛肿痛,瘿气,目痛。

〔操作〕直刺0.5～0.8寸。

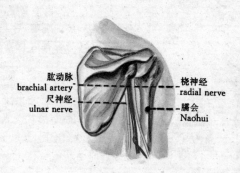

肱动脉 brachial artery
尺神经 ulnar nerve
桡神经 radial nerve
臑会 Naohui

Method of locating the point:

(1) This point is located 3 cun below Jianliao point(SJ 14), on the line connecting Jianliao (SJ 14) and the olecranon, on the posterior border of m. deltoideus.

(2) When patient sits erect with the shoulders dropped, it is found 3 cun below the Jianliao (SJ 14) point posterior to the acromion, at the level of Tianjing point (SJ 10).

Actions and indications: Dredge channels and activate blood flow in the collaterals, subdue swelling and dissipate blood stasis, used to treat pain of the shoulder and arm, swelling and pain of the scapular region, thyroid enlargement and pain of eyes.

Manipulation: Puncture perpendicularly 0.5—0.8 cun.

肩髎 Jiānliáo（SJ 14）

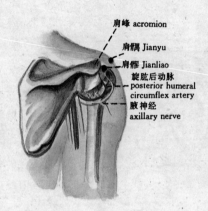

肩峰 acromion
肩髃 Jianyu
肩髎 Jianliao
旋肱后动脉 posterior humeral circumflex artery
腋神经 axillary nerve

〔取穴法〕（1）在肩部，肩髃穴后方，当臂外展时，于肩峰后下方呈现凹陷处。

（2）垂肩，于锁骨肩峰端后缘直下约2寸，当肩峰与肱骨大结节之间处定穴。

〔功效与主治〕祛风湿，通经络。肩臂痛不得举，中风偏瘫。

〔操作〕直刺0.5～0.8寸。

Method of locating the point:

(1) This point is located posterior to Jianyu point (LI 15), in the depression below the acromion when the arm is abducted.

(2) When the shoulder drops, it is found 2 cun below the posterior border of the acrominal extremity of clavicle, between the acromion and the greater tuberosity of humerus.

Actions and indications: Expel wind-dampness, activate blood flow in the channels and collaterals, used to treat pain and motor impairment of the shoulder and arm, hemiplegia in apoplexy.

Manipulation: Puncture perpendicularly 0.5—0.8 cun.

天髎 Tiānliáo (SJ 15)

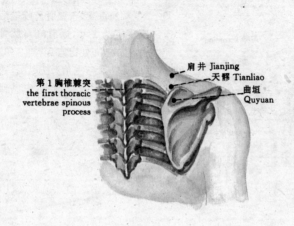

肩井 Jianjing
天髎 Tianliao
曲垣 Quyuan

第1胸椎棘突
the first thoracic
vertebrae spinous
process

〔取穴法〕(1)在肩胛部,肩井与曲垣的中间,当肩胛骨上角处。

(2)正坐垂肩,于肩胛骨的内上角端取穴。

〔功效与主治〕祛风湿,通经络。颈项强痛,肩背酸痛。

〔操作〕直刺0.3~0.5寸。

〔备注〕手、足少阳经与阳维脉交会穴。

Method of locating the point:

(1) This point is located in the midway between Jianjing (G 21) and Quyuan (SI 13), on the superior angle of the scapula.

(2) When patient sits erect with the shoulder dropped, it is found in the superior angle of the scapula of the inner side.

Actions and indications: Expel wind-dampness, promote flow of Qi and blood in the channels and collaterals, used to treat rigidity and pain of neck, aching sensation of the shoulder and back.

Manipulation: Puncture perpendicularly 0.5-0.8 cun.

Notes: Tianliao (SJ 15) is a crossing point of the Hand-Shaoyang and Foot-Shaoyang Meridians and the Yangwei Meridian.

天牖 Tiānyǒu (SJ 16)

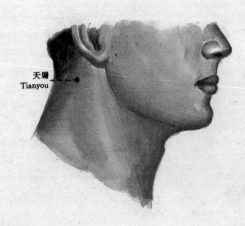

天牖
Tianyou

〔取穴法〕(1)在
颈侧部,当乳突的后
方直下,平下颌角,胸
锁乳突肌的后缘。
　(2)正坐,在乳突
下方,胸锁乳突肌后
缘近发际处取穴。
　〔功效与主治〕
清头明目,活络利耳。
头晕,头痛,暴聋。
　〔操作〕直刺 0.3
～0.5 寸。

Method of locating the point:

(1) This point is located on the lateral aspect of the neck, posterior and inferior to the mastoid process, on the posterior border of m. sternocleidomastoideus, level with the angle of jaw.

(2) When patient takes a sitting position, it is found inferior to the mastoid process, on the posterior border of the sternocleidomastoideus, near the hairline.

Actions and indications: Clear away heat from the head to improve vision, activate flow of blood in the collaterals to benefit the ear, used to treate dizziness, headache and sudden deafness.

Manipulation: Puncture perpendicularly 0.3—0.5 cun.

翳风 Yìfēng (SJ 17)

〔取穴法〕(1)在耳垂后方,当乳突与下颌角之间的凹陷处。

(2)正坐或侧伏,耳垂微向内折,于乳突前方凹陷处取穴。

〔功效与主治〕散风活络,聪耳启闭。耳鸣,耳聋,口眼㖞斜。

〔操作〕直刺0.5～0.8寸。

〔备注〕手、足少阳交会穴。

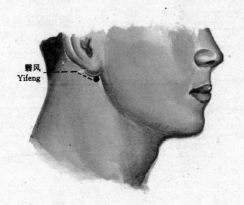

翳风
Yifeng

Method of locating the point:

(1) This point is posterior to the lobule of the ear, in the depression between the mandile and mastoid process.

(2) When patient takes a sitting or a lying position on his side and his lobule of ear is folded forward, it is found in the depression anterior to the mastoid process.

Actions and indications: Disperse wind, activate flow of blood in the collaterals, improve hearing, used to treat tinnitus, deafness and distortion of the eyes and mouth.

Manipulation: Puncture perpendicularly 0.5—0.8 cun.

Notes: Yifeng (SJ 17) is a crossing point of the Hand-Shaoyang Meridian and Foot-Shaoyang Meridian.

颅息 Lúxī（SJ 19）

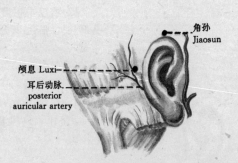

角孙 Jiaosun

颅息 Luxi

耳后动脉. posterior auricular artery

〔取穴法〕（1）在头部，当角孙至翳风之间，沿耳轮连线的上、中 1/3 的交点处。

（2）正坐或侧伏，于耳后发际，当瘈脉穴与角孙穴沿耳轮连线的中点处取穴。

〔功效与主治〕通窍熄风，镇惊止痛。头痛，耳痛，耳鸣，小儿惊痫。

〔操作〕平刺 0.1～0.2 寸。

Method of locating the point：

(1) This point is located posterior to the ear, at the junction of the upper and middle third of the curve formed by Yifeng (SJ 17) and Jiaosun (SJ 20) behind the helix.

(2) When patient takes a sitting or a lying position on his side, it is found in the middle of the curve formed by Chimai point (Extra) and Jiaosun point (SJ 20) behind the helix.

Actions and indications：Restore consciousness, calm wind, relieve convulsion and stop pain, used to treat headache, earache, tinnitus, infantile convulsion and epilepsy.

Manipulation：Puncture subcutaneously 0.1—0.2 cun.

角孙 Jiǎosūn (SJ 20)

〔取穴法〕(1)在头部,折耳廓向前,当耳尖直上入发际处。

(2)若以手按着耳尖头部,使口张合,其处牵动者是穴。

〔功效与主治〕清头明目,疏风活络。耳部肿痛,目赤肿痛,痄腮,头痛。

〔操作〕斜刺 0.1～0.2寸。

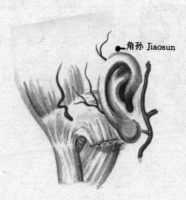

●—角孙 Jiaosun

Method of locating the point:

(1) When the lobule of the ear is folded forward, it is located directly above the ear apex, within the hair line.

(2) When patient opens and shuts his mouth while his head and ear apex are pressed by doctor's hand, the point is found where a dragging movement is felt.

Actions and indications: Clear away heat from the head, improve vision, disperse wind and activate flow of blood in the collaterals, used to treat swelling and pain of the ear, redness, swelling and pain of the eye, mumps, and headache.

Manipulation: Puncture obliquely 0.1—0.2 cun.

210

耳门 Ermén (SJ 21)

〔取穴法〕(1)在面部,当耳屏上切迹的前方,下颌骨髁突后缘,张口有凹陷处。

(2)正坐或侧伏,微张口,当听宫穴直上0.5寸之凹陷处取穴。

〔功效与主治〕疏通经络,开窍益聪。耳聋,耳鸣。

〔操作〕微张口,直刺0.3～0.5寸。

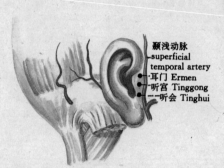

颞浅动脉
superficial
temporal artery
耳门 Ermen
听宫 Tinggong
听会 Tinghui

Method of locating the point:

(1) This point is located in the depression anterior to the the supratragic notch and on the border posterior to the condyloid process when the mouth is open.

(2) Ask patient to take a sitting or a lying position on one side with his mouth slightly opened, locate the point in the depression 0.5 cun directly above the Tinggong point (SI 19).

Actions and indications: Dredge channels and collaterals, induce resuscitation and improve intelligence, used to treat deafness and tinnitus.

Manipulation: Puncture perpendicularly 0.3—0.5 cun with the mouth open.

耳和髎 Erhéliáo（SJ 22）

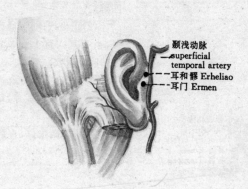

颞浅动脉
superficial
temporal artery
耳和髎 Erheliao
耳门 Ermen

〔取穴法〕(1)在头侧部，当鬓发后缘，平耳廓根之前方，颞浅动脉的后缘处。

(2)正坐或侧伏，在耳门前上方，平耳廓根前，鬓发后缘之动脉搏动处取穴。

〔功效与主治〕祛风活络，消肿止痛。头重痛，耳鸣，牙关拘急。

〔操作〕斜刺 0.1～0.3寸。

〔备注〕手、足少阳、手太阳经交会穴。

Method of locating the point：

(1) This point is located on the posterior border of the hairline of the temple where the superficial temporal artery passes, at the level with the root of the auricle.

(2) Ask patient to take a sitting or a lying position on his side, locate the point anterior and superior to Ermen (SJ 21), at the level with the root of the auricle, on the posterior border of the hairline of the temple where the superficial temporal artery passes.

Actions and indications：Expel wind, activate flow of blood in the collaterals, subdue swelling and relieve pain, used to treat heaviness and pain of the head, tinnitus, lockjaw.

Manipulation：Puncture obliquely 0.1—0.3 cun.

Notes：Erheliao is a crossing point of the Hand-Shaoyang Meridian, the Foot-Shaoyang Meridian and the Hand-Taiyang Meridian.

丝竹空 Sīzhúkōng（SJ 23）

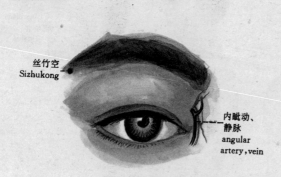

丝竹空
Sizhukong

内眦动、
静脉
angular
artery, vein

〔取穴法〕（1）在面部，当眉梢凹陷处取穴。

（2）正坐或侧伏，于额骨颧突外缘，眉梢外侧凹陷处取穴。

〔功效与主治〕平肝熄风，明目镇痛。头痛，偏头痛，目眩，目赤肿痛。

〔操作〕沿皮刺 0.5～0.8 寸。

〔备注〕禁灸。

Method of locating the point:

(1) This point is located in the depression at the lateral end of the eyebrow.

(2) Ask patient to take a sitting or a lying position on his side, locate the point in the depression at the lateral end of the eyebrow, on the lateral border of the zygomatic bone.

Actions and indications: Suppress the hyperactive liver to calm wind, improve vision and relieve pain, used to treat headache, migraine, redness, swelling and pain of the eye.

Manipulation: Puncture subcutaneously 0.5—0.8 cun.

Notes: Moxibustion is contraindicated.

十一、足少阳胆经

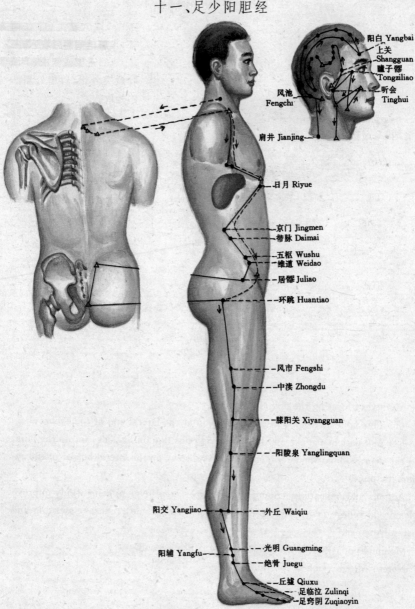

阳白 Yangbai
上关 Shangguan
瞳子髎 Tongziliao
听会 Tinghui

风池 Fengchi
肩井 Jianjing
日月 Riyue
京门 Jingmen
带脉 Daimai
五枢 Wushu
维道 Weidao
居髎 Juliao
环跳 Huantiao
风市 Fengshi
中渎 Zhongdu
膝阳关 Xiyangguan
阳陵泉 Yanglingquan
阳交 Yangjiao
外丘 Waiqiu
阳辅 Yangfu
光明 Guangming
绝骨 Juegu
丘墟 Qiuxu
足临泣 Zulinqi
足窍阴 Zuqiaoyin

起于目外眦(瞳子髎),向上到达额角部(颔厌),下行至耳后(风池),沿着颈部行于手少阳经的前面,到肩上交出手少阳经的后面,向下进入缺盆部。耳部的支脉:从耳后进入耳中,出走耳前,到目外眦后方;外眦部的支脉:从目外眦处分出,下走大迎,会合于手少阳经到达目眶下,下行经颊车,由颈部向下会合前脉于缺盆,然后向下进入胸中,通过横膈,联络肝脏,属于胆,沿着胁肋内,出于少腹两侧腹股沟动脉部,经过外阴部毛际,横行入髋关节部(环跳)。缺盆部直行的脉:下行腋部,沿着侧胸部,经过季胁,向下会合前脉于髋关节部,再向下沿着大腿的外侧,出于膝外侧,下行经腓骨前面,直下到达腓骨下段,再下到外踝的前面,沿足背部,进入足第4趾外侧端(足窍阴);足背部支脉:从足临泣处分出,沿着第一二跖骨之间,出于大趾端,穿过趾甲,回过来到趾甲后的毫毛部(大敦,属肝经),与足厥阴肝经相接。

11. The Gallbladder Meridian of Foot-Shaoyang

The Gallbladder Meridian of Foot-Shaoyang originates from the outer canthus (Tongziliao, GB1), goes upwards to the corner of the forehead (Hanyan, GB 4), then curves to the retroauricular region (Fengchi, GB 20) and runs along side of the neck in front of the Sanjiao Meridian of Hand-Shaoyang to the shoulder, where it crosses with and then goes behind the Hand-Shaoyang Meridian down to the supraclavicular fossa. The retroauricular branch arises from the retroauricular region and enters the ear. Emerging in front of the ear, it reaches the posterior aspect of the outer canthus. The branch arising from the outer canthus descends to Daying (St 5), meeting the Sanjiao Meridian of Hand-Shaoyang there and then reaching the infraorbital region. Passing through Jiache (St 6), it travels downwards to the neck and enters the supraclavicular fossa, where it meets the main meridian. From there, it enters the thoracic cavity, passes through the diaphragm and connects with the liver and pertains to the gallbladder in the abdominal cavity. Then, it runs inside the hypochondriac region and emerges on lateral side of the lower abdomen near the femoral artery at the inguinal region. Passing around the margin of the pubic hair, it goes transversely into the hip region (Huantiao, GB 30). The straight portion of the meridian runs downwards from the supraclavicular fossa, passes in front of the axilla along the side of the chest and through the free ends of the floating ribs to the hip region, meeting the previous meridian there. Then, along the lateral aspect of the thigh, it descends to the lateral side of the knee. Going further downwards along the anterior aspect of the fibula, it reaches the lower part of the fibula. From there, it descends to the anterior aspect of the external malleolus, and then reach the lateral side of the tip of the 4th toe (Zuqiaoyin, GB 44) following the dorsum of the foot. The branch arising from the dorsum of the foot originates from Zulinqi (GB 41), runs between the 1st and the 2nd metacarpal bones to the distal portion of the greater toe and ends at its hairy region, where it links with the Liver Meridian of Foot-Jueyin.

瞳子髎 Tóngzǐliáo (GB 1)

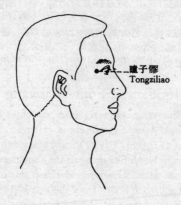

瞳子髎
Tongziliao

〔取穴法〕(1)在面部,目外眦旁,当眶外侧缘处取穴。

(2)正坐仰靠,令患者闭目,当眼外角纹之止处取穴。

〔功效与主治〕疏风散热,清头明目,消肿止痛。头痛,目痒,目赤肿痛,视力下降。

〔操作〕向后平刺 0.2～0.4 寸,或用三棱针点刺出血。

〔备注〕手太阳、手足少阳经交会穴。

Method of locating the point:

(1) This point is located beside the outer canthus, on the lateral border of the outer canthus.

(2) Ask patient to sit erect with the back supported and the eye closed, locate the point at the end of the wrinkle of the outer canthus.

Actions and indications: Expel wind, clear away heat, purge fire to improve vision, subdue swelling and relieve pain, used to treat headache, itching of eyes, redness, swelling and pain of the eyes, and poor vision.

Manipulation: Puncture subcutaneously 0.2－0.4 cun, or prick with a three-edged needle to cause bleeding.

Notes: Tongziliao (GB 1) is a crossing point of the Hand-Taiyang Meridian and Hand-Shaoyang and Foot-Shaoyang Meridians.

216

听会 Tīnghuì（GB 2）

〔取穴法〕（1）在面部，当耳屏间切迹的前方，下颌骨髁突的后缘，张口有凹陷处。

（2）正坐仰靠或侧伏，在耳屏间切迹前，当听宫（小肠经）直下，下颌骨髁状突后缘，张口有空处。

〔功效与主治〕疏经活络，开窍益聪。耳鸣，耳聋，口㖞，腮肿。

〔操作〕微张口，直刺 0.3～0.5 寸。

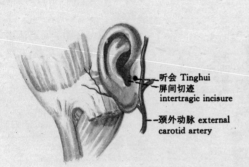

听会 Tinghui
屏间切迹 intertragic incisure
颈外动脉 external carotid artery

Method of locating the point：

(1) This point is located anterior to the intertragic notch, at the posterior border of the condyloid process of the mandible, or in the depression when the mouth is opened.

(2) Ask patient to sit erect with the back supported or lies on his one side, locate the point in the depression while the mouth is open, anterior to the intertragic notch, right below Tinggong (SI 19) and at the posterior border of the condyloid process of the mandible.

Actions and indications：Dredge channels and activate collaterals, induce resuscitation and benefit intelligence, used to treat tinnitus, deafness, distortion of mouth and mumps.

Manipulation：Puncture perpendicularly 0.3—0.5 cun.

Notes：Tinghui (GB 2) is a crossing point of the Hand- and Foot-Shaoyang Meridians and the Foot-Yangming Meridian.

上关 Shàngguān (GB 3)

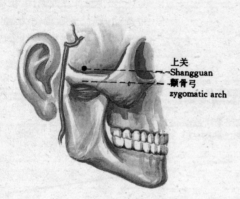

上关
Shangguan
颧骨弓
zygomatic arch

〔取穴法〕(1)在耳前,下关直上,当颧弓的上缘凹陷处。

(2)正坐仰靠或侧伏,按取耳前颧骨弓上侧,张口时有孔处取穴。

〔功效与主治〕通经活络,开窍益聪。偏头痛,耳聋,耳鸣,齿痛。

〔操作〕直刺 0.3～0.5寸。

〔备注〕手足少阳、足阳明经交会穴。

Method of locating the point:

(1) This point is anterior to the ear, directly above Xiagguan (ST 7), in the depression above the upper border of zygomatic arch.

(2) Ask patient to take a sitting position with his back supported or a lateral recumbent position, locate the point where a foramen is felt when the mouth is open in the upper border of the zygomatic arch.

Actions and indications: Promote blood flow in the channels and collaterals, restore consciousness and improve hearing, used to treat migraine, deafness, tinnitus, and toothache.

Manipulation: Puncture 0.3—0.5 cun perpendicularly.

Notes: This is the crossing point of the Hand Shaoyang meridians, the Foot Shaoyang meridian and the foot Yangming meridian.

颔厌 Hànyàn (GB 4)

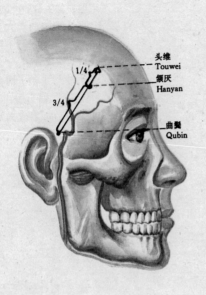

〔取穴法〕(1)在头部鬓发上,当头维与曲鬓弧形连线的上 1/4 与下 3/4 交点处。

(2)正坐仰靠或侧伏,先定头维和曲鬓穴,从头维向曲鬓凸向前作一弧线,于弧线之中点定悬颅,再在头维与悬颅之间取颔厌。试作咀嚼食物状,其处随咀嚼而微动。

〔功效与主治〕疏风活络,止痛益聪。头晕,目眩,偏头痛。

〔操作〕向下或向后平刺 0.5～1 寸。

〔备注〕手足少阳、足阳明经交会穴。

Method of locating the point:

(1) This point is located within the hairline of the temporal region, at the junction of the upper 1/4 and the lower 3/4 of the curve line formed by Touwei (St 8) and Qubin (GB 7).

(2) Ask patient to take a sitting position with the back supported or a lying position on his one side, locate Touwei (St 8) and Qubin (GB 7) first, then draw a curve line from Touwei (St 8) to Qubin (GB 7) and locate Xuanlu (GB 5) and finally locate the Hanyan (GB 4) between Touwei (St 8) and Xuanlu (GB 5). The region where Hanyan (GB 4) is located will do mild movement when patient chews.

Actions and indications: Expel wind, activate blood flow in the collaterals, relieve pain and improve intelligence, used to treat headache, vertigo, and migraine.

Manipulation: Puncture subcutaneously downwards or backwards 0.5—1 cun.

Notes: Hanyan (GB 4) is a crossing point of the Hand- and Foot-Shaoyang Meridians and the Foot-Yangming Meridian.

悬颅 Xuánlú (GB 5)

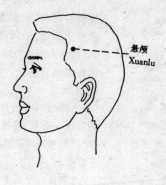

悬颅
Xuanlu

〔取穴法〕(1)在头部鬓发上,当头维与曲鬓穴弧形连线的中点处。

(2)见颔厌穴。

〔功效与主治〕清热止痛,散风消肿。偏头痛,面肿。

〔操作〕向下或向后平刺0.5～1寸。

Method of locating the point:

(1) This point is lcoated within the hairline of the temporal region, at the mid-point of the curve formed by Touwei (St 8) and Qubin (GB 7).

(2) See Hanyan point (GB 4).

Actions and indications: Clear away heat to relieve pain, expel wind and subdue swelling, used to treat migraine and swelling of face.

Manipulation: Puncture subcutaneously downwards or backwards 0.5—1 cun.

220

悬厘 Xuánlí (GB 6)

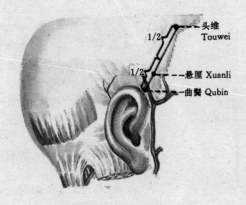

头维 Touwei
1/2

1/2
悬厘 Xuanli
曲鬓 Qubin

〔取穴法〕(1)在头部鬓发上,当头维与曲鬓穴弧形连线的上 3/4 与下 1/4 交点处。

(2)正坐仰靠或侧伏,在鬓角之上际,当悬颅穴与曲鬓穴之中点处。

〔功效与主治〕清热止痛,散风消肿。偏头痛,面肿,目外眦痛。

〔操作〕向下或向后平刺 0.5～0.8 寸。

〔备注〕手足少阳、足阳明经交会穴。

Method of locating the point:

(1) This point is located within the hairline of the temporal region, at the junction of the upper 3/4 and the lower 1/4 of the curve formed by Touwei (St 8) and Qubin (GB 7).

(2) Ask patient to take a sitting position with his back supported, locate the point in the upper border of the hairline of the temporal region, at the mid-point of Xuanlu (GB 5) and Qubin (GB 7).

Actions and indications: Clear away heat to relieve pain, expel wind and subdue swelling, used to treat migraine, swelling of face, and pain in the outer canthus.

Manipulation: Puncture subcutaneously downwards or backwards 0.5 — 0.8 cun.

Notes: Xuanli (GB 8) is a crossing point of the Hand- and Foot-Shaoyang Meridian and the Foot-Yangming Meridian.

曲鬓 Qūbìn (GB 7)

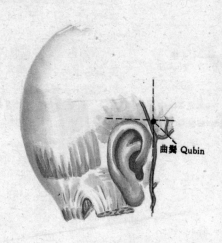

曲鬓 Qubin

〔取穴法〕(1)在头部,当耳前鬓角发际后缘的垂线与耳尖水平线交点处。

(2)正坐或侧伏,于耳上前入发际 1 寸,当角孙穴(三焦经)之前方约 1 寸处取穴。

〔功效与主治〕止痛消肿,祛风开噤。头痛连齿,颊颔肿,口噤。

〔操作〕向下或向后平刺 0.5～0.8 寸。

〔备注〕足少阳与足太阳经交会穴。

Method of locating the point:

(1) This point is on the head, at a crossing point of the vertical posterior border of the temple and horizontal line through the ear apex.

(2) Ask patient to take a sitting position or a lateral recumbent position, locate the point 1 cun within the hairline above the ear, 1 cun anterior to Jiaosun (SJ 20).

Actions and indications: Relieve pain, subdue swelling, disperse wind and treat trismus, used to treat headache referring to the teeth, swelling of cheeks and trismus.

Manipulation: Puncture perpendicularly downwards or backwards 0.5 — 0.8 cun.

Notes: This is a crossing point of the foot Shaoyang meridian and the foot Taiyang meridian.

率谷 Shuàigǔ (GB 8)

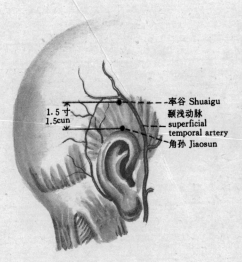

1.5寸
1.5cun

率谷 Shuaigu
颞浅动脉
superficial
temporal artery
角孙 Jiaosun

〔取穴法〕(1)在头部，当耳尖直上入发际1.5寸，角孙直上方处。

(2)正坐或侧伏，将耳部向前折曲，于耳翼尖直上入发际1.5寸处取穴。

〔功效与主治〕疏泄肝胆，清热熄风。偏头痛，目痛，疟腮。

〔操作〕平刺0.3～0.5寸。

〔备注〕足少阳与足太阳经交会穴。

Method of locating the point：

(1) This point is located 1.5 cun within the hairline, directly superior to the ear apex, just above Jiaosun (SJ 20).

(2) Ask patient to take a sitting position or a lying position on his one side, locate the point 1.5 cun within the hairline directly superior to the apex of the auricle when the ear is folded forwards.

Actions and indications：Soothe flow of the liver-Qi, purge heat from the liver and gallbladder, clear away heat and calm wind, used to treat migraine, pain of eyes and mumps.

Manipulation：Puncture subcutaneously 0.3—0.5 cun.

Notes：Shuaigu (GB 8) is a crossing point of the Foot-Shaoyang Meridian and the Foot-Taiyang Meridian.

天冲 Tiánchōng （GB 9）

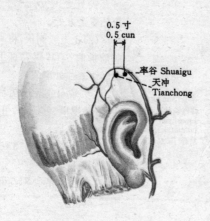

0.5 寸
0.5 cun

率谷 Shuaigu
天冲 Tianchong

〔取穴法〕(1)在头部,当耳根后缘直上入发际 2 寸,率谷后 0.5 寸处。

(2)正坐或侧伏,先取率谷穴,向后约 0.5 寸处取本穴。

〔功效与主治〕祛风定惊。头痛,眩晕,惊恐,痫证。

〔操作〕平刺 0.3～0.5 寸。

〔备注〕足少阳与足太阳经交会穴。

Method of locating the point:

(1) This point is located directly above the posterior border of the auricle, 2 cun within the hairline, about 0.5 cun posterior to Shuaigu (GB 8).

(2) Ask patient to take a sitting position or a lying position on his one side, locate Shuaigu (GB 8) first, then find the Tianchong point (GB 9) 0.5 cun posterior to Shuaigu (GB 8).

Actions and indications: Expel wind and relieve convulsion, used to treat headache, dizziness, being frightened and epilepsy.

Manipulation: Puncture subcutaneously 0.3—0.5 cun.

Notes: Tianchong (GB 9) is a crossing point of the Foot-Shaoyang Meridian and the Foot-Taiyang Meridian.

完骨 Wángǔ (GB 12)

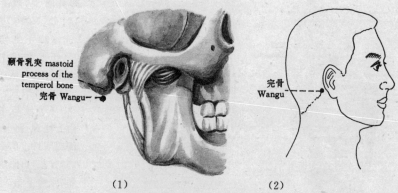

顧骨乳突 mastoid process of the temperol bone
完骨 Wangu

完骨 Wangu

(1)   (2)

〔取穴法〕(1)在头部,当耳后乳突的后下方凹陷处。

(2)正坐或侧伏,医者用手指从耳后乳突由上向下滑动,当滑至乳突下凹陷处是穴。

〔功效与主治〕祛风清热,止痛明目。头痛,眩晕,颈项强痛。

〔操作〕向下斜刺 0.3～0.5 寸。

〔备注〕足少阳与足太阳经交会穴。

Method of locating the point:

(1) This point is located in the depression posterior and inferior to the mastoid process.

(2) Ask patient to take a sitting or a lying position on his one side, move the finger up and down around the mastoid process, locate the point in the depression felt.

Actions and indications: Expel wind, clear away heat, relieve pain and improve vision, used to treat headache, dizziness and rigidity of the neck.

Manipulation: Puncture obliquely downwards 0.3－0.5 cun.

Notes: Wangu is a crossing point of Foot-Shaoyang Meridian and Foot-Taiyang Meridian.

阳白 Yángbái (GB 14)

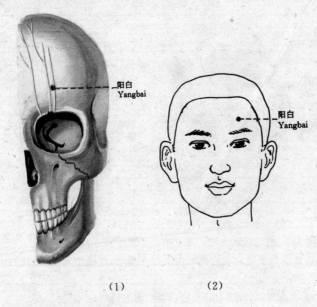

阳白 Yangbai

阳白 Yangbai

(1)　　　　　(2)

〔取穴法〕

(1)在前额部,当瞳孔直上,眉上1寸处。

(2)正坐仰靠,于前额目中线即眉毛中点直上1寸处取穴。

〔功效与主治〕祛风泄火,清头明目。前头痛,目眩,口眼㖞斜,眼睑下垂。

〔操作〕向下沿皮刺 0.3～0.5寸。

〔备注〕足少阳与阳维脉交会穴。

Method of locating the point:

(1) This point is located on the forehead, 1 cun directly above the midpoint of the eyebrow.

(2) Ask patient to take a sitting position with his back supported, locate the point 1 cun above the midpoint of the eyebrow, or 1 cun above the eyebrow on the midline of the eye on the forehead.

Actions and indications: Expel wind, purge fire, clear away heat from the head, improve vision, used to treat headache, dizziness, deviation of the eye and mouth and ptosis of the eyelids.

Manipulation: Puncture downward subcutaneously 0.3—0.5 cun.

Notes: Yangbai (GB 14) is a crossing point of the Foot-Shaoyang Meridian and Yangwei Meridian.

头临泣 Tóulínqì (GB 15)

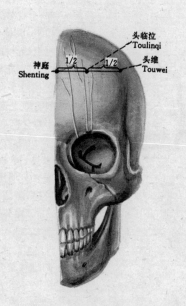

神庭 Shenting　1/2　1/2　头临泣 Toulinqi　头维 Touwei

〔取穴法〕(1)在头部,当瞳孔直上入前发际0.5寸,神庭与头维连线的中点处。

(2)正坐仰靠,于阳白穴直上,入发际0.5寸处,于神庭穴与头维穴之间。

〔功效与主治〕清头明目,安神定志。头痛,目眩,目翳,流泪。

〔操作〕向上沿皮刺0.3～0.5寸。

〔备注〕足少阳、足太阳经与阳维脉交会穴。

Method of locating the point:

(1) This point is located on the head, 0.5 cun within the anterior hairline directly above the pupil, midway between Shenting (DU 24) and Touwei (St 8).

(2) Ask patient to take a sitting position with his back supported, locate the point 0.5 cun within the hairline directly above Yangbai (GB 14), in the midway between Shenting (DU 24) and Touwei (St 8).

Actions and indications: Purge fire, improve vision, tranquilize mind and sedate emotional state, used to treat headache, dizziness, cataract and lacrimation.

Manipulation: Puncture upwards subcutaneously 0.3—0.5 cun.

Notes: Toulinqi (GB 15) is a crossing point of the Foot-Shaoyang Meridian, Foot-Taiyang Meridian and Yangwei Meridian.

风池 Fēngchí (GB 20)

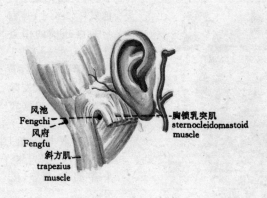

风池
Fengchi
风府
Fengfu
斜方肌
trapezius
muscle
胸锁乳突肌
sternocleidomastoid
muscle

〔取穴法〕(1)在项部,当枕骨之下,与风府穴相平,胸锁乳突肌与斜方肌上端之间的凹陷处。

(2)正坐或俯伏,于项后枕骨下两侧凹陷处,当斜方肌上部与胸锁乳突肌上端之间取穴。

〔功效与主治〕疏风解热,清头开窍,明目益聪。头项强痛,眩晕,目赤肿痛,鼻渊,感冒。

〔操作〕向鼻尖方向刺0.5~0.8寸。

〔备注〕足少阳经与阳维脉交会穴。

Method of locating the point:

(1) This point is located on the nape, at the same level with Fengfu (DU 16) below the pillow bone, in the depression between the upper portion of m. sternocleidomastoideus and that of m. trapezius.

(2) Ask patient to take a sitting position or a prone position, locate the point in the depressions inferior to the pillow bone, at the midpoint of the line connecting the upper portion of m. sternocleidomastoideus and that of m. trapezius.

Actions and indications: Expel wind, clear away heat, purge fire, induce resuscitation, improve vision and intelligence, used to treat headache, rigidity of nape, dizziness, redness, pain and swelling of the eye, rhinorrhea, and common cold.

Manipulation: Puncture 0.5—0.8 cun towards the tip of the nose.

Notes: Fengchi (GB 20) is a crossing point of the Foot-Shaoyang Meridian and Yangwei Meridian.

肩井 Jiānjǐng (GB 21)

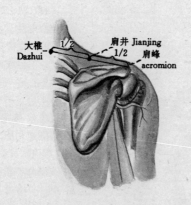

大椎 Dazhui 1/2 肩井 Jianjing 1/2 肩峰 acromion

〔取穴法〕(1)在肩上，前直乳中，当大椎与肩峰连线的中点上取之。

(2)医生以手掌后第1横纹按在病人肩胛冈下缘，拇指按在第7颈椎下，其余四指并拢按在肩上，食指靠于颈部，中指屈曲，中指尖处是穴。

〔功效与主治〕通经理气，豁痰开郁。头项肩背疼痛，手臂不举，乳痈。

〔操作〕直刺 0.3～0.5 寸，勿深刺。

〔备注〕手、足少阳与阳维脉交会穴。

Method of locating the point：

(1) This point is located at the highest point of the shoulder, in the midpoint of the line joining Dazhui (DU 14) and the acrimion.

(2) Doctor may locate the point below the tip of his middle finger when he places the first transverse crease of his wrist in the lower border of the patient's spine of scapula, presses the area inferior to the 7th cervical vertebra with his thumb and put his rest closed four fingers on the shoulder, with the index finger touching the neck and the middle finger silghtly flexed.

Actions and indications：Promote flow of blood in the channels, regulate flow of Qi, dissolve phlegm and relieve depression, used to treat pain of the head, nape, shoulder and back, inability to lift arm, and acute mastitis.

Manipulation：Puncture perpendicularly 0.3—0.5 cun. Deep needling is not advisable.

日月 Riyuè (GB 24)

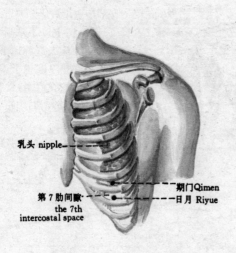

乳头 nipple

第 7 肋间隙
the 7th
intercostal space

期门 Qimen
日月 Riyue

〔取穴法〕(1)在上腹部,当乳头直下,第 7 肋间隙,前正中线旁开 4 寸处。

(2)正坐或仰卧,于锁骨中线之第 7 肋间隙取穴。

〔功效与主治〕开郁止痛,降逆利胆。胁肋痛,胀满,呕吐,黄疸。

〔操作〕沿肋间隙斜刺 0.5～0.8 寸。

〔备注〕胆之募穴;足少阳与足太阴经交会穴。

Method of locating the point:

(1) This point is located in the upper abdomen, directly inferior to the nipple, in the 7th intercostal space, 4 cun lateral to the anterior midline.

(2) Ask patient to take a sitting position or lie on his back, locate the point on the midclavicular line in the 7th intercostal space.

Actions and indications: Relieve liver depression and pain, lower upward adverse flow of Qi and benefit gallbladder, used to treat pain and fullness in the hypochondriac region, vomiting and jaundice.

Manipulation: Puncture 0.5－0.8 cun along the intercostal space.

Notes: Riyue (GB 24) is the Front-Mu point of the Gallbladder Meridian of Foot-Shaoyang and a crossing point of the Foot-Shaoyang Meridian and the Foot-Taiyin Meridian.

京门 Jingmén (GB 25)

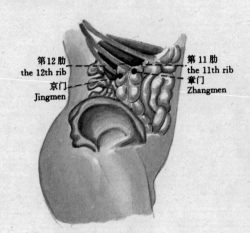

第12肋 the 12th rib
京门 Jingmen
第11肋 the 11th rib
章门 Zhangmen

〔取穴法〕(1)在侧腰部,章门后1.8寸,当第12肋骨游离端的下方处取穴。

(2)侧卧或俯卧,于侧腰部第12肋骨游离端下方取穴。

〔功效与主治〕益肾利水。肾绞痛,石淋。

〔操 作〕斜刺0.3～0.5寸。

〔备注〕肾之"募"穴。

Method of locating the point:

(1) This point is on the lateral side of the lumbar region, 1.8 cun posterior to Zhangmen (Li 13), on the lower border of the free end of the 12th rib.

(2) Ask patient to lie on one side or take a prone position, locate the point on the lower border of the free end of the 12th rib on the lateral side of the lumbar region.

Actions and indications: Benefit the kidney and induce diuresis, used to treat renal colic, stranguria caused by the passage of the urinary stone.

Manipulation: Puncture obliquely 0.3—0.5 cun.

Notes: Jingmen (GB 25) is the Front-Mu point of the kidney.

231

带脉 Dàimài (GB 26)

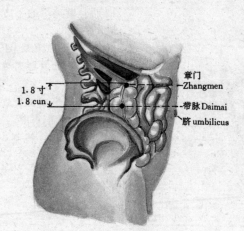

1.8寸
1.8 cun

章门 Zhangmen
带脉 Daimai
脐 umbilicus

〔取穴法〕(1)在侧腹部,章门下1.8寸,当第11肋骨游离端下方垂线与脐水平线的交点上取穴。

(2)侧卧,于腋中线与平脐横线之交点处取穴。

〔功效与主治〕清热利湿,通经止带。赤白带下,月经不调。

〔操作〕直刺0.5～0.8寸。

〔备注〕足少阳经与带脉交会穴。

Method of locating the point:

(1) This point is located on the lateral side of the abdomen, 1.8 cun inferior to Zhangmen (Li 13), at the junction of the vertical line passing through the region below the free end of the 11th rib and the transverse line at the level with the umbilus.

Actions and indications: Clear away heat, remove dampness, regulate blood flow in the channels and relieve leukorrhea, used to treat leukorrhea white or red in colour, and irregular menstruation.

Manipulation: Puncture perpendicularly 0.5—0.8 cun.

Notes: Daimai (GB 26) is a crossing point of the Foot-Shaoyang Meridian and the Dai Meridian.

五枢 Wǔshū (GB 27)

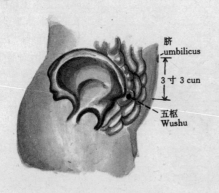

脐
umbilicus

3 寸 3 cun

五枢
Wushu

〔取穴法〕(1)在侧腹部,当髂前上嵴的前方,横平脐下 3 寸处。

(2)侧卧,在髂前上嵴之前 0.5 寸,约平脐下 3 寸处。

〔功效与主治〕调理经带。小腹痛,月经不调,赤白带下。

〔操作〕直刺 0.5～1 寸。

〔备注〕足少阳经与带脉交会穴。

Method of locating the point:

(1) This point is located in the lateral side of the abdomen, anterior to the suppine illiac spine, 3 cun below the level of the umbilicus.

(2) Ask patient to lie on his one side, locate the point 0. 5 cun anterior to the superior illiac spine, about 3 cun below the level of the umbilicus.

Actions and indications: Regulate menstruation and leukorrhea, used to treat pain in the lower abdomen, irregular menstruation and leukorrhea white or red in colour.

Manipulation: Puncture perpendicularly 0. 5—1 cun.

Notes: Wushu (GB 27) is a crossing point of the Foot-Shaoyang Meridian and the Daimai Meridian.

维道 Wéidào（GB 28）

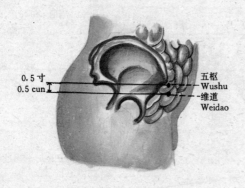

0.5 寸
0.5 cun

五枢
Wushu
维道
Weidao

〔取穴法〕（1）在侧腹部，当髂前上嵴的前下方，五枢前下 0.5 寸处取穴。

（2）侧卧，于五枢穴前下 0.5 寸，对腹股沟处取穴。

〔功效与主治〕调经固冲，理肠通便。小腹痛，带下，阴挺。

〔操作〕向前下斜刺 0.5～1 寸。

〔备注〕足少阳经与带脉交会穴。

Method of locating the point：

(1) This point is located on the lateral side of the abdomen, anterior and inferior to the superior illiac spine, 0.5 cun anterior and inferior to Wushu (GB 27).

(2) Ask patient to lie on his one side, locate the point 0.5 cun anterior and inferior to Wushu point (GB 27), at the level of the groin.

Actions and indications：Regulate menstruation, consolidate the Chong Meridian, regulate the bowel movement and relax the bowels, used to treat pain in the lower abdomen, leukorrhea and prolapse of the uterus.

Manipulation：Puncture 0.5—1 cun forwards and downwards obliquely.

Notes：Weidao (GB 28) is a crossing point of the Foot-Shaoyang Meridian and the Dai Meridian.

居髎 Jūliáo（GB 29）

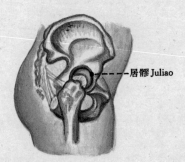

------居髎 Juliao

〔取穴法〕（1）在髋部，当髂前上嵴与股骨大转子最凸点连线的中点处。

（2）侧卧，于维道穴后下方3寸，髂骨旁，当髂前上嵴与大转子高点连线之中点处。

〔功效与主治〕舒筋活络，强健腰腿。腰髋腿痹痛、麻木，下肢瘫痪。

〔操作〕直刺或斜刺0.6～1.2寸。

〔备注〕足少阳经与阳蹻脉交会穴。

Method of locating the point:

(1) This point is located in the buttock, at the midpoint of the line connecting the superior illiac spine and the lowest point of the great trochanter.

(2) Ask patient to lie on his one side, locate the point 3 cun postero-inferior to Weidao (GB 28), at the midpoint of the line connecting the superior illiac spine and the lowest point of the great trochanter.

Actions and indications: Relax muscles and tendones and activate flow of Qi and blood in the channels and collaterals, strengthen the loins and the legs, used to treat pain and numbness of the buttock and legs, paralysis of the lower limbs.

Manipulation: Puncture perpendicularly or obliquely 0.6—1.2 cun

Notes: Juliao (GB 29) is a crossing point of the Foot-Shaoyang Meridian and the Yangqiao Meridian.

环跳 Huántiào (GB 30)

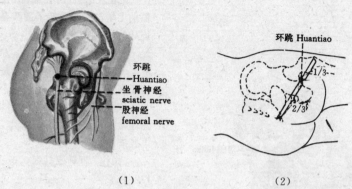

环跳
—Huantiao
坐骨神经
sciatic nerve
股神经
femoral nerve

环跳 Huantiao

(1)　　　　　　　　　　(2)

〔取穴法〕(1)在股外侧部,侧卧屈股,当股骨大转子最凸点与骶管裂孔连线的外1/3与中1/3交点处。

(2)侧卧,屈上腿(呈90度)以拇指关节横纹按在大转子头上,拇指指脊柱,当拇指尖止处是穴。

〔功效与主治〕通经活络,驱风散寒,强健腰腿。下肢痿、痹证,中风偏瘫。

〔操作〕直刺1.5~2寸,使针感至足。

〔备注〕足少阳经与足太阳经交会穴。

Method of locating the point:
(1) This point is in the lateral side of the buttock, at the junction of the lateral 1/3 and the medial 2/3 of the distance between the great trochanter and the hiatus of the sacrum when patient takes a lateral recumber position with the thigh flexed.

(2) Ask patient to take a lateral recumber position with his thigh flexed at an angle of 90°, locate the point at where the tip of the thumb is by placing the thumbs on the head of the great trachanter with the tip directing at the spinal column.

Actions and indications: Promote flow of Qi and blood in the channels and collaterals, expel wind and cold, strengthen the loins and legs, used to treat arthralgia and atrophy of the lower limbs, hemiplegia.

Manipulation: Puncture 1. 5 — 2 cun perpendicularly until the sensation of needling is transmitted to the foot.

Notes: Huantiao (GB 30) is a crossing point of the Foot-Shaoyang Meridian and Foot-Taiyang Meridian.

风市 Fengshì (GB 31)

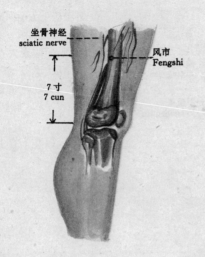

坐骨神经
sciatic nerve

风市
Fengshì

7 寸
7 cun

〔取穴法〕(1)在大腿外侧部的中线上,当腘横纹上 7 寸处。

(2)直立垂手时,中指尖所到处是穴。

〔功效与主治〕通经活络,疏风除湿。中风半身不遂,下肢痿、痹证,遍身瘙痒。

〔操作〕直刺 0.5～1 寸。

Method of locating the point:

(1) This point is on the midline of the lateral aspect of the thigh, 7 cun above the transverse popliteal crease.

(2) When the patient stands erect with his hands close to the sides of his body, the point is where the tip of the middle finger touches.

Actions and indications: Promote flow of Qi and blood in the channels and collaterals, expel wind and remove dampness, used to treat hemiplegia, atrophy or arthritis of the lower limbs, and general pruritus.

Manipulation: Puncture perpendicularly 0.5—1 cun.

膝阳关 Xīyángguān (GB 33)

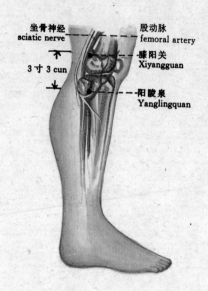

坐骨神经
sciatic nerve

3寸 3 cun

股动脉
femoral artery

膝阳关
Xiyangguan

阳陵泉
Yanglingquan

〔取穴法〕(1)在膝外侧,当阳陵泉上 3 寸,股骨外上髁上方的凹陷处。

(2)屈膝,于大腿外侧中线,阳陵泉穴直上 3 寸处定取。

〔功效与主治〕疏筋脉,利关节。膝髌肿痛,腘筋挛急。

〔操 作〕直刺 0.3～0.5寸。

Method of locating the point:

(1) This point is on the lateral aspect of the knee, 3 cun above Yanglingquan (GB 34), in the depression supero-lateral to the external epicondyle of femur.

(2) Ask patient to flex his knee, locate the point in the midline of the lateral aspect of the thigh, 3 cun directly above Yanglingquan (GB 34).

Actions and indications: Relax muscles and tendons and benefit joints, used to treat swelling and pain of the knee joint, spasm of tendons in the popliteal fossa.

Manipulation: Puncture perpendicularly 0. 3－0. 5 cun.

阳陵泉 Yánglíngquán（GB 34）

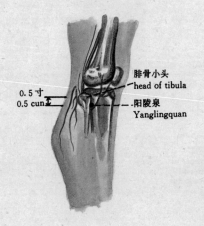

腓骨小头
head of tibula

0.5 寸
0.5 cun

阳陵泉
Yanglingquan

〔取穴法〕（1）在小腿外侧，当腓骨头前下方凹陷处。

（2）屈膝，先取腓骨小头，向前下 0.5 寸处取本穴。

〔功效与主治〕舒肝利胆，清泄湿热，舒筋活络。半身不遂，下肢痿、痹证，胁痛，破伤风，小儿惊风。

〔操作〕直刺 0.5～1.2 寸。

〔备注〕足少阳经"合"穴；胆之"下合"穴；八会穴之一，筋之会穴。

Method of locating the point：

(1) This point is located in the lateral aspect of the lower leg, in the depression anterior and inferior to the head of fibula.

(2) Ask patient to flex his leg, find out the head of the fibula first, then locate the point 0.5 cun anterior and inferior to the head of the fibula.

Actions and indications：Promote flow of the liver-Qi, normalize functioning of gallbladder, purge damp-heat, relax muscles and tendons and activate flow of Qi and blood in the channels and collaterals, used to treat hemiplegia, atrophy and arthralgia of the lower limbs, hypochondriac pain, tetanus, and infantile convulsion.

Manipulation：Puncture perpendicularly 0.5—1.2 cun.

Notes：Yanglingquan (GB 34) is the He-Sea point of the Foot Shaoyang Meridian, the Lower He-Sea point of the gallbladder and the confluent point of tendon.

阳交 Yángjiāo (GB 35)

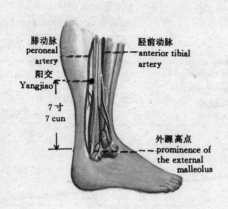

腓动脉
peroneal artery

阳交
Yangjiao

7寸
7 cun

胫前动脉
anterior tibial artery

外踝高点
prominence of the external malleolus

〔取穴法〕(1)在小腿外侧,当外踝尖上7寸,腓骨后缘处。

(2)正坐或侧卧,先取外踝尖,再向上7寸,腓骨后缘处取穴。

〔功效与主治〕疏肝利胆,定惊安神。胸胁胀满,下肢痿、痹证,癫狂。

〔操作〕直刺0.5～0.8寸。

〔备注〕阳维脉之"郄"穴。

Method of locating the point:

(1) This point is located in the lateral aspect of the lower leg, 7 cun above the tip of the external malleolus, on the posterior border of the fibula.

(2) Ask patient to take a sitting position or lie on his one side, find out the tip of the external malleolus first, then locate the point 7 cun above the tip on the posterior border of the fibula.

Actions and indications: Promote flow of the liver-Qi, normalize functions of the gallbladder, and tranquilize the mind, used to treat fullness in the chest and hypochondriac region, atrophy and arthralgia of the lower limbs, epilepsy and mania.

Manipulation: Puncture perpendicularly 0.5—0.8 cun.

Notes: Yangjiao (GB 35) is the Xi-Cleft point of the Yangwei Meridian.

外丘 Wàiqiū (GB 36)

〔取穴法〕(1)在小腿外侧,当外踝尖上7寸,腓骨前缘,平阳交穴。

(2)正坐或侧卧,先取外踝尖上绝骨穴,再向上4寸,腓骨前缘处。

〔功效与主治〕疏肝利胆,清热利湿。胸胁支满,下肢痿、痹证。

〔操作〕直刺0.5～0.8寸。

〔备注〕足少阳胆经"郄"穴。

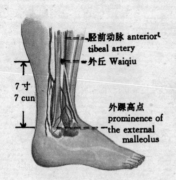

胫前动脉 anterior tibeal artery

外丘 Waiqiu

7寸
7 cun

外踝高点 prominence of the external malleolus

Method of locating the point:

(1) This point is on the lateral aspect of the lower leg, 7 cun above the tip of the external malleolus, on the anterior border of the fibula, at the level of Yangjiao (GB 35).

(2) Ask patient to take a sitting position or a lying position on his one side, locate Juegu (GB 39) above the tip of the external malleolus first, then locate the Waiqiu point (GB 36) 4 cun above the Juegu (GB 39).

Actions and indications: Promote flow of the liver-Qi, normalize functions of the gallbladder, clear away heat and remove dampness, used to treat fullness of the chest and hypochondrium, atrophy and arthralgia of the lower limbs.

Manipulation: Puncture perpendicularly 0.5—0.8 cun.

Notes: This point is the Xi-Cleft point of the Gallbladder Meridian of Foot-Shaoyang.

光明 Guāngmíng (GB 37)

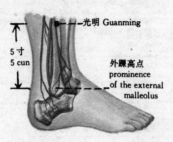

光明 Guanming

5寸
5 cun

外踝高点
prominence
of the external
malleolus

〔取穴法〕(1)在小腿外侧,当外踝尖上 5 寸,腓骨前缘处。

(2)正坐或侧卧,绝骨穴向上 2 寸,腓骨前缘处。

〔功效与主治〕通经活络,调肝明目。目视不明,目痛,夜盲,乳痈。

〔操作〕直刺 0.6～1寸。

〔备注〕足少阳胆经"络"穴。

Method of locating the point:

(1) This point is located on the lateral aspect of the lower leg, 5 cun above the tip of the external malleolus, on the anterior border of the fibula.

(2) Ask patient to take a sitting position or a lying position on his one side, locate the point 2 cun above Juegu (GB 39), on the anterior border of the fibula.

Actions and indications: Activate flow of Qi and blood in the channels and collaterals, regulate functions of the liver and improve vision, used to treat blurred vision, pain of the eyes, night blindness and acute mastitis.

Manipulation: Puncture perpendicularly 0.6—1 cun.

Notes: Guangming (GB 37) is the Luo-Connecting point of the Gallbladder Meridian of Foot-Taiyang.

阳辅 Yángfǔ (GB 38)

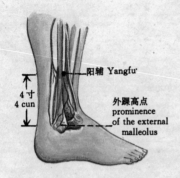

阳辅 Yangfu'

外踝高点
prominence
of the external
malleolus

4 寸
4 cun

〔取穴法〕（1）在小腿外侧，当外踝尖上 4 寸，腓骨前缘稍前方处。

（2）正坐或侧卧，绝骨穴向上 1 寸，腓骨前缘处。

〔功效与主治〕清肝利胆，行气开郁。偏头痛，胸胁及下肢外侧痛。

〔操作〕直刺 0.5～0.8 寸。

〔备注〕足少阳胆经"经"穴。

Method of locating the point:

(1) This point is located on the lateral aspect of the lower leg, 4 cun above the tip of the external malleolus, and silghtly anterior to the anterior border of the fibula.

(2) Ask patient to take a sitting or a lying position on his one side, locate the point 1 cun above Juegu (GB 39), on the anterior border of the fibula.

Actions and indications: Clear away heat from the liver, normalize the functions of gallbladder, promote flow of Qi and relieve stagnation of Qi, used to treat migraine, pain in the hypochondrium or on the lateral aspect of the lower limbs.

Manipulation: Puncture perpendicularly 0.5—0.8 cun.

Notes: Yangfu (GB 38) is the Jing-Well point of the Gallbladder Meridian of Foot-Shaoyang.

悬钟 Xuánzhōng(又名绝骨 Juégǔ)(GB 39)

〔取穴法〕在小腿外侧,当外踝尖上3寸,腓骨前缘处。按压本穴时,足背动脉暂绝。

〔功效与主治〕通经活络,坚筋壮骨。半身不遂,颈项强痛,脑转耳鸣。

〔操作〕直刺或向后内斜刺0.8～1.2寸。

〔备注〕八会穴之一,髓之会穴。

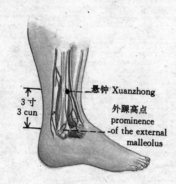

悬钟 Xuanzhong

外踝高点 prominence of the external malleolus

3 寸
3 cun

Method of locating the point: This point is located on the lateral aspect of the lower leg, 3 cun above the tip of the external malleolus, on the anterior border of the fibula. When this point is pressed, the pulse beats of dorsal artery of the foot will be absent temporarily.

Actions and indications: Promote flow of Qi and blood in the channels and collaterals, strengthen the tendons and bones, used to treat hemiplegia, rigidity and pain of the neck and nape, dizziness and tinnitus.

Manipulation: Puncture 0.8 — 1.2 cun perpendicularly or backwards and inwards.

Notes: Xuanzhong (GB 39) is the confluence point of marrow, which is one of the eight confluence points.

244

丘墟 Qiūxū (GB 40)

〔取穴法〕（1）在足外踝的前下方，当趾长伸肌腱的外侧凹陷处取穴。

（2）正坐或侧卧，于外踝前下方，趾长伸肌腱外侧凹陷处取穴。

〔功效与主治〕活络化瘀，舒肝利胆。头颈项强，胁痛，外踝肿痛。

〔操作〕直刺 0.3～0.5 寸。

〔备注〕足少阳胆经"原"穴。

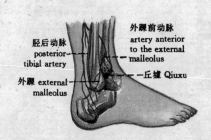

胫后动脉 posterior-tibial artery

外踝前动脉 artery anterior to the external malleolus

外踝 external malleolus

丘墟 Qiuxu

Method of locating the point:

(1) This point is located anterior and inferior to the external malleolus, in the depression on the lateral side of the tendon of m. extensor digitorium longus.

(2) Ask patient to take a sitting position or a lying position on his one side, locate the point anterior and inferior to the external malleolus, in the depression on the lateral side of the tendon of m. extensor digitorium longus.

Actions and indications: Activate flow of Qi and blood in the collaterals, remove blood stasis, promote flow of the liver-qi and normalize functions of the gallbladder, used to treat headache, rigidity of the nape, hypochondriac pain, swelling and pain of the external malleolus.

Manipulation: Puncture perpendicularly 0.3—0.5 cun.

Notes: Qiuxu (GB 40) is the Yuan-Primary point of the Gallbladder Meridian of Foot-Shaoyang.

足临泣 Zúlíngqì (GB 41)

〔取穴法〕(1)在足背外侧,当第4跖趾关节的后方,小趾伸肌腱的外侧陷处。

(2)正坐垂足着地,于第四五跖骨底前方,第5趾前伸肌腱外侧凹陷处取穴。

〔功效与主治〕舒肝利胆,聪耳明目。头痛,眩晕,乳痈。

〔操作〕直刺 0.3～0.5寸。

〔备注〕足少阳胆经"输"穴;八脉交会穴之一,通于带脉。

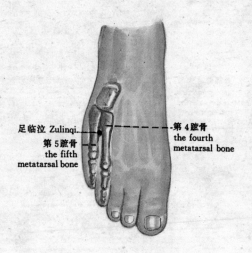

足临泣 Zulinqi
第5跖骨
the fifth
metatarsal bone

第4跖骨
the fourth
metatarsal bone

Method of locating the point:

(1) This point is located in the lateral side of the dorsum of foot, anterior to the 4th metatarsal joint, in the depression on the lateral side of the tendon of m. extensor digiti minimi of the foot.

(2) Ask patient to sit with his foot touching the ground, locate the point in the area posterior to the junction of the fourth and fifth metatarsal bones, in the depression on the lateral side of the tendon of the fifth anterior digital flexor muscle.

Actions and indications: Promote flow of the liver-Qi, normalize functions of the gallbladder, improve hearing and vision, used to treat headache, dizziness, acute mastitis.

Manipulation: Puncture perpendicularly 0.3—0.5 cun.

Notes: Zulinqi (GB 41) is the Shu-Stream point of the Gallbladder Meridian of Foot-Shaoyang and one of the eight confluence points, connecting with the Dai Meridian.

侠溪 Xiàxī (GB 43)

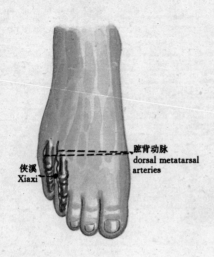

侠溪
Xiaxi

踱背动脉
dorsal metatarsal
arteries

〔取穴法〕(1)在足背外侧,当第四五趾间,趾蹼缘后方赤白肉际处。

(2)正坐垂足着地,于足背第四五趾趾缝端取穴。

〔功效与主治〕清头明目,熄风通络。头痛,眩晕,耳聋耳鸣,乳痈初起。

〔操作〕直刺或斜刺0.2~0.3寸。

〔备注〕足少阳胆经"荥"穴。

Method of locating the point:

(1) This point is located on the dorsum of foot, between the fourth and the fifth toes, proximal to the margin of the web.

(2) Ask patient to take a sitting position with his foot touching the ground, locate the point in the web of the fourth and fifth toes on the dorsum.

Actions and indications: Clear away heat from the head, improve vision, calm wind and promote flow of Qi and blood in the collaterals, used to treat headache, dizziness, tinnitus, deafness, and early acute mastitis.

Manipulation: Puncture perpendicularly or obliquely 0.2—0.3 cun.

Notes: Xiaxi (GB 43) is the Ying-Spring point of the Gallbladder Meridian of Foot-Shaoyang.

足窍阴 Zúqiàoyīn (GB 44)

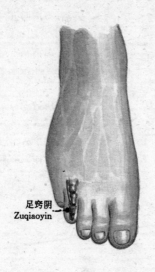

足窍阴
Zuqiaoyin

〔取穴法〕(1)在足第 4 趾末节外侧,距趾甲角 0.1 寸(指寸)。

(2)正坐垂足着地,于第 4 趾爪甲外侧缘与基底部各作一线,两线交点处取穴。

〔功效与主治〕开窍泄热,聪利耳目。头痛目眩,目赤肿痛,耳聋耳鸣。

〔操作〕浅刺 0.1 寸,或三棱针点刺出血。

〔备注〕足少阳胆经"井"穴。

Method of locating the point:

(1) This point is located on the lateral side of the fourth toe, 0.1 cun away from the corner of the nail.

(2) Ask patient to take a sitting position with his foot touching the ground, locate the point at the junction of the line drawn along the lateral border of the lateral side of the nail of the fourth toe and that drawn along the base of the nail.

Actions and indications: Induce resuscitation, purge heat, improve hearing and vision, used to treat headache, dizziness, redness, swelling and pain of the eye, deafness and tinnitus.

Manipulation: Puncture superficially 0.1 cun, or prick with a three-edged needle to cause bleeding.

Notes: Zuqiaoyin (GB 44) is the Ying-Spring point of the Gallbladder Meridian of Foot-Shaoyang.

十二、足厥阴肝经

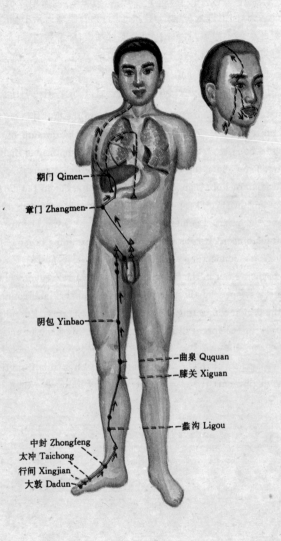

期门 Qimen —

章门 Zhangmen —

阴包 Yinbao —

曲泉 Ququan

膝关 Xiguan

蠡沟 Ligou

中封 Zhongfeng
太冲 Taichong
行间 Xingjian
大敦 Dadun

起于足大趾上毫毛部(大敦),沿着足跗部向上,经过内踝前1寸处(中封),向上至内踝上8寸处交出于足太阴经的后面,上行膝内侧,沿着股部内侧,进入阴毛中,绕过阴部,上达小腹,挟着胃旁,属于肝脏,联络胆腑,向上通过横膈,分布于胁肋,沿着喉咙的后面,向上进入鼻咽部,连接于"目系"(眼球连系于脑的部位),向上出于前额,与督脉会合于巅顶。目系的支脉:下行颊里,环绕唇内;肝部的支脉:从肝分出,通过横膈,向上流注于肺,与手太阴肺经相接。

12. The Liver Meridian of Foot-Jueyin

The Liver Meridian of Foot-Shaoyang starts from the dorsal hairy region of the great toe (Dadun, LR 1). Running upwards along the dorsum of the foot and passing through Zhongfeng (LR 4), 1 cun in front of the medial malleolus, it ascends to an area 8 cun above the medial malleolus, where it runs across and behind the Spleen Meridian of Foot-Taiyin. Then, it runs further to the medial aspect of the knee and along the medial aspect of the thigh to the pubic hair region. Then, it curves around the external genital and goes up to the lower abdomen. Going upward around the stomach, it runs to the liver, its pertaining organ, and further to the gallbladder, its connecting organ. From there, it passes through the diaphragm and branches out in the hypochondriac and costal region. Then it ascends along the posterior aspect of the throat to the nasopharynx and connects with the eye system (the region connecting the eyeball and the brain). Running further upward, it emerges in the forehead and meets the Du Meridian at the vertex. The branch arising from the eye system goes downwards into the cheek and curves around the inner surface of the lips. Its another branch arising from the liver passes through the diaphragm, travels into the lung and links with the Lung Meridian of Hand-Taiyin.

大敦 Dàdūn (LR 1)

〔取穴法〕（1）在足大趾末节外侧，距趾甲角 0.1 寸(指寸)。

（2）伸足，从踇趾爪甲外侧缘与基底部各作一线，于交点处取穴。

〔功效与主治〕理气调血，泄热解痉。疝气，阴缩，阴部肿痛。

〔操作〕浅刺 0.1 寸，或用三棱针点刺出血。

〔备注〕足厥阴肝经"井"穴。

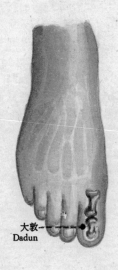

大敦
Dadun

Method of locating the point：

（1）This point is located in the lateral side of the dorsum of the terminal phalanx of the great toe, 0.1 cun away from to the corner of the nail.

（2）Ask patient to stretch his foot, located the point at the junction of the line along the lateral side of the nail of the great toe and the line along the base of the nail.

Actions and indications：Regulate flow of Qi and blood, purge heat and relieve convulsion, used to treat hernia, contraction of the external genital, swelling and pain of the external genital.

Manipulation：Puncture superficially 0.1 cun, or prick with a three-edged needle to cause bleeding.

Notes：Dadun (LR 1) is the Jing-Well point of the Liver Meridian of Foot-Jueyin.

行间 Xíngjiān (LR 2)

〔取穴法〕(1)在足背侧,当第一二趾间,趾蹼缘的后方赤白肉际处。

(2)正坐垂足,于足背第一二趾缝端凹陷处取穴。

〔功效与主治〕舒肝理气,清热镇惊。胁痛,头痛,目眩,目赤肿痛。

〔操作〕直刺或斜刺0.2～0.3寸。

〔备注〕足厥阴肝经"荥"穴。

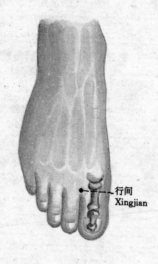

行间
Xingjian

Method of locating the point:

(1) This point is located on the dorsum of the foot, between the first and the second toes, posterior to the border of the web.

(2) Ask patient to take a sitting position with his foot suspected naturally, locate the point in the depression proximal to the margin of the web between the first and the second toes on the dorsum.

Actions and indications: Relieve liver-depression, regulate flow of Qi, clear away heat and tranquilize the mind, used to treat hypochondriac pain, headache, dizziness, redness, swelling and pain of the eyes.

Manipulation: Puncture perpendicularly or obliquely 0.2—0.3 cun.

Notes: Xingjian (LR 2) is the Ying-Spring point of the liver Meridian of Foot-Jueyin.

太冲 Tàichōng （LR 3）

〔取穴法〕（1）在足背侧，当第1
跖骨间隙的后方凹陷处。

（2）正坐垂足，于足背第一二跖
骨之间，跖骨底结合部前方凹陷处，
当蹈长伸肌腱外缘处取穴。

〔功效与主治〕舒肝理气，泄热
镇惊。头痛，眩晕，小儿惊风，口喎。

〔操作〕直刺 0.3～0.5 寸。

〔备注〕足厥阴肝经"输"、"原"
穴。

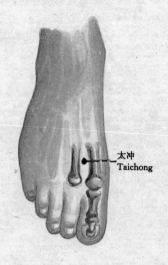

太冲
Taichong

Method of locating the point:

(1) This point is located on the dorsum of the foot, in the depression proximal
to the junction of the first and the second metatarsal bones.

(2) Ask patient to take a sitting position with his foot suspended naturally, locate the point between the first and the second metatarsal bones, in the depression
anterior to the junction of the first and the second metatarsal bones, on the lateral
border of the tendon of the long extensor muscle of the great toe.

Actions and indications: Promote flow of the liver-Qi, regulate flow of Qi,
purge heat and relieve convulsion, used to treat headache, dizziness, infantile convulsion and deviation of the mouth and eyes.

Manipulation: Puncture perpendicularly 0.3—0.5 cun.

Notes: Taichong (LR 3) is both the Shu-Stream point and the Yuan-Primary
point of the Liver Meridian of Foot-Jueyin.

中封 Zhōngfēng (LR 4)

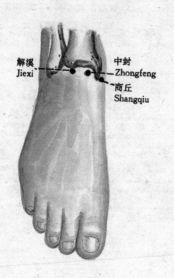

解溪 Jiexi
中封 Zhongfeng
商丘 Shangqiu

〔取穴法〕(1)在足背侧，当足内踝前，商丘与解溪连线之间，胫骨前肌腱的内侧凹陷处。

(2)足背屈时，于内踝前下方，当胫骨前肌腱与踇长伸肌腱之间凹陷处取穴。

〔功效与主治〕舒肝通络。疝气，阴茎痛，内踝肿痛。

〔操作〕直刺 0.3～0.5 寸。

〔备注〕足厥阴肝经"经"穴。

Method of locating the point:

(1) This point is located on the dorsum of the foot, anterior to the medial malleolus, in the midway of the line connecting Shangqiu (SP 5) and Jiexi (ST 41), in the depression of the medial side of the tendon of m. tibialis anterior.

(2) Locate the point in an area anterior and inferior to the medial malleolus, in the depression of the tendon of m. tibialis anterior and the tendon of long extensor muscle of the great toe.

Actions and indications: Promote flow of the liver-qi and remove obstructions from the collaterals, used to treat hernia, pain of the penis, swollen and painful medial malleolus.

Manipulation: Puncture perpendicularly 0.3—0.5 cun.

Notes: Zhongfeng (LR 4) is the Jing-Well point of the Liver Meridian of Foot-Jueyin.

254

蠡沟 Lígōu (LR 5)

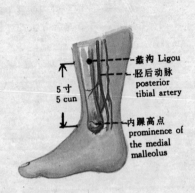

5 寸
5 cun

蠡沟 Ligou

胫后动脉
posterior
tibial artery

内踝高点
prominence of
the medial
malleolus

〔取穴法〕(1)在小腿内侧,当足内踝尖上 5 寸,胫骨内侧面的中央取穴。

(2)正坐或仰卧,先在内踝尖上 5 寸的胫骨内侧面上作一平线,当胫骨内侧的后中 1/3 交点处取穴。

〔功效与主治〕疏肝理气,调经活络。小便不利,遗尿,睾丸肿痛,阴痒。

〔操作〕平刺 0.3～0.5 寸。

〔备注〕足厥阴肝经"络"穴。

Method of locating the point:

(1) This point is located in the medial aspect of the lower leg, 5 cun above the tip of the medial malleolus, in the centre of the medial aspect of the tibia.

(2) Ask patient to take a sitting position or a supine position, draw a horizontal line 5 cun above the tip of the medial malleolus in the medial aspect of the lower leg, locate the point at the junction of the middle and the later 1/3 of the line.

Actions and indications: Soothe flow of the liver-Qi, regulate flow of Qi, activate collaterals to treat menstrual disorders, used to treat oliguria, enuresis, swelling and pain of the scrotum and pruritus of the external genital.

Manipulation: Puncture subcutaneously 0.3—0.5 cun.

Notes: Ligou (LR 5) is the Luo-Connecting point of the Liver Meridian of Foot-Jueyin.

膝关 Xīguān (LR 7)

〔取穴法〕(1)在小腿内侧,当胫骨内上髁后下方,阴陵泉后1寸,腓肠肌内侧头的上部。

(2)屈膝,先取胫骨内侧髁下缘的阴陵泉穴,再于其后方1寸处取穴。

〔功效与主治〕散寒除湿,通经利节。膝髌肿痛,历节风痛。

〔操作〕直刺0.3～0.5寸。

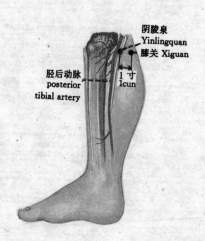

阴陵泉
Yinlingquan
膝关 Xiguan

胫后动脉
posterior
tibial artery

1寸
1cun

Method of locating the point:

(1) This point is located in the medial aspect of the lower leg, posterior and inferior to the medial condyle of the tibia, 1 cun posterior to Yanglingquan (Sp 9), in the upper portion of the medial head of m. gastrocnemius.

(2) Ask patient to flex his leg, locate Yinlingquan (Sp 9) first on the lower border of the medial malleolus, then locate Xiguan (LR 7) 1 cun posterior to Yinlingquan (Sp 9).

Actions and indications: Expel wind, remove dampness, promote flow of Qi and blood in the channels and collaterals, and benefit the joints, used to treat pain of the knee, general arthralgia due to wind.

Manipulation: Puncture subcutaneously 0.3—0.5 cun.

曲泉 Qūquán（LR 8）

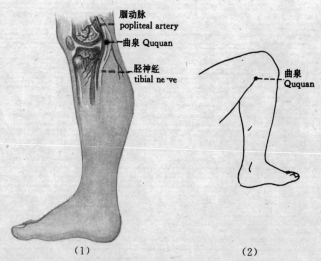

膕动脉 popliteal artery
曲泉 Ququan
胫神经 tibial nerve

曲泉 Ququan

（1）　　　　　　　　　　　（2）

〔取穴法〕（1）在膝内侧，屈膝，当膝关节内侧面横纹内侧端，股骨内侧髁的后缘，半腱肌、半膜肌止端的前缘凹陷处。

（2）屈膝，于膝内侧横纹端凹陷处取穴。

〔功效与主治〕舒筋活络，清湿热，利下焦。阴痒，阴痛，痛经，遗精，阳痿，膝髌内侧痛。

〔操作〕直刺 0.3～0.6 寸。

〔备注〕足厥阴肝经"合"穴。

Method of locating the point:

(1) This point is located in the medial aspect of the knee. When the knee is flexed, it is at the medial end of the transverse popliteal crease, on the posterior border of the medial epicondyle of the femur, on the anterior part of the depression of m. semimembranosus and m. semitendinosus.

(2) Ask patient to flex his knee, locate the point at the medial end of the transverse popliteal crease.

Actions and indications: Relax muscles and tendons, promote flow of Qi and blood in the channels and collaterals, clear away damp-heat, and benefit the lower-jiao, used to treat pruritus vulvae, pain of the vulvae, dysmenorrhea, nocturnal emission, impotence and pain in the medial aspect of the knee.

Manipulation: Puncture subcutaneously 0.3—0.6 cun.

Notes: Ququan (LR 8) is the He-Sea point of the Liver Meridian of Foot-Jueyin.

章门 Zhāngmén (LR 13)

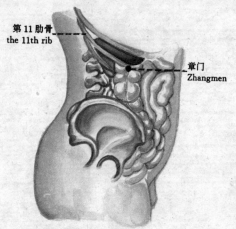

第11肋骨
the 11th rib

章门
Zhangmen

（1）

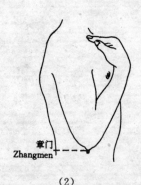

章门
Zhangmen

（2）

〔取穴法〕（1）在侧腹部，当第11肋游离端的下方取穴。

（2）侧卧，在腋中线，上肢合腋屈肘时，当肘尖所止处是穴。

〔功效与主治〕疏肝理气，活血化瘀。胁痛，腹胀，肠鸣，痞块。

〔操作〕斜刺 0.5～0.8 寸。

〔备注〕脾之"募"穴；八会穴之一，脏之会穴；足厥阴经与足少阳经交会穴。

Method of locating the point:

(1) This point is located in the lateral side of the abdomen, below the free end of the 11th floating rib.

(2) Ask patient to lie on his one side, locate the point in the midaxillary line, and where the tip of the elbow touches when he closes his arm to the trunk with the elbow flexed.

Actions and indications: Soothe flow of the liver-Qi, activate blood flow and remove blood stasis, used to treat hypochondriac pain, abdominal distension, borborygmus, and abdominal masses due to stagnation of qi.

Manipulation: Puncture obliquely 0.5—0.8 cun.

Notes: Zhangmen (LR 13) is the Front-Mu point of the spleen, the confluence point of zang organs and a crossing point of the Foot-Jueyin Meridian and the Foot-Shaoyang Meridian.

期门 Qímén (LR 14)

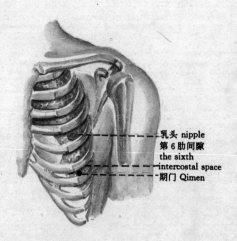

乳头 nipple
第 6 肋间隙
the sixth
intercostal space
期门 Qimen

〔取穴法〕(1)在胸部,当乳头直下,第 6 肋间隙,前正中线旁开 4 寸处。

(2)仰卧,乳中穴直下 2 肋处取穴。如妇女则应以锁骨中线的第 6 肋间隙处定取。

〔功效与主治〕疏肝理气,活血化瘀。胸胁胀满疼痛,呕逆吞酸,奔豚喘咳。

〔操作〕沿肋间隙斜刺 0.3～0.5 寸。

〔备注〕肝之"募"穴;足厥阴经、足太阴经与阴维脉交会穴。

Method of locating the point:

(1) This point is located in the chest, directly below the nipple, in the 6th intercostal space, 4 cun lateral to the anterior midline.

(2) Ask patient to lie on his back, located the point two ribs below the Ruzhong point (St 17). In females, it is located in the 6th intercostal space on the midclavicular line.

Actions and indications: Soothe the liver-Qi, activate blood flow and remove blood stasis, used to treat fullness and pain of the chest and hypochondrium, vomiting, acid regurgitation, asthma and cough caused by rushing up of Qi from the lower abdomen.

Manipulation: Puncture obliquely 0.3 — 0.5 cun along the border of the intercostal space.

Notes: Qimen (LR 14) is the Front-Mu point of the liver, and a crossing point of the Foot-Taiyin Meridian and Yinwei Meridian.

十三、任　脉

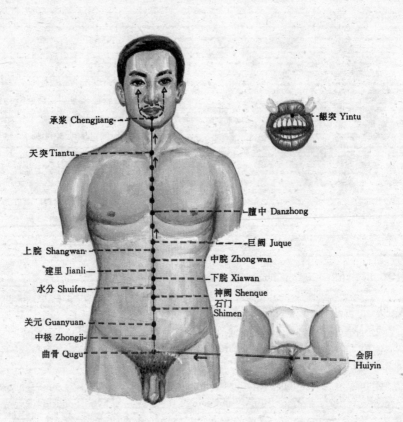

承浆 Chengjiang

龈突 Yintu

天突 Tiantu

膻中 Danzhong

巨阙 Juque

上脘 Shangwan

中脘 Zhongwan

建里 Jianli

下脘 Xiawan

水分 Shuifen

神阙 Shenque

石门
Shimen

关元 Guanyuan

中极 Zhongji

曲骨 Qugu

会阴
Huiyin

起于小腹内,下出会阴部,向上行于阴毛部,沿着腹内,向上经过关元等穴,到达咽喉部,再上行环绕口唇,经过面部,进入目眶下(承泣,属足阳明胃经)。

13. The Ren Meridian

The Ren Meridian starts inside the lower abdomen. Emerging in·the perineum, it goes upwards to the pubic region and ascends along the interior part of the abdomen, passing through Guanyuan (RN 4) and other points, to the throat. Then it goes upwards further to curve around the lips, pass through the cheek and enter the infraorbital region (Chengqi, St 1).

会阴 Huìyīn（RN 1）

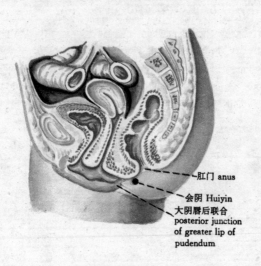

肛门 anus

会阴 Huiyin
大阴唇后联合
posterior junction
of greater lip of
pudendum

〔取穴法〕患者取截石位,在会阴部,男性当阴囊根部与肛门连线的中点处;女性当大阴唇后联合与肛门连线的中点处。

〔功效与主治〕调经强肾,清利湿热。二便不利,痔疮,脱肛。

〔操作〕直刺0.2~0.3寸。

〔备注〕任脉、督脉与冲脉交会穴。

Method of locating the point: Put patient in a knee—chest position, locate the point in the midpoint of the line connecting the root of scrotum and the anus in male or in the midpoint of the posterior labial commissure and the anus in female.

Actions and indications: Regulate menstruation, strengthen the kidney, clear away heat and induce diuresis, used to treat oliguria, constipation, haemorrhoid, prolapse of the rectum.

Manipulation: Puncture perpendicularly 0.2—0.3 cun.

Notes: Huiyin (RN 1) is a crossing point of the Ren Meridian, the Du Meridian and the Chong Meridian.

曲骨 Qūgǔ (RN 2)

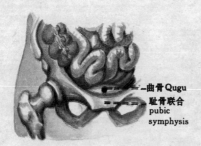

曲骨Qugu

耻骨联合
pubic
symphysis

〔取穴法〕(1)在下腹部,当前正中线上,耻骨联合上缘的中点处。

(2)仰卧,于耻骨联合上缘中点,腹白线上取穴。

〔功效与主治〕温补肾阳,调经止带。遗精,阳痿,带下,尿闭。

〔操作〕直刺 0.5～0.8寸。针前令患者排尿,尿闭者宜沿皮刺。

〔备注〕足厥阴经与任脉交会穴。孕妇不宜针。

Method of locating the point:

(1) This point is located in the lower abdomen, on the anterior midline, in the midpoint of the upper border of the symphysis pubis.

(2) Ask patient to lie on his back, locate the point at the midpoint of the upper border of the symphysis pubis, on the linea alba.

Actions and indications: Warm up the kidney-yang, regulate menstruation and relieve leukorrhea, used to treat emission, impotence, leukorrhea, and retention of urine.

Manipulations: Puncture perpendicularly 0.5 — 0.8 cun. Before needling, patient should pass urine first. In the case of retention of urine, puncturing subcutaneously is contraindicated.

Notes: Qugu (RN 2) is a crossing point of the Foot-Jueyin Meridian and the Ren Meridian. Puncture at this point is not advisable in the pregnant woman.

中极 Zhōngjí (RN 2)

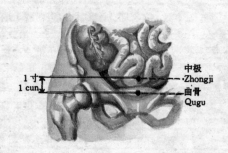

1 寸
1 cun

中极
Zhongji
曲骨
Qugu

〔取穴法〕(1)在下腹部；前正中线上，当脐下 4 寸处。

(2)仰卧，在腹白线上，当曲骨穴直上 1 寸处。

〔功效与主治〕培元固本，清热利湿。遗精，阳痿，遗尿，尿闭，不孕，月经不调。

〔操作〕直刺 0.5～1 寸，孕妇不宜针，针前排尿。

〔备注〕膀胱之"募"穴；任脉与足三阴经交会穴。

Method of locating the point:

(1) This point is located in the lower abdomen, on the anterior midline, 4 cun below the umbilicus.

(2) Ask patient to take a supine position, locate the point 1 cun directly above the Qugu point (RN 2) on the linea alba.

Actions and indications: Build up the primordial Qi and consolidate basis, clear away heat and remove dampness, used to treat emission, impotence, enuresis, retention of urine, sterility, and irregular menstruation.

Manipulations: Puncture perpendicularly 0.5－1 cun. Tell patient to urinate before needling and puncture at this point is not advisable in pregnant woman.

Notes: Zhongji (RN 3) is the Front-Mu point of bladder, and a crossing point of the Ren Meridian and the three Yin meridians of foot.

关元 Guānyuán（RN 4）

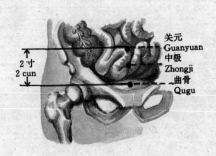

2 寸
2 cun

关元
Guanyuan
中极
Zhongji
曲骨
Qugu

〔取穴法〕（1）在下腹部，前正中线上，当脐中下 3 寸处。

（2）仰卧，于脐与耻骨联合上缘中点连线的下 2/5 与上 3/5 的交点处取穴。

〔功效与主治〕培肾固本，补益元气，回阳固脱。遗精，阳痿，遗尿，尿频，痛经，不孕，中风脱证，泄泻。

〔操作〕直刺 0.5～1 寸，针前排尿。

〔备注〕小肠之"募"穴；任脉与足三阴经交会穴。孕妇慎用。

Method of locating the point：

（1）This point is located in the lower abdomen, on the anterior midline of the body, 3 cun below the umbilicus.

（2）Ask patient to take a supine position, locate the point at the junction of the lower 2/5 and the upper 3/5 of the line joining the umbilicus and the pubic symphysis.

Actions and indications：Cultivate and consolidate the kidney, supplement the primordial Qi, and recuperate the depleted yang, used to treat emission, impotence, enuresis, frequent urine, dysmenorrhea, sterility, prostration syndrome of the apoplexy, and diarrhea.

Manipulation：Puncture perpendicularly 0.5—1 cun. Ask patient to pass urine before puncture.

Notes：Guanyuan (RN 4) is the Front-Mu point of the small intestine and the crossing point of the Ren Meridian and the three Yin meridians of foot. When puncture is applied at this point in pregnant woman, great care must be taken.

石门 Shímén (RN 5)

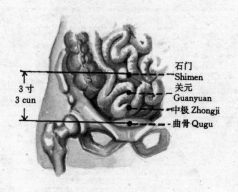

3 寸
3 cun

石门
Shimen
关元
Guanyuan
中极 Zhongji
曲骨 Qugu

〔取穴法〕(1)在下腹部，前正中线上，当脐中下2寸处。

(2)仰卧，于脐与耻骨联合上缘中点连线的上2/5与下3/5的交点处取穴。

〔功效与主治〕补肾培元，清热利湿。腹胀，泄泻，绕脐腹痛，小便不利。

〔操作〕直刺0.5～1寸。

〔备注〕三焦之"募"穴。孕妇慎用。

Method of locating the point:

(1) This point is located in the lower abdomen, on the anterior midline of the body, 2 cun below the umbilicus.

(2) Ask patient to take a supine position, locate the point at the junction of the upper 2/5 and the lower 3/5 of the line connecting the umbilicus and the upper border of the pubic symphysis.

Actions and indications: Tonify the kidney, consolidate the primordial Qi, clear away heat and induce diuresis, used to treat abdominal distension, diarrhea, pain around the umbilicus and oliguria.

Manipulation: Puncture perpendicularly 0.5—1 cun.

Notes: Shimen (RN 5) is the Front-Mu point of triple jiao. It must be very carefully adopted for puncture in pregnant woman.

气海 Qìhǎi（RN 6）

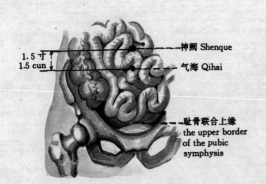

1.5 寸
1.5 cun

神阙 Shenque
气海 Qihai
耻骨联合上缘 the upper border of the pubic symphysis

〔取穴法〕（1）在下腹部，前正中线上，当脐中下 1.5 寸处。

（2）仰卧，当脐中与关元穴连线之中点处。

〔功效与主治〕补肾培元，益气活血。绕脐腹痛，遗尿，遗精，月经不调，中风脱证。

〔操作〕直刺 0.5～1 寸。

〔备注〕肓之原，出于脐映，即气海穴。

Method of locating the point：

(1) This point is located in the lower abdomen, on the anterior midline of the body, 1.5 cun below the umbilicus.

(2) Ask patient to take a supine position, locate the point at the midpoint of the line connecting the umbilicus and Guanyuan (RN 4).

Actions and indications：Tonify the kidney, build up the primordial Qi, supplement Qi and activate blood circulation, used to treat pain around the umbilicus, enuresis, emission, irregular menstruation, prostration syndrome of apoplexy.

Manipulation：Puncture perpendicularly 0.5—1 cun.

Notes：The primordial Qi of Gaohuang (BL 53) emerges in this point.

阴交 Yīnjiāo（RN 7）

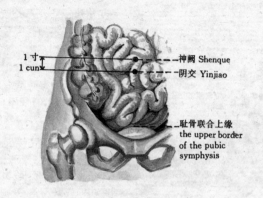

1寸
1 cun

神阙 Shenque
阴交 Yinjiao

耻骨联合上缘
the upper border
of the pubic
symphysis

〔取穴法〕(1)在下腹部，前正中线上，当脐下1寸处。

(2)仰卧，于脐中与石门穴的连线之中点处。

(3)于脐与耻骨联合上缘中点连线的上1/5与下4/5的交点处是穴。

〔功效与主治〕补肾培元，清热利湿。水肿，疝气，经闭。

〔操作〕直刺0.5～1寸。

〔备注〕任脉、足少阴经与冲脉交会穴。

Method of locating the point：

(1) This point is located in the lower abdomen, on the anterior midline of the body, 1 cun below the umbilicus.

(2) Ask patient to take a supine position, locate the point between umbilicus and Shimen (RN 5).

(3) Locate this point at the junction of the upper 1/5 and the lower 4/5 of the line joining the umbilicus and the pubic symphysis.

Actions and indications：Tonify the kidney and consolidate the primordial Qi, clear away heat and remove dampness, used to treat edema, hernia and amenorrhea.

Manipulation：Puncture perpendicularly 0.5－1 cun.

Notes：Yinjiao (RN 7) is a crossing point of the Ren Meridian, the Foot-Shaoyin Meridian and the Chong Meridian.

神阙 Shánquè (RN 8)

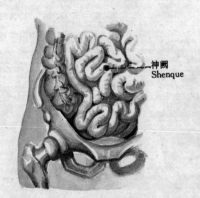

神阙
Shenque

〔取穴法〕仰卧,在腹中部,脐中央处取穴。

〔功效与主治〕健脾和胃,温阳开窍。泄泻,腹胀,腹痛,腹中虚冷,中风脱证,不孕,阳痿。

〔操作〕隔盐灸5～15壮,严禁起泡。

〔备注〕禁针。

Method of locating the point: Ask patient to take a supine position, locate the point in the centre of the abdomen or the centre of the umbilicus.

Actions and indications: Strengthen the spleen, regulate the function of the stomach, warm up yang and induce resuscitation, used to treat diarrhea, abdominal distension, abdominal pain, cold feeling of abdomen due to deficiency, prostration syndrome of apoplexy, sterility, and impotence.

Manipulation: Moxibustion with salt is applied to this point for a period of 5—15 cones being ignited. Bluster must be avoided.

Notes: Puncture at this point is prohibited.

水分 Shuǐfēn (RN 9)

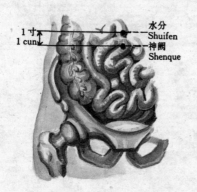

1 寸
1 cun

水分
Shuifen
神阙
Shenque

〔取穴法〕(1)在上腹部,前正中线上,当脐上1寸处。

(2)仰卧,于(胸)岐骨至脐中连线的下 1/8 与 7/8 的交点处取穴。

〔功效与主治〕和中理气,分利水湿。腹胀肠鸣,水肿膨胀,小便不通。

〔操作〕直刺 0.5～1寸。

Method of locating the point:

(1) This point in the upper abdomen, on the anterior midline of the body, 1 cun directly above the umbilicus.

(2) Ask patient to take a supine position, locate the point at the junction of the upper 7/8 and the lower 1/8 of the line connecting the xiphoid process and the umbilicus.

Actions and indications: Normalize the function of the middle-jiao, regulate flow of Qi, induce diuresis, used to treat abdominal distension, borborygmus, ascites, oliguria.

Manipulation: Puncture perpendicularly 0.5—1 cun.

下脘 Xiàwǎn (RN 10)

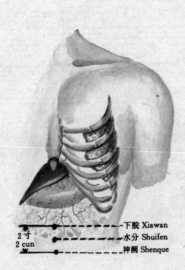

2寸 下脘 Xiawan
2 cun 水分 Shuifen
神阙 Shenque

〔取穴法〕(1)在上腹部,前正中线上,当脐上2寸处。

(2)仰卧,于(胸)歧骨至脐孔连线的下 1/4 与上 3/4 的交点处取穴。

(3)于水分穴直上 1寸处取穴。

〔功效与主治〕和中理气,消积化滞。腹痛肠鸣,饮食不化,呕吐反胃。

〔操作〕直刺 0.5～1寸。

Method of locating the point:

(1) This point is located in the upper abdomen, on the anterior midline of the body, 2 cun above the umbilicus.

(2) Ask patient to take a supine position, locate the point at the junction of the lower 1/4 and the upper 3/4 of the line connecting the xiphoid process and the umbilicus.

(3) Locate the point 1 cun directly above Shuifen (RN 9).

Actions and indications: Normalize the functions of the middle-jiao, regulate the flow of Qi, promote digestion and eliminate retained food, used to treat abdominal pain, borborygmus, indigestion, vomiting and acid regurgitation.

Manipulation: Puncture perpendicularly 0.5—1 cun.

建里 Jiànlǐ (RN 11)

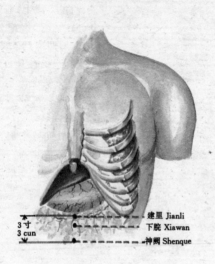

建里 Jianli
下脘 Xiawan
神阙 Shenque

3寸
3 cun

〔取穴法〕(1)在上腹部,前正中线上,当脐上3寸处。

(2)仰卧,当(胸)歧骨至脐中连线的下与上的交点处。

(3)当下脘穴直上1寸处。

〔功效与主治〕和中理气,消积化滞。胃痛,呕吐,腹胀肠鸣。

〔操作〕直刺0.5~1寸。

Method of locating the point:

(1) This point is located in the upper abdomen, on the anterior midline of the body, 3 cun directly above the umbilicus.

(2) Ask patient to take a supine position, locate the point at the junction of the lower 3/8 and the upper 5/8 of the line joining the xiphoid process and the umbilicus.

(3) Locate the point 1 cun above Xiawan (RN 10).

Actions and indications: Normalize the function of the middle-jiao, regulate the flow of Qi, promote digestion and eliminate retained food, used to treat stomachache, vomiting, abdominal distension and borborygmus.

Manipulation: Puncture perpendicularly 0.5—1 cun.

中脘 Zhōngwǎn (RN 12)

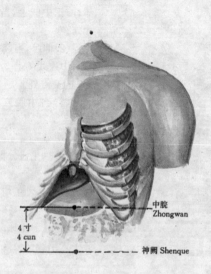

中脘 Zhongwan

4 寸
4 cun

神阙 Shenque

〔取穴法〕(1)在上腹部,前正中线上,当脐上4寸处。

(2)仰卧,当(胸)歧骨与脐中连线的中点处。

〔功效与主治〕调理中焦,行气活血,清热化滞。胃痛,腹胀肠鸣,脾胃虚弱,痫证。

〔操作〕直刺0.5～0.8寸。

〔备注〕胃之"募"穴;八会穴之一,腑之会穴;任脉、手太阳、手少阳与足阳明经交会穴。

Method of locating the point:

(1) This point is located in the upper abdomen, on the anterior midline of the body, 4 cun above the umbilicus.

(2) Ask patient to take a supine position, locate the point in the midpoint of the line connecting the xiphoid process and the umbilicus.

Actions and indications: Regulate functions of the middle-jiao, promote flow of Qi, activate blood circulation, clear away heat and promote digestion, used to treat stomachache, abdominal distension, borborygmus, deficiency of both the spleen and the stomach, and epilepsy.

Manipulation: Puncture perpendicularly 0.5—0.8 cun.

Notes: Zhongwan (RN 12) is the Front-Mu point of the stomach, the confluence point of the fu organs and the crossing point of the Ren Meridian, Hand-Taiyang Meridian, Hand-Shaoyang Meridian and the Foot-Yangming Meridian.

上脘 Shàngwǎn (RN 13)

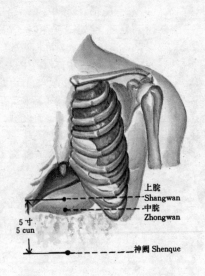

上脘
Shangwan
中脘
Zhongwan

5寸
5 cun

神阙 Shenque

〔取穴法〕（1）在上腹部，前正中线上，当脐上 5 寸处。

（2）仰卧，当（胸）歧骨与脐中连线的上 3/8 与下 5/8 的交点处。

（3）当中脘穴直上 1 寸处。

〔功效与主治〕和中降逆，清热化痰。胃痛，腹胀，呕吐。

〔操作〕直刺 0.5～0.8 寸。

〔备注〕任脉、足阳明与手太阳经交会穴。

Method of locating the point:

(1) This point is located in the upper abdomen, on the anterior midline of the body, 5 cun above the umbilicus.

(2) Ask patient to take a supine position, locate the point at the junction of the upper 3/8 and the lower 5/8 of the line connecting the xiphoid process and the umbilicus.

(3) Locate the point 1 cun directly above Zhongwan point (RN 12).

Actions and indications: Regulate the function of the middle-jiao, lower the upward adverse flow of Qi, clear away heat and dissolve phlegm, used to treat stomachache, abdominal distension, vomiting.

Manipulation: Puncture perpendicularly 0.5—0.8 cun.

Notes: Shangwan (RN 13) is a crossing point of the Ren Meridian, Foot-Yangming Meridian and Hand-Taiyang Meridian.

274

巨阙 Jùquè (RN 14)

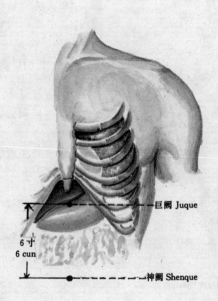

巨阙 Juque

6 寸
6 cun

神阙 Shenque

〔取穴法〕(1)在上腹部,前正中线上,当脐中上6寸处。

(2)仰卧,当(胸)歧骨至脐中连线的上1/4与下3/4的交点处取穴。

(3)当上脘穴直上1寸处取穴。

〔功效与主治〕和中降逆,宁心安神。心胸痛,反胃,心悸。

〔操作〕向下斜刺0.3~0.5寸。

〔备注〕心之"募"穴。

Method of locating the point:

(1) This point is located in the upper abdomen, on the anterior midline of the body, 6 cun above the umbilicus.

(2) Ask patient to take a supine position, locate the point at the junction of the upper 1/4 and the lower 3/4 of the line connecting the xiiphoid process and the umbilicus.

(3) Locate the point 1 cun directly above Shangwan (RN 13).

Actions and indications: Regulate function of the middle-jiao, lower down upward adverse flow of Qi, tranquilize the mind, used to treat pain in the precardial region, acid regurgitation and palpitation.

Manipulation: Puncture obliquely downwards 0.3—0.5 cun.

Notes: Juque (RN 14) is the Front-Mu point of the heart.

鸠尾 Jiūwěi (RN 15)

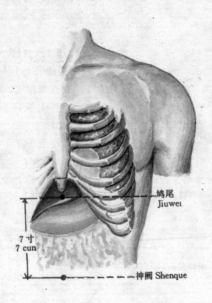

鸠尾
Jiuwei

7寸
7 cun

神阙 Shenque

〔取穴法〕(1)在上腹部,前正中线上,当胸剑结合部下1寸处。

(2)仰卧,当(胸)歧骨至脐中连线的上1/8与下7/8的交点处取穴。

(3)当巨阙穴直上1寸处取穴。

〔功效与主治〕和中降逆,清热化痰。心胸痛,癫狂,痫证。

〔操作〕向下斜刺0.3～0.5寸。

〔备注〕任脉络穴;膏之原,出于鸠尾穴。

Method of locating the point:

(1) This point is lcoated in the upper abdomen, on the anterior midline of the body, 1 cun below the xiphoid process.

(2) Ask patient to take a supine position, locate the point at the junction of the upper 1/8 and the lower 7/8 of the line connecting the xiphoid process and the umbilicus.

(3) Locate the point 1 cun directly above Juque (RN 14).

Actions and indications: Regulate the function of the middle-jiao, lowering the upward adverse flow of Qi, clear away heat and dissolve phlegm, used to treat pain in the precardial region, depressive psychosis, mania and epilepsy.

Manipulation: Puncture downward obliquely 0.3—0.5 cun.

Notes: Jiuwei (RN 15) is the Luo-Connecting point of the Ren Meridian and the primordial Qi of Gaohuang (BL 53) emerges from it.

276

膻中 Dànzhōng (RN 17)

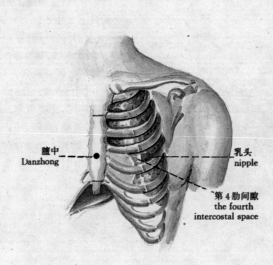

膻中
Danzhong

乳头
nipple

第4肋间隙
the fourth
intercostal space

〔取穴法〕（1）在胸部，当前正中线上，平第4肋间，两乳头连线的中点。

（2）仰卧，男性于胸骨中线与两乳头连线之交点处定取；女性则于胸骨中线平第4肋间隙处定取。

〔功效与主治〕宽胸理气，降逆化痰。气喘，咳嗽，心痛，胸闷，乳少。

〔操作〕下向沿皮刺0.3～0.5寸。

〔备注〕心包之"募"穴；八会穴之一，气之会穴。

Method of locating the point：

(1) This point is located in the chest, on the anterior midline of the body, at the level with the fourth intercostal space, at the midpoint of the two nipples.

(2) Ask patient to take a supine position, locate the point at the midpoint of the line connecting the two nipples in males and at the level with the fourth intercostal space on the midline of the sternum in females.

Actions and indications：Promote and regulate flow of Qi in the chest, lower down upward adverse flow of Qi and dissolve phlegm, used to treat asthma, cough, cardiac pain, chest stuffiness and aglactation.

Manipulation：Puncture subcutaneously downwards 0.3—0.5 cun.

Notes：Danzhong (RN 17) is the Front-Mu point of the heart, and the confluence point of Qi.

璇玑 Xuánjī（RN 21）

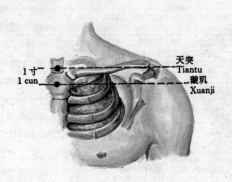

天突 Tiantu
璇玑 Xuanji
1 寸 1 cun

〔取穴法〕（1）在胸部，当前正中线上，天突下1寸处。

（2）仰卧或仰靠，于胸骨中线，第1胸肋关节之间处取穴。

〔功效与主治〕宽胸理气，化痰消食。咳嗽，气喘，胸痛。

〔操作〕沿皮刺0.2～0.3寸。

Method of locating the point：

（1）This point is located in the chest, on the anterior midline of the body, 1 cun below Tiantu (RN 22).

（2）Ask patient to take a supine position or a sitting position with his back supported, locate the point on the midline of the sternum, in the middle of the sternocostal joint.

Actions and indications：Soothe flow of Qi in the chest, dissolve phlegm and promote digestion, used to treat cough, asthma and chest pain.

Manipulation：Puncture subcutaneously 0.2－0.3 cun.

天突 Tiāntū (RN 22)

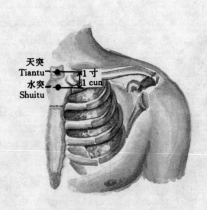

天突
Tiantu
水突
Shuitu

1寸
1 cun

〔取穴法〕(1)在颈部,当前正中线上,胸骨上窝中央。

(2)正坐仰靠,当胸骨切迹上缘中点直上五分凹陷处。

(3)当璇玑穴上1寸,胸骨上窝正中处。

〔功效与主治〕宽胸理气,清热化痰。气喘,咳嗽,呃逆,吞咽困难。

〔操作〕微仰头,针尖向下方,沿胸骨后刺入0.3~0.5寸,不可直刺,以免伤及气管。

〔备注〕任脉与阴维脉交会穴。

Method of locating the point:

(1) This point is located in the neck, on the anterior midline, in the centre of the suprasternal fossa.

(2) Ask patient to take a sitting position with his back supported, locate the point in the depression 0.5 cun above the midpoint of the upper border of the sternal notch.

(3) Locate the point 1 cun above Xuanji (RN 21), in the centre of the suprasternal fossa.

Actions and indications: Soothe flow of Qi in the chest, clear away heat and dissolve phlegm, used to treat asthma, cough, hiccup, dysphagia.

Manipulation: Ask patient to lift his head slightly, then insert the needle 0.3—0.5 cun downward along the posterior aspect of the sternum. Perpendicular puncture must be avoided lest the trachea be injuried.

Notes: Tiantu (RN 22) is a crossing point of the Ren Meridian and Yinwei Meridian.

廉泉 Liánquán (RN 23)

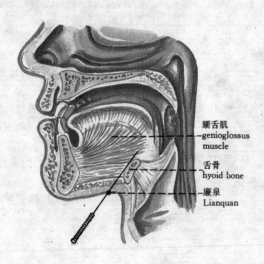

颏舌肌
-genioglossus
 muscle

舌骨
 hyoid bone

廉泉
 Lianquan

〔取穴法〕(1)在颈部,当前正中线上,结喉上方,舌骨下缘凹陷处。

(2)正坐仰靠,当喉结上方,舌骨体下缘与甲状软骨切迹之间处。

〔功效与主治〕通利舌咽,清热化痰。舌下肿痛,流涎,中风舌强不语,咽食困难。

〔操作〕向舌根方向斜刺 0.3~0.5 寸。

〔备注〕任脉与阴维脉交会穴。

Method of locating the point:

(1) This point is located in the neck, on the anterior midline, superior to the Adam's apple, in the depression of the lower border of the hyoid bone.

(2) Ask patient to take a sitting position with his body supported, locate the point above the Adam's apple, in the midway of the lower border of the hyoid bone and the superior thyroid notch.

Actions and indications: Benefit swallowing, clear away heat and dissolve phlegm, used to treat swelling and pain of the subglossal region, salivation, aphasia with stiffness of tongue by apoplexy, difficulty in swallowing.

Manipulation: Puncture 0.3—0.5 cun towards the tongue root.

Notes: Lianquan (RN 23) is a crossing point of Ren Meridian and Yinwei Meridian.

承浆 Chéngjiāng（RN 24）

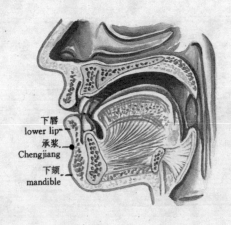

下唇
lower lip
承浆
Chengjiang
下颔
mandible

〔取穴法〕（1）在面部，当颏唇沟的正中凹陷处。

（2）正坐仰靠，在颌下正中线，下唇缘下方凹陷处。

〔功效与主治〕开窍醒神，祛风通络。口眼㖞斜，面肿，龈肿，流涎，小便不禁。

〔操作〕向上斜刺0.2～0.3寸。

〔备注〕任脉、督脉、手阳明与足阳明经交会穴。

Method of locating the point：

(1) This point is located on face, in the depression at the centre of the mento-labial groove.

(2) Ask patient to take a sitting position with his back supported, locate the point in the midline of the jaw, in the depression inferior to the lower border of the lower lip.

Actions and indications: Induce resuscitation, restore consciousness, expel wind and activate flow of Qi and blood in the collaterals, used to treat deviation of the mouth and eye, swollen gum, salivation, incontinence of urine.

Manipulation: Puncture upward obliquely 0.2—0.3 cun.

Notes: Chengjiang (RN 24) is a crossing point of the Ren Meridian, the Du Meridian, the Hand-Yangming Meridian and the Foot-Yangming Meridian.

十四、督　脉

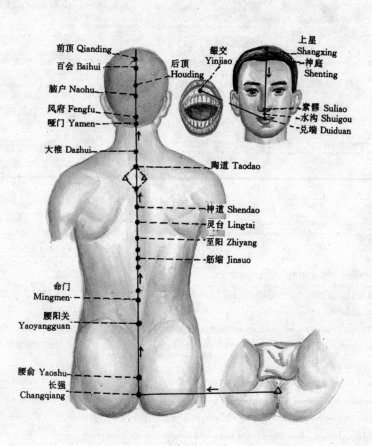

前顶 Qianding
百会 Baihui
脑户 Naohu
风府 Fengfu
哑门 Yamen
大椎 Dazhui

后顶 Houding
龈交 Yinjiao

上星 Shangxing
神庭 Shenting
素髎 Suliao
水沟 Shuigou
兑端 Duiduan

陶道 Taodao
神道 Shendao
灵台 Lingtai
至阳 Zhiyang
筋缩 Jinsuo

命门 Mingmen
腰阳关 Yaoyangguan
腰俞 Yaoshu
长强 Changqiang

起于小腹内，下出于会阴部，向后行于脊柱的内部，上达项后风府，进入脑内，上行巅顶，沿前额下行鼻柱。

14. The Du Meridian

The Du Meridian arises from the lower abdomen and emerges from the perineum. Then it runs posteriorly along the interior of the spinal column to Fengfu (DU 16) at the nape, where it enters the brain. It further goes upward to the vertex and winds along the forehead to the columnella of the nose.

长强 Chángqiáng (DU 1)

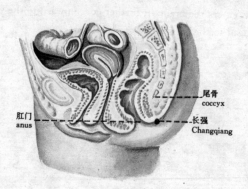

〔取穴法〕跪伏或胸膝位,在尾骨端下,当尾骨端与肛门连线的中点处。

〔功效与主治〕清热利湿,调理下焦。泄泻,便血,痔疮,脱肛。

〔操作〕紧靠尾骨前面斜刺 0.3～0.5 寸,不得刺穿直肠,防止感染。

〔备注〕督脉络穴;督脉、足少阴经与足少阳经交会穴。

Method of locating the point: Ask patient to knee with both hands put forwards or take a knee-chest position, locate the point below the tip of the coccyx, in the midway of the tip of the coccyx and the anus.

Actions and indications: Clear away heat, remove dampness, regulate the function of the lower-jiao, used to treat diarrhea, hematochezia, hemorrhoid and prolapse of retum.

Manipulation: Puncture obliquely 0.3—0.5 cun proximal to the anterior aspect of the coccyx. Avoid penetrating the retum and prevent infection.

Notes: Changqiang (DU 1) is the Luo-Connecting point of the Du Meridian, and the crossing point of the Du Meridian, Foot-Shaoyin Meridian and Foot-Shaoyang Meridian.

腰俞 Yāoshū (DU 2)

〔取穴法〕（1）在骶部，当后正中线上，适对骶管裂孔处。

（2）在第 4 骶椎下，骶管裂孔中取穴。

（3）俯卧或侧卧，先按取尾骨上方左右的骶角，与两骶角下缘平齐的后正中线上取穴。

〔功效与主治〕培补下焦，清利湿热。痔疾，痫证，腰脊强痛。

〔操作〕向上斜刺 0.5～1 寸。

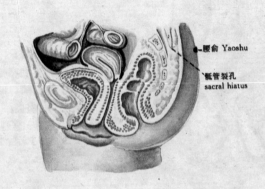

腰俞 Yaoshu

骶管裂孔 sacral hiatus

Method of Locating the point:

(1) This point is located in the sacral region, on the posterior midline, in the hiatus of the sacrum.

(2) Locate the point below the fourth sacral vertebra, in the hiatus of the sacrum.

(3) Ask patient to take a prone position or a lying position on one side, firstly find out the sacral horn above the sacrum, then locate the point on the posterior midline at the level with the lower border of the two sacral horns.

Actions and indications: Tonify the lower-jiao, clear away heat and remove dampness, used to treat hemorrhoid, epilepsy, rigidity and pain of the lumbar region and the spine.

Manipulation: Puncture upwards obliquely 0.5—1 cun.

285

腰阳关 Yāoyángguān (DU 3)

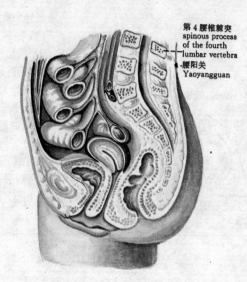

第4腰椎棘突
spinous process
of the fourth
lumbar vertebra
腰阳关
Yaoyangguan

〔取穴法〕(1)在腰部,当后正中线上,第4腰椎棘突下凹陷中。

(2)俯卧,当髂嵴平线与后正中线交点处。

〔功效与主治〕调补肾气,利腰膝,祛寒湿。腰骶痛,月经不调,遗精,阳痿。

〔操作〕直刺0.5～1寸。

Method of locating the point:

(1) This point is located in the lumbar region, on the posterior midline, in the depression below the spinous process of the fourth lumbar vertebra.

(2) Ask patient to take a prone position, locate the point at the junction of the line formed by the upper border of the crista illica and the posterior midline.

Actions and indications: Regulate and tonify the kidney-Qi, benefit the loins and knee, expel cold-dampness, used to treat pain in the lumbosacral region, irregular menstruation, emission, and impotence.

Manipulation: Puncture perpendicularly 0.5—1 cun.

命门 Mingmén (DU 4)

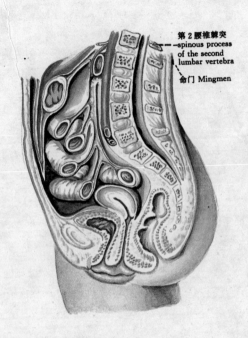

第2腰椎棘突
—spinous process
of the second
lumbar vertebra

命门 Mingmen

〔取穴法〕(1)在腰部,当后正中线上,第2腰椎棘突下凹陷中。

(2)俯卧,腰阳关穴向上摸取两个棘突上方的凹陷处是穴。

(3)在与脐中相对的棘突下缘处取穴。

〔功效与主治〕补肾固精壮阳,强健腰脊。脊强腰痛,痛经,阳痿,遗精,遗尿,早泄。

〔操作〕直刺或向上斜刺0.5~0.8寸。

Method of locating the point:

(1) This point is located in the lumbar region, on the posterior midline, in the depression below the spinous process of the 2nd lumbar vertebra.

(2) Ask patient to take a prone position, locate the point in the depression two spinous processes above Yaoyangguan (DU 3).

(3) Locate the point below the spinous process opposite to the umbilicus.

Actions and indications: Tonify the kidney, consolidate essence, invigorate yang, strengthen the loins and column, used to treat rigidity and pain of the spine and the loin, dysmenorrhea, impotence, emission, enuresis, and premature ejaculation.

Manipulation: Puncture perpendicularly or upwards obliquely 0.5−0.8 cun.

筋缩 Jīnsuō (DU 8)

〔取穴法〕(1)在背部,当后正中线上,第9胸椎棘突下凹陷中。

(2)俯卧至阳穴向下摸取两个棘突,其下方凹陷中是穴。

〔功效与主治〕镇惊熄风,通络止痉,痫证,小儿惊风,脊强。

〔操作〕向上斜刺0.3～0.5寸。

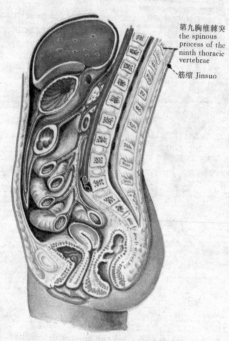

第九胸椎棘突
the spinous process of the ninth thoracic vertebrae

筋缩 Jinsuo

Method of locating the point:

(1) This point is located on the back, on the posterior midline, below the spinous process of the 9th thoracic vertebra.

(2) Ask patient to take a prone position, locate the point in the depression two spinous processes below the Zhiyang point (DU 9).

Actions and indications: Relieve convulsion, calm wind, activate flow of Qi and blood in the collaterals, used to treat epilepsy, infantile convulsion, and rigidity of the spine.

Manipulation: Puncture upward obliquely 0.3—0.5 cun.

至阳 Zhìyáng（DU 9）

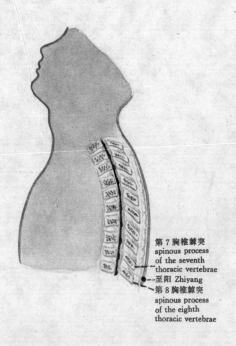

第7胸椎棘突
spinous process
of the seventh
thoracic vertebrae
--至阳 Zhiyang
第8胸椎棘突
spinous process
of the eighth
thoracic vertebrae

〔取穴法〕（1）在背部，当后正中线上，第7胸椎棘突下凹陷中。

（2）俯伏或俯卧，当后正中线与两肩胛骨下角连线的交点处。

〔功效与主治〕宽胸利气，健脾调中。咳嗽，气喘，胸痛彻背，胸闷。

〔操作〕向上斜刺0.3～0.5寸。

Method of locating the point：

（1）This point is located on the back，on the posterior midline，in the depression below the spinous process of the 7th thoracic vertebra.

（2）Ask patient to take a prone position with his hands close or not close to his trunk，locate the point at the junction of the posterior midline and the line connecting the two inferior angles of scapula.

Actions and indications：Soothe flow of Qi in the chest，strengthen the spleen and regulate function of the middle-jiao，used to treat cough，asthma，pain of the chest radiating to the back，and chest distension.

Manipulation：Puncture upward obliquely 0.3—0.5 cun.

灵台 Língtái (DU 10)

〔取穴法〕(1)在背部，当后正中线上，第6胸椎棘突下凹陷中。

(2)俯伏或俯卧，从至阳向上1个棘突下之陷中是穴。

〔功效与主治〕宣肺通络，清热解毒。咳嗽，气喘，疔疮，脊痛项强。

〔操作〕向上斜刺0.3～0.5寸。

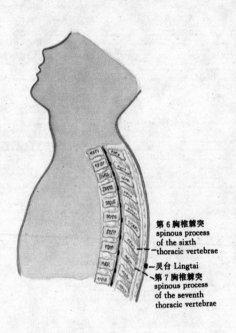

第6胸椎棘突
spinous process
of the sixth
thoracic vertebrae

灵台 Lingtai

第7胸椎棘突
spinous process
of the seventh
thoracic vertebrae

Method of locating the point：

(1) This point is located on the back, on the posteror midline, in the depression of the spinous process of the 6th thoracic vertebra.

(2) Ask patient to take a prone position with his hands close or not close to his trunk, locate the point in the depression one process above Zhiyang (DU 9).

Actions and indications：Facilitate flow of the lung-Qi, activate flow of Qi and blood in the collaterals, clear away heat and detoxicate, used to treat cough, asthma, furuncles; pain of the spine and rigidity of the nape.

Manipulation：Puncture upward obliquely 0.3—0.5 cun.

神道 Shéndào（DU 11）

〔取穴法〕（1）在背部，当后正中线上，第5胸椎棘突下凹陷中。

（2）俯伏或俯卧，从至阳向上摸两个棘突下之凹陷处是穴。

〔功效与主治〕镇惊宁神，通经止痛。心痛，惊悸，怔忡，失眠健忘。

〔操作〕向上斜刺0.3～0.5寸。

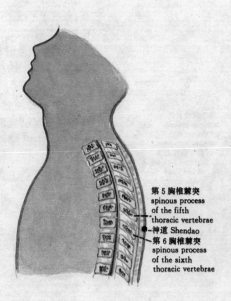

第5胸椎棘突
spinous process
of the fifth
thoracic vertebrae
神道 Shendao
第6胸椎棘突
spinous process
of the sixth
thoracic vertebrae

Method of locating the point：

（1）This point is located in the back, on the posterior midline, in the depression below the spinous process of the 5th thoracic vertebra.

（2）Ask patient to take a prone position with his hands close or not close to his trunk, locate the point in the depression two spinous processes above Zhiyang (DU 9).

Actions and indications：Relieve convulsion, calm the mind, activate flow of Qi and blood in the channels and collaterals to alleviate pain, used to treat cardiac pain, palpitation, insomnia and amnesia.

Manipulation：Puncture upward obliquely 0.3—0.5 cun.

身柱 Shēnzhù (DU 12)

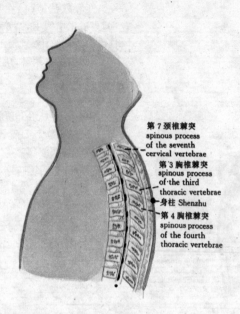

第7颈椎棘突
spinous process
of the seventh
cervical vertebrae

第3胸椎棘突
spinous process
of the third
thoracic vertebrae

身柱 Shenzhu

第4胸椎棘突
spinous process
of the fourth
thoracic vertebrae

〔取穴法〕（1）在背部，当后正中线上，第3胸椎棘突下凹陷中。

（2）俯伏或俯卧，当后正中线与两肩胛冈高点连线之交点处。

〔功效与主治〕理气降逆，止咳喘，镇静安神。胸背痛，咳嗽，哮喘，小儿惊风。

〔操作〕向上斜刺0.3～0.5寸。

Method of locating the point:

(1) This point is located on the back, on the posterior midline, in the depression below the spinous process of the 3rd thoracic vertebra.

(2) Ask patient to take a prone position with his hands close or not close to his trunk, locate the point at the junction of the posterior midline and the line connecting the two highest points of the spine of the bilateral scapula.

Actions and indications: Regulate flow of Qi, lower down upward adverse flow of Qi, relieve cough and asthma, sedate and calm the mind, used to treat pain in the chest and back, cough, asthma and infantile convulsion.

Manipulation: Puncture obliquely upward 0.3—0.5 cun.

陶道 Táodào (DU 13)

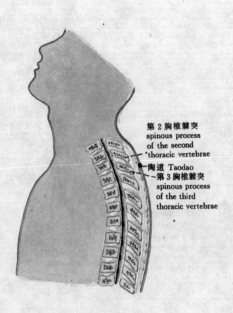

第2胸椎棘突
spinous process
of the second
thoracic vertebrae
陶道 Taodao
第3胸椎棘突
spinous process
of the third
thoracic vertebrae

〔取穴法〕（1）在背部，当后正中线上，第1胸椎棘突下凹陷中。

（2）俯伏或俯卧，从大椎穴向下摸1个棘突下之陷中是穴。

〔功效与主治〕解表，退热，安神。发热恶寒，疟疾，脊强。

〔操作〕向上斜刺0.3～0.5寸。

〔备注〕足太阳经与督脉交会穴。

Method of locating the point:

(1) This point is located on the back, on the posterior midline, in the depression of the spinous process of the first thoracic vertebra.

(2) Ask patient to take a prone position with his hands close or not close to his trunk, locate the point in the depression one spinous process below Dazhui (DU 14).

Actions and indications: Relieve exterior syndrome, reduce fever and tranquilize the mind, used to treat fever and chills, malaria, rigidity of the spinal column.

Manipulation: Puncture upwards obliquely 0.3—0.5 cun.

Notes: Taodao (DU 13) is the crossing point of the Foot-Taiyang Meridian and the Du Meridian.

大椎 Dàzhuī (DU 14)

〔取穴法〕在后正中线上,第7颈椎棘突下凹陷中。

〔功效与主治〕散寒解表,理气降逆,镇静安神。感冒,热病,疟疾,咳嗽,气喘,癫狂痫。

〔操作〕向上斜刺0.3~0.5寸。

〔备注〕手、足三阳经与督脉交会穴。

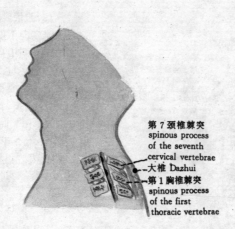

第7颈椎棘突
spinous process
of the seventh
cervical vertebrae
大椎 Dazhui
第1胸椎棘突
spinous process
of the first
thoracic vertebrae

Method of locating the point: This point is located on the posterior midline, in the depression below the spinous process of the 7th cervical vertebra.

Actions and indications: Expel cold, relieve exterior syndrome, regulate flow of Qi, lower upward adverse flow of Qi, tranquilize the mind, used to treat common cold, febrile diseases, malaria, cough, mania, depressive psychosis and epilepsy.

Manipulation: Puncture upwards obliquely 0.3—0.5 cun.

Notes: Dazhui (DU 14) is a crossing point of the three Yin meridians of hand, three Yin meridians of foot and the Du Meridian.

哑门 Yǎmén (DU 15)

〔取穴法〕（1）在项部，当后发际正中直上0.5寸，第1颈椎下。

（2）正坐，头稍前倾，于后正中线入发际5分处取穴。

〔功效与主治〕疏风通络，开窍醒脑。暴喑，中风，舌强不语，癫狂痫。

〔操作〕向下颌方向缓慢刺入0.3～0.5寸，不宜大幅度捻转、提插。

〔备注〕督脉与阳维脉交会穴。禁灸。

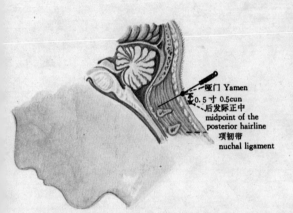

哑门 Yamen
0.5 寸 0.5cun
后发际正中
midpoint of the posterior hairline
项韧带
nuchal ligament

Method of locating the point：

（1）This point is located on the nape，0.5 cun within the posterior hairline，on the posterior midline，below the first cervical vertebra.

（2）Ask patient to take a sitting position with the head slightly put forward，locate the point 0.5 cun within the posterior hairline on the midline.

Actions and indications：Expel wind，activate flow of Qi and blood in the channels and collaterals，induce resuscitation and restore consciousness，used to treat sudden hoarseness，apoplexy，aphasia due to rigidity of the tongue，mania，depressive psychosis，and epilepsy.

Manipulation：Puncture 0.3－0.5 cun slowly toward the jaw.

Notes：This point is a crossing point of the Du Meridian and Yangwei Meridian. Moxibustion is prohibited.

风府 Fēngfǔ (DU 16)

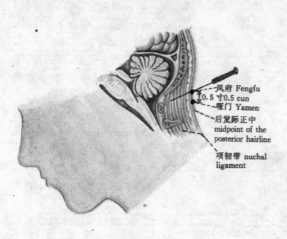

风府 Fengfu
0.5 寸 0.5 cun
哑门 Yamen
后发际正中
midpoint of the
posterior hairline
项韧带 nuchal
ligament

〔取穴法〕(1)正坐，头微前倾，在项部，当后发际正中直上 1 寸，枕外隆凸直下，两侧斜方肌之间凹陷中。

(2)在哑门穴上 0.5 寸处取穴。

〔功效与主治〕清热散风，通关开窍。项强，眩晕，中风不语，半身不遂。

〔操作〕向下斜刺 0.3 ～0.5 寸，针尖不可向上刺太深，以免刺入枕骨大孔，误伤延髓。

〔备注〕足太阳经、督脉与阳维脉交会穴。禁灸。

Method of locating the point：

(1) Ask patient to take a sitting position with his head slightly put forward, locate the point in the nape, 1 cun within the posterior hairline, directly below the the external occipital protruberance, in the depression between m. trapezius of both sides.

(2) Locate the point 0.5 cun above Yamen (DU 15).

Actions and indications：Clear away heat, expel wind, indcue resuscitation, used to treat rigidity of the nape, dizziness, aphasia by apoplexy, and hemiplegia.

Manipulation：Puncture downward obliquely 0.3 — 0.5 cun. The tip of needle cannot be inserted upwards too deep, otherwise it may enter the great occipital foramen and injury the medullary bulb.

Notes：This point is a crossing point of the Foot-Taiyang Meridian, Du Meridian and Yangwei Meridian. Moxibustion is prohibited.

脑户 Nǎohù (DU 17)

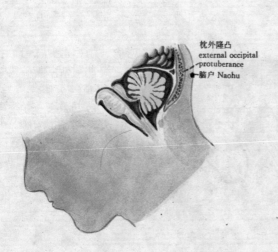

枕外隆凸
external occipital
protuberance
脑户 Naohu

〔取穴法〕（1）在头后部，后发际正中直上2.5寸，枕外隆凸的上缘凹陷处。

（2）在风府穴上1.5寸，枕外隆凸的上缘凹陷处。

〔功效与主治〕散风清热，开窍镇痉。痫证，喑不能言。头痛项强。

〔操作〕沿皮刺0.3～0.5寸。

〔备注〕足太阳经与督脉交会穴。

Method of locating the point:

(1) This point is located on the back of head, 2.5 cun directly above midpoint of the posterior hairline, in the depression of the upper border of the external occipital protuberance.

(2) Locate the point 1.5 cun above the Fengfu point (DU 16), in the depression of the upper border of the external occipital protruberance.

Actions and indications: Expel wind, clear away heat, induce resuscitation and relieve convulsion, used to treat epilepsy, aphasia, headache and rigidity of the nape.

Manipulation: Puncture subcutaneously 0.3—0.5 cun.

Notes: This point is a crossing point of the Foot-Taiyang Meridian and the Du Meridian.

后顶 Hòudǐng（DU 19）

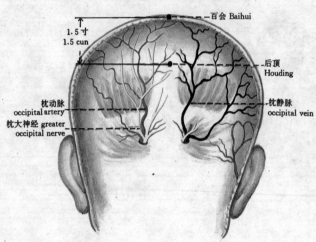

百会 Baihui

1.5 寸
1.5 cun

后顶
Houding

枕动脉
occipital artery

枕大神经 greater
occipital nerve

枕静脉
occipital vein

〔取穴法〕(1)在头部,当后发际正中直上5.5寸（脑户穴上3寸）。

(2)正头,于后正中线,当前、后发际连线中点向后5分处。

〔功效与主治〕清头散风,镇静安神。头痛,目眩,失眠。

〔操作〕沿皮刺0.3~0.5寸。

Method of locating the point:

(1) This point is located on the head, 5.5 cun above the midpoint of the posterior hairline, or 3 cun above Naohu (DU 17).

(2) Ask patient to put his head straight, locate the point on the posterior midline, 5 cun posterior to the midpoint of the line connecting the anterior and posterior hairline.

Actions and indications: Clear away heat from the head, disperse wind, sedate and tranquilize the mind, used to treat headache, dizziness and insomnia.

Manipulation: Puncture subcutaneously 0.3—0.5 cun.

百会 Bǎihuì (DU 20)

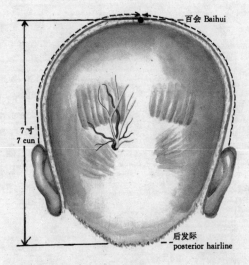

百会 Baihui

7 寸
7 cun

后发际
posterior hairline

〔取穴法〕(1)在头顶部,当前发际正中线直上5寸处。

(2)正坐,于两耳尖连线的中点处。

(3)正坐,于前、后发际连线中点向前1寸处取穴。

〔功效与主治〕清热开窍,健脑宁神,回阳固脱,平肝熄风。头痛,眩晕,中风半身不遂,失语,癫狂痫,脱肛,健忘。

〔操作〕沿皮刺0.3~0.5寸。

〔备注〕足三阳经与督脉交会穴。

Method of locating the point:

(1) This point is located in the vertex, 5 cun directly above the midpoint of the anterior hairline.

(2) Ask patient to take a sitting position, locate the point at the midpoint of the line connecting the apexes of the bilateral ears.

(3) Ask patient to take a sitting position, locate the point 1 cun anterior to the midpoint of the line joining the anterior and posterior hairlines.

Actions and indications: Clear away heat, induce resuscitation, strengthen the brain, tranquilize the mind, recuperate the depleted yang, suppress the hyperactive liver and relieve convulsion, used to treat headache, dizziness, hemiplegia by apoplexy, aphasia, mania, depressive psychosis, epilepsy, prolapse of the retum and amnesia.

Manipulation: Puncture subcutaneously 0.3—0.5 cun.

Notes: This point is a crossing point of the three Yang meridians of foot and the Du Meridian.

前顶 Qiándǐng (DU 21)

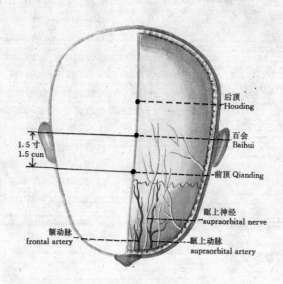

后顶
Houding

百会
Baihui

前顶 Qianding

1.5 寸
1.5 cun

眶上神经
supraorbital nerve

额动脉
frontal artery

眶上动脉
supraorbital artery

〔取穴法〕(1)在头部,当前发际正中直上 3.5 寸(百会前1.5 寸)处。

(2)正坐,于前、后发际连线的前 1/4 折点向后 0.5 寸处。

〔功效与主治〕清头散风。痫证,头痛,头晕,小儿惊风。

〔操作〕沿皮刺0.3～0.5 寸。

Method of locating the point:

(1) This point is located on the head, 3.5 cun directly above the midpoint of the anterior hairline, or 1.5 cun anterior to Baihui (Du 20)

(2) Ask patient to take a sitting position, 0.5 cun posterior to the junction of the anterior 1/4 of the line connecting the anterior and the posterior hairline.

Actions and indications: Clear away heat from the head and dissipate wind, used to treat epilepsy, headache, dizziness, and infantile convulsion.

Manipulation: Puncture subcutaneously 0.3—0.5 cun.

300

上星 Shàngxīng (DU 23)

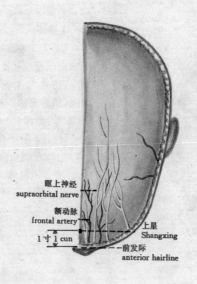

眶上神经
supraorbital nerve

额动脉
frontal artery

1寸 1 cun

上星
Shàngxing

一前发际
anterior hairline

〔取穴法〕（1）在头部，当前发际正中直上1寸处。

（2）正坐，于神庭穴向后0.5寸处取穴。

（3）若无发际时，当百会穴向前4寸处。

〔功效与主治〕清头散风，通窍明目。头痛，目痛，鼻渊，癫狂痫。

〔操作〕沿皮刺0.3～0.5寸，小儿囟门未闭者禁针。

Method of locating the point：

(1) This point is located on the head，1 cun directly above the midpoint of the anterior hairline.

(2) Ask patient to take a sitting position，locate the point 0.5 cun posterior to Shenting (DU 24).

(3) Locate the point 4 cun anterior to Baihui (DU 20) in patients without anterior hairline.

Actions and indications：Clear away heat from head，expel wind，induce resuscitation and improve vision，used to treat headache，pain of the eye，rhinorrhea，mania，depressive psychosis and epilepsy.

Manipulation：Puncture subcutaneously 0.3—0.5 cun. Puncture is prohibited in infants whose fontanels are not closed.

神庭 Shéntíng (DU 24)

〔取穴法〕（1）在头部，当前发际正中直上 0.5 寸处。

（2）若无发际时，当百会穴向前量取 4.5 寸处。

〔功效与主治〕清头散风，镇静安神。痫证，头痛，眩晕，鼻渊。

〔操作〕沿皮刺 0.2～0.3 寸，或点刺出血。

〔备注〕督脉、足太阳经与足阳明经交会穴。

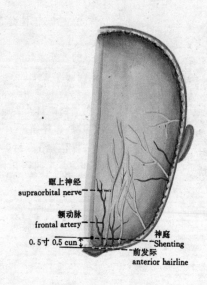

眶上神经
supraorbital nerve

额动脉
frontal artery

0.5 寸 0.5 cun

神庭
Shenting

前发际
anterior hairline

Method of locating the point：

(1) This point is located on the head，0. 5 cun directly above the midpoint of the anterior hairline.

(2) In patients without the hairline，locate the point 4. 5 cun anterior to Baihui (DU 20).

Actions and indications：Clear away heat from head，expel wind，sedate and tranquilize the mind，used to treat epilepsy，headache，dizziness and rhinorrhea.

Manipulation：Puncture subcutaneously 0. 3 — 0. 5 cun，or prick with a three edged needle to cause bleeding.

Notes：This point is a crossing point of the Du Meridian，the Foot-Taiyang Meridian and the Foot-Yangming Meridian.

素髎 Sùliáo (DU 25)

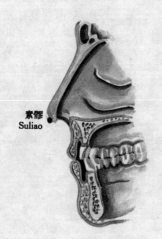

素髎
Suliao

〔取穴法〕正坐仰靠或仰卧,在面部,当鼻尖的正中央。

〔功效与主治〕泄热开窍,回阳救逆。鼻塞,鼻衄,虚脱。

〔操作〕向上斜刺0.1~0.2寸。

〔备注〕禁灸。

Method of locating the point: Ask patient to take a sitting position with his back supported and bent backwards or take a supine position, locate the point on the face, in the centre of the nose tip.

Actions and indications: Purge heat, induce resuscitation, and recuperate depleted yang, used to treat stuffy nose, epistaxis and syncope.

Manipulation: Puncture upward obliquely 0.1—0.2 cun.

Notes: Moxibustion is prohibited.

水沟 Shuǐgōu (DU 26)

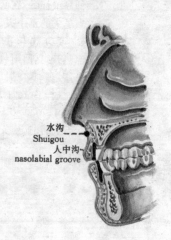

水沟
Shuigou
人中沟
nasolabial groove

〔取穴法〕正坐仰靠或仰卧,在面部,当人中沟的上 1/3 与中 1/3 交点处。

〔功效与主治〕清热开窍,镇痛宁神,回阳救逆。癫狂痫证,小儿惊风,昏迷,口眼㖞斜,面肿,腰脊强痛。

〔操作〕向上斜刺 0.2～0.3 寸。

〔备注〕督脉、手阳明经与足阳明经交会穴。

Method of locating the point: Ask patient to take a sitting position with his back supported and bent backwards or take a supine position, locate the point on the face, at the junction of the upper 1/3 and the middle 1/3 of the nasolabial groove.

Actions and indications: Clear away heat, induce resuscitation, sedate and tranquilize the mind, recuperate depleted yang, used to treat mania, depressive psychosis, epilepsy, infantile convulsion, coma, deviation of mouth and eye, swollen face, rigidity and pain of the loins and spinal column.

Manipulation: Puncture upward obliquely 0.2—0.3 cun.

Notes: This point is a crossing point of the Du Meridian, Hand-Yangming Meridian and Foot-Yangming Meridian.

兑端 Duìduān (DU 27)

兑端
Duiduan

〔取穴法〕正坐仰靠或仰卧,在面部,当上唇的尖端,人中沟下端的皮肤与唇的移行部。

〔功效与主治〕清热利湿,定惊止痛。癫狂,口喎唇动,遗尿。

〔操作〕向上斜刺0.2～0.3寸,或点刺出血。禁灸。

Located method: Ask patient to take a sitting position with his back supported and slightly bent backward or take a supine position, locate the point on the face on the medial tubercle of the upper lip, at the junction of the skin of the nasolabial groove and the upper lip.

Actions and indications: Clear away heat, remove dampness, relieve convulsion and relieve pain, used to treat depressive psychosis, mania, deviation of mouth, tremor of the lips, and enuresis.

Manipulation: Puncture upward obliquely 0.2—0.3 cun or prick with a three-edged needle to cause bleeding. Moxibustion is prohibited.

龈交 Yínjiāo (DU 28)

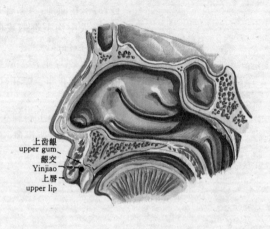

上齿龈
upper gum
龈交
Yinjiao
上唇
upper lip

〔取穴法〕(1)在上唇内,唇系带与上齿龈的相接处。

(2)正坐仰靠,提起上唇,于上唇系带与齿龈之移行陷凹处。

〔功效与主治〕清热利湿,开窍醒神。癫狂痫证,齿龈肿痛,口喁。

〔操作〕向上斜刺0.1~0.2寸,或点刺出血。

〔备注〕督脉、任脉与足阳明经交会穴。禁灸。

Method of locating the point:

(1) This point is located within the upper lip, at the junction of the gum and the frenulum of the upper lip.

(2) Ask patient to sit straight with the back bent backward, pull the upper lip upward and locate the point in the depression at the junction of the frenulum of the upper lip and the gum.

Actions and indications: Clear away heat, remove dampness, induce resuscitation and restore the consciousness, used to treat mania, depressive psychosis, epilepsy, swollen and painful gums, and lockjaw.

Manipulation: Puncture upwards obliquely 0.1—0.2 cun, or prick with a three edged needle to cause bleeding.

Notes: This point is a crossing point of the Du Meridian, the Ren Meridian and the Foot-Yangming Meridian. Moxibustion at this point is prohibited.

十五、经外穴

15. The extraordinary points

四神聪 Sìshéncōng (EX—HN1)

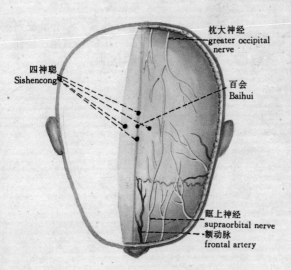

枕大神经
greater occipital nerve

四神聪
Sishencong

百会
Baihui

眶上神经
supraorbital nerve

额动脉
frontal artery

〔取穴法〕在头顶部，当百会前后左右各1寸，共4穴。

〔功效与主治〕安神聪脑，疏通经络。头痛，眩晕，失眠，健忘。

〔操作〕沿皮刺向百会穴0.3～0.5寸。

Method of locating the point: These are a group of points on the vertex, which are located 1 cun respectively posterior, anterior and lateral to Baihui (DU 20).

Actions and indications: Tranquilize the mind, improve mentality, remove obstructions in the channels and collaterals, used to treat headache, dizziness, insomnia and amnesia.

Manipulation: Puncture toward Baihui (DU 20) subcutaneously 0.3—0.5 cun.

印堂 Yìntáng（EX—HN3）

〔取穴法〕（1）在额部，当两眉头之中间取穴。

（2）仰靠或仰卧，当两眉头连线与前正中线的交点处是穴。

〔功效与主治〕活络疏风，镇痉安神。小儿急、慢惊风，头痛，眩晕。

〔操作〕向下沿皮刺0.3～0.5寸，或用三棱针点刺出血。

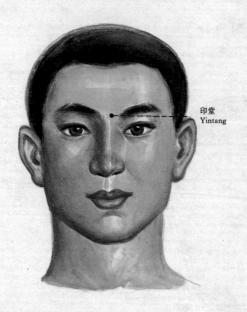

印堂
Yintang

Method of locating the point:

(1) This point is located between the inner ends of the bilateral eyebrows.

(2) Ask patient to take a sitting position with the body supported and bent backwards or take a supine position, locate the point at the junction of the line connecting the bilateral eyebrows and the anterior midline.

Actions and indications: Activate flow of Qi and blood in the collaterals, expel wind, relieve convulsion and tranquilize the mind, used to treat actue or chronic infantile convulsion, headache and dizziness.

Manipulation: Puncture 0.3—0.5 cun downward subcutaneously, or prick with a three edged needle to cause bleeding.

鱼腰 Yúyāo（EX—HN4）

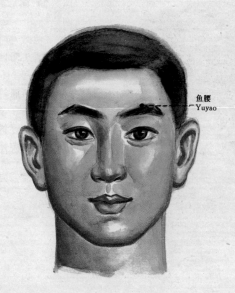

鱼腰
Yuyao

〔取穴法〕正坐平视，在额部，瞳孔直上，眉毛中取穴。

〔功效与主治〕祛风清热，清头明目。目赤肿痛，眉棱骨痛，面痛。

〔操作〕沿皮刺向攒竹或丝竹空 0.2～0.3 寸。

〔备注〕禁灸。

Method of locating the point: Ask patient to sit straight with the eye seeing straight forward, locate the point on the forehead directly above the pupil, at the midpoint of the eyebrow.

Actions and indications: Expel wind, clear away heat, clear away heat from the head and improve vision, used to treat redness, swelling and pain of the eye, pain of the supraorbital region, and facial pain.

Manipulation: Puncture 0.2—0.3 cun subcutaneously toward Zanzhu (B 2) or Sizhukong (SJ 23).

Notes: Moxibustion is prohibited.

太阳 Tàiyáng (EX—HN5)

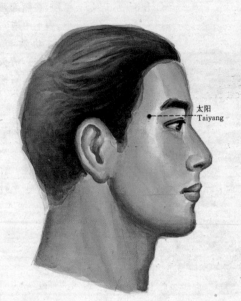

太阳
Taiyang

〔取穴法〕正坐或仰卧,在颞部,当眉梢与目外眦之间,向后约一横指的凹陷处。

〔功效与主治〕疏风散热,清头明目。头痛,偏头痛,头晕,目赤肿痛,口眼㖞斜,面痛,视力减退。

〔操作〕直刺 0.2～0.3 寸;向后斜刺 0.5～1 寸,或用三棱针点刺出血。

〔备注〕禁灸。

Method of locating the point: Ask patient to take a sitting position or a supine position, locate the point in the depression about one-finger-width posterior to the midpoint of the line connecting the lateral end of the eyebrow and the outer canthus.

Actions and indications: Expel wind, clear away heat from head and improve vision, used to treat headache, migraine, dizziness, redness, swelling and pain of the eye, deviation of the eye and mouth, facial pain, and decline of vision.

Manipulation: Puncture perpendicularly 0.2—0.3 cun, or puncture posteriorly 0.5—1 cun, or prick with a three edged needle to cause bleeding.

Notes: Moxibustion is prohibited.

310

球后 Qiúhòu（EX—HN7）

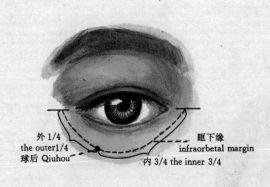

外 1/4
the outer1/4
球后 Qiuhou
内 3/4 the inner 3/4
眶下缘
infraorbetal margin

〔取穴法〕（1）在面部，当眶下缘外 1/4 与内 3/4 交点处。

（2）正坐平视，由眼内、外角向下引一垂线，两线之间分成四等分，其外 1/4 与内 3/4 交界处，眼眶下缘处。

〔功效与主治〕活血明目。目疾：视神经炎、视神经萎缩、青光眼、近视等。

〔操作〕轻压眼球向上，针沿眼眶下缘缓慢刺入 0.5～1 寸，不捻转提插。

〔备注〕禁灸。

Method of locating the point：

（1）This point is located on the face, at the junction of lateral 1/4 and medial 3/4 of the infraobital margion.

（2）Ask patient to sit straight with the eyes seeing forward, locate the point at the junction of the lateral 1/4 and the medial 3/4 of the distance between the outer and inner canthus.

Actions and indications：Activate blood flow and improve vision, used to treat eye disorders, including optic neuritis, atrophy of the optic nerve, glaucoma, myopia.

Manipulation：Push the eyeball gently upward, then puncture perpendicularly 0.5－1 cun along the orbital margin slowly without lifting, thrusting, twisting and rotating the needle.

Notes：Moxibustion is prohibited.

金津 Jīnjīn（EX−HN12）

〔取穴法〕仰靠坐位,张口,舌尖向上反卷,在口腔内,当舌下系带左侧的静脉上取穴。

〔功效与主治〕清热开窍。舌肿痛,喉痹,失语。

〔操作〕三棱针点刺出血。

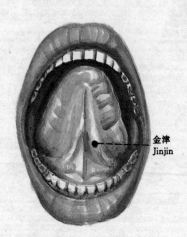

金津
Jinjin

Method of locating the point：Ask patient to take a sitting position with the back bent backwards, the mouth open and the tougue tip curled up, locate the point in the oral cavity, on the left vein of the frenulum of the tongue.

Actions and indications：Clear away heat and induce resuscitation, used to treat swelling and pain of the tongue, sore throat, aphasia.

Manipulation：Prick with a three edged needle to cause bleeding.

312

玉液 Yùyè (EX—HN13)

〔取穴法〕仰靠坐位,张口,舌尖向上反卷,在口腔内,当舌下系带右侧的静脉上取穴。

〔功效与主治〕清热开窍。舌肿痛,喉痹,失语。

〔操作〕三棱针点刺出血。

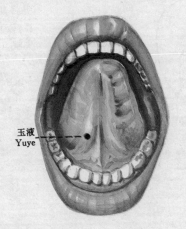

玉液
Yuye

Method of locating the point: Ask patient to take a sitting position with the back bent backwards, the mouth open and the tougue tip curled up, locate the point in the oral cavity, on the right vein of the frenulum of the tongue.

Actions and indications: Clear away heat and induce resuscitation, used to treat swelling and pain of the tongue, sore throat, aphasia.

Manipulation: Prick with a three edged needle to cause bleeding.

翳明 Yìmíng (EX—HN14)

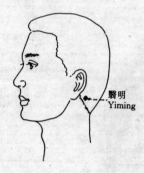

翳明
Yiming

〔取穴法〕正坐，头略前倾，在项部，当翳风穴后1寸处取穴。

〔功效与主治〕明目聪耳。目疾：近视、夜盲、青盲；耳鸣，失眠。

〔操作〕直刺0.5～0.8寸。

Method of locating the point: Ask patient to take a sitting position with the head slightly bent forwards, locate the point on the nape, 1 cun posterior to Yifeng (SJ 17).

Actions and indications: Improve vision and hearing, used to treat eye disorders such as myopia, night blindness and blindness due to glaucoma, and tinnitis and insomnia.

Manipulation: Puncture perpendicularly 0.5—0.8 cun.

颈百劳 Jǐngbǎiláo (EX—HN15)

〔取穴法〕正坐，头微前倾，或俯伏，在项部，当大椎穴直上2寸，后正中线旁开1寸处。

〔功效与主治〕理肺降逆，舒筋活络。咳嗽，气喘，颈项强痛。

〔操作〕直刺0.3～0.5寸。

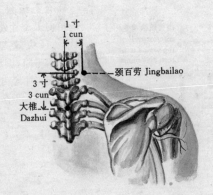

Method of locating the point: Ask patient to take a sitting position with the head slightly bent forwards or take a prone position, locate the point on the nape, 2 cun directly above Dazhui (DU 20), 1 cun lateral to the posterior midline.

Actions and indications: Facilitate flow of the lung-Qi, relax muscles and tendons, and activate flow of Qi and blood in the channels and collaterals, used to treat cough, asthma, rigidity and pain of the nape.

Manipulation: Puncture perpendicularly 0.3—0.5 cun.

315

子宫 Zǐgōng (EX—CA1)

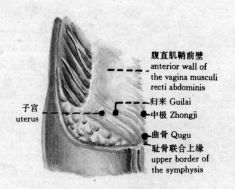

腹直肌鞘前壁
anterior wall of
the vagina musculi
recti abdominis

子宫
uterus

归来 Guilai

中极 Zhongji

曲骨 Qugu

耻骨联合上缘
upper border of
the symphysis

〔取穴法〕(1)在下腹部,当脐中下 4 寸,中极旁开 3 寸处。

(2)仰卧,于耻骨联合上缘旁开 3 寸,再向上 1 寸处。

〔功效与主治〕升阳举陷,调经止痛。阴挺,月经不调,痛经,带下,不孕。

〔操作〕直刺 0.5~1 寸。

Method of locating the point:

(1) This point is located in the lower abdomen, 4 cun inferior to the umbilicus, 3 cun lateral to Zhongji (RN 3).

(2) Ask patient to take a supine position, 1 cun above a point 3 cun lateral to the midpoint of the upper border of the pubic symphysis.

Actions and indications: Lift Yang and treat prolapse, regulate menstruation and relieve pain, used to treat prolapse of the uterus, irregular menstruation, dysmenorrhea, leukorrhea and sterility.

Manipulation: Puncture perpendicularly 0.5—1 cun.

316

定喘 Dìngchuǎn (EX—B1)

〔取穴法〕（1）俯伏，在背上部，第7颈椎棘突下旁开 0.5 寸处。

（2）俯伏，大椎穴左右各旁开 0.5 寸处。

〔功效与主治〕宣肺定喘，祛风活血。哮喘，咳嗽，落枕，青年痤疮。

〔操作〕针尖向脊柱方向斜刺 0.5～1 寸。

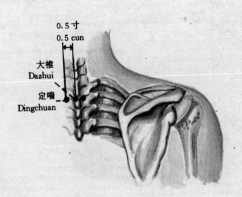

0.5 寸
0.5 cun

大椎
Dazhui

定喘
Dingchuan

Method of locating the point：

（1）When patient takes a prone position，the points are located in the upper part of the back，0.5 cun respectively lateral to the the area below spinous process of the 7th cervical vertebra.

（2）When patient takes a prone position，locate the points respectively lateral to Dazhui (DU 20).

Actions and indications：Facilitate flow of the lung-Qi，expel wind and activate flow of blood，used to treat asthma，cough，stiff neck，and acne in young people.

Manipulation：Puncture 0.5—1 cun obliquely with the needle tip pointing at the spinal column.

317

夹脊 Jiájǐ (EX—B2)

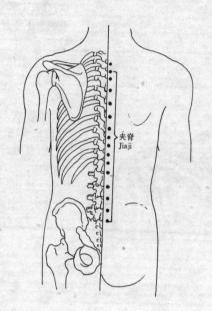

夹脊
Jiaji

〔取穴法〕俯伏或俯卧,在背腰部,当第 1 胸椎至第 5 腰椎棘突下两侧,后正中线旁开 0.5 寸,一侧 17 穴,共 34 穴。

〔功效与主治〕通利关节,调理脏腑。咳嗽,哮喘,胸胁痛,背腰酸痛,上、下肢痿、痹证。

〔操作〕向脊柱方向斜刺 0.3～0.5 寸。可灸。

Method of locating the point: When patient takes a prone position or a lateral recubent position, the point is lcoated in the back and lumbar region, on the bilateral sides of the spinous processes between the first and the fifth lumbar vertebra, 0.5 cun lateral to the posterior midline, 17 points on each side, 34 points in all.

Actions and indications: Smooth the articulations, regulate functions of zang-fu organs, used to treat cough, asthma, pain in the chest and hypochondrium, aching pain of the lumbar region and back, atrophy and arthralgia of the limbs.

Manipulations: Puncture 0.3 — 0.5 cun obliquely toward the spinal column. Moxibustion is applicable.

胃脘下俞 Wèiwǎnxiàshù (EX—B3)

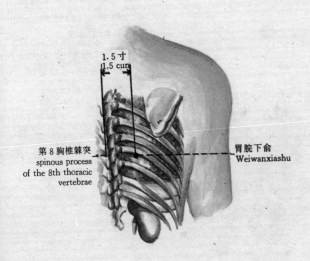

1.5寸
1.5 cun

第8胸椎棘突
spinous process
of the 8th thoracic
vertebrae

胃脘下俞
Weiwanxiashu

〔取穴法〕俯伏或俯卧,在背部,当第8胸椎棘突下,旁开1.5寸处。

〔功效与主治〕宽胸理气,和中降逆。胃脘痛,呕吐,胸胁痛,消渴。

〔操作〕斜刺0.5～0.8寸。

Method of locating the point: Ask patient to take a prone position or a lateral recubent position, locate the points below the spinous process of the 8th thoracic vertebra, 1.5 cun lateral to the midline.

Actions and indications: Soothe flow of the Qi in the chest, regulate functions of the middle-jiao, lower down upward adverse flow of Qi, used to treat stomachache, vomiting, hypochondriac pain, and diabetes.

Manipulation: Puncture obliquely 0.5—0.8 cun.

319

腰眼 Yāoyǎn（EX－B7）

〔取穴法〕俯卧，在腰部，当第 4 腰椎棘突下，旁开约 3.5 寸凹陷中取穴。

〔功效与主治〕补肾壮腰，活血祛瘀。腰痛，腰扭伤。

〔操作〕直刺 0.5～1 寸。

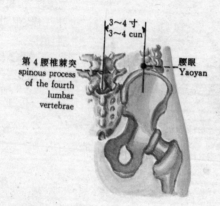

第 4 腰椎棘突
spinous process
of the fourth
lumbar
vertebrae

3～4 寸
3～4 cun

腰眼
Yaoyan

Method of locating the point: Ask patient to take a prone position, locate the point below the spinous process of the 4th lumbar vertebra, in the depression 3.5 cun lateral to the midline.

Actions and indications: Tonify the kidney, strengthen the loins, activate blood flow and remove blood stasis, used to treat lumbago and lumbar sprains.

Manipulation: Puncture perpendicularly 0.5－1 cun.

十七椎 Shíqīzhuī（EX—B8）

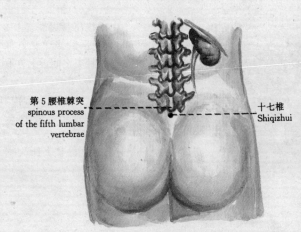

第5腰椎棘突
spinous process
of the fifth lumbar
vertebrae

十七椎
Shiqizhui

〔取穴法〕（1）俯卧，在腰部，当后正中线上，第5腰椎棘突下凹陷中取穴。

（2）俯卧，先取与髂嵴相平的腰阳关穴，再向下摸一个棘突，其棘突下凹陷中是穴。

〔功效与主治〕补肾壮腰。腰痛，腿痛，崩漏，痛经。

〔操作〕直刺0.5～1寸。

Method of locating the point:

(1) Ask patient to take a prone position, locate the point in the lumbar region on the posterior midline, in the depression of the spinous process of the 5th lumbar vertebra.

(2) Ask patient to take a prone position, locate Yaoyangguan (DU 3) which is at the level of the superior illiac spine, then locate Shiqizhui (EX-B 8) in the depression one process below Yaoyangguan (DU 3).

Actions and indications: Tonify the kidney, strengthen the loin, used to treat lumbago, pain of the legs, metrostaxis and metrorrhagia, and dysmenorrhea.

Manipulation: Puncture perpendicularly 0.5—1 cun.

腰奇 Yāoqī (EX—B9)

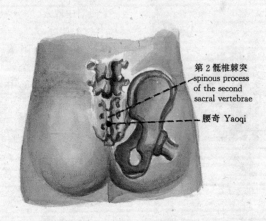

第2骶椎棘突
spinous process
of the second
sacral vertebrae

腰奇 Yaoqi

〔取穴法〕(1)在骶部,当尾骨端直上2寸,骶角之间凹陷中取穴。

(2)俯卧,于后正中线尾骨尖端直上2寸处,约当第二三骶椎棘突之间近上方取穴。

〔功效与主治〕宁神通络。痫证,头痛。

〔操作〕针尖向上平刺1~2寸。可灸。

Method of locating the point:

(1) This point is located in the lumbar region, 2 cun directly above the tip of coccyx, in the depression between the sacral horns.

(2) Ask patient to take a prone position, locate the point 2 cun directly above the tip of the sacrum on the posterior midline, about the upper part of the depression between the spinous processes of the second and third lumbar vertebra.

Actions and indications: Tranquilize the mind, promote flow of Qi and blood in the collaterals, used to treat epilepsy and headache.

Manipulation: Puncture 1—2 cun upwards subcutaneously. Moxibustion is applicable.

二白 Erbái (EX—UE2)

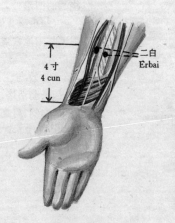

4寸
4 cun

二白
Erbai

〔取穴法〕(1)在前臂掌侧,腕横纹上4寸,桡侧腕屈肌腱的两侧,一侧2穴。

(2)伸臂仰掌,于曲泽穴与大陵穴连线的中1/3与下1/3交界处相平,桡侧腕屈肌腱左右两侧各1穴,两手共4穴。

〔功效与主治〕活血通经,理肛肠。痔疮,脱肛。

〔操作〕直刺0.5～0.8寸。

Method of locating the point: These are a group of points located on the palmar side of the forearm, 4 cun superior to the transverse crease of the wirst, on the bilateral sides of the tendon of m. flexor carpi radialis, 2 points on one hand.

(2) Ask patient to stretch out his arm with the palm placed upward, locate the points at the level with the the junction of the middle 1/3 and the lower 1/3 of the line connecting Quze (PC 3) and Daling (PC 70), 2 points on bilateral sides of the tendon of m. flexor carpi radialis, 4 points on both hands.

Actions and indications: Activate flow of blood in the channels and collaterals, regulate anus and rectum, used to treat hemorrhoid and prolapse of rectum.

Manipulation: Puncture perpendicularly 0.5—0.8 cun.

中泉 Zhōngquán（EX—UE3）

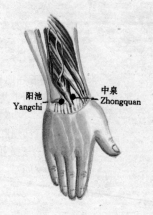

阳池
Yangchi

中泉
Zhongquan

〔取穴法〕（1）在腕背侧横纹中，当指总伸肌腱桡侧的凹陷处。

（2）手腕背侧横纹上，阳溪与阳池穴连线的中点处取穴。

〔功效与主治〕宽胸和胃，舒筋活络。腕痛，腕下垂，胸闷，胃痛。

〔操作〕直刺 0.3～0.5 寸。

Method of locating the point：

（1）This point is located on the dorsal transverse crease of the wrist, in the depression of the radial side of the tendon of flexor digital muscle.

（2）Locate the point on the dorsal transverse crease of the wrist, between Yangxi (LI 5) and Yangchi (SJ 4).

Actions and indications：Soothe flow of Qi in the chest, regulate the function of the stomach, relax muscles and tendons and activate flow of Qi and blood in the channels and collaterals, used to treat pain of the wrist, ptosis of the wrist, suffocation of the chest and stomachache.

Manipulation：Puncture perpendicularly 0.3—0.5 cun.

中魁 Zhōngkuí（EX—UE4）

〔取穴法〕握拳，在手中指背侧近侧指间关节的中点处。

〔功效与主治〕和胃降逆。翻胃，呕吐，呃逆。

〔操作〕艾炷灸3～5壮，或艾条灸10分钟。

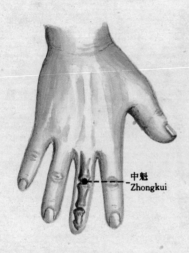

中魁
Zhongkui

Method of locating the point: When a fist is clenched, this point is located at the midpoint of the proximal interphalangeal joint of the middle finger at the dorsal aspect.

Actions and indications: Regulate the function of the stomach and lower down upward adverse flow of Qi, used to treat acid regurgitation, vomiting, and hiccup.

Manipulation: Moxibustion is applied with three moxa cones or 10 minutes with moxa roll.

大骨空 Dàgǔkōng (EX—UE5)

〔取穴法〕屈曲大拇指,在拇指背侧近指间关节的中点处。

〔功效与主治〕清热明目。目痛,目翳。

〔操作〕艾炷灸3～5壮,或艾条灸5～10分钟。

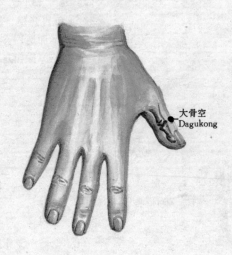

大骨空
Dagukong

Method of locating the point: When the thumb is flexed, the point is located at the midpoint proximal to the interphalangeal joint of the thumb at the dorsal aspect.

Actions and indications: Clear away heat, improve vision, used to treat pain of eyes, cloudy substance of the eye.

Manipulation: Moxibustion is applied with 3 to 5 moxa cones or 5—10 minutes with moxa rolls.

小骨空 Xiǎogǔkōng （EX—UE6）

〔取穴法〕屈曲小拇指，在小指背侧近侧指间关节的中点处。

〔功效与主治〕清热明目。眼肿痛，目翳，喉痛。

〔操作〕艾炷灸3～5壮，或艾条灸5～10分钟。

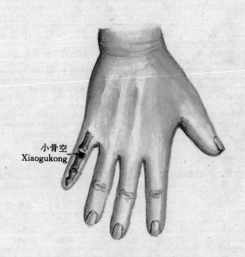

小骨空
Xiaogukong

Method of locating the point: When the small finger is flexed, the point is located at the midpoint proximal to the interphalangeal joint of the small finger at the dorsal aspect.

Actions and indications: Clear away heat and improve vision, used to treat swelling and pain of the eyes, glaucoma, and sore throat.

Manipulation: Moxibustion is applied with 3 to 5 moxa cones or 5—10 minutes with moxa rolls.

八邪 Báxié（EX—UE9）

〔取穴法〕微握拳,在手背侧,第1~5指间,指蹼缘后方赤白肉际处,左右共8穴。

〔功效与主治〕祛瘀通络,清热解毒。手指麻木,手指拘急,手背红肿。

〔操作〕斜刺 0.3~0.5寸,或点刺出血。

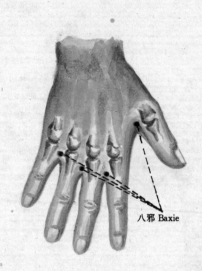

八邪 Baxie

Method of locating the point: When the fist is loosely clenched, this point is located on the dorsal aspect of the hand, at the junction of the white and red skin between the first and the fifth fingers, 8 points in all on both hands.

Actions and indications: Remove blood stasis, activate flow of Qi and blood in the channels and collaterals, clear away heat and remove toxic materials, used to treat numbness or convulsion of the fingers, swelling and redness of the dorsum of hand.

Manipulation: Puncture obliquely 0.3—0.5 cun, or prick with a three-edged needle to cause bleeding.

四缝 Sìfèng (EX—UE10)

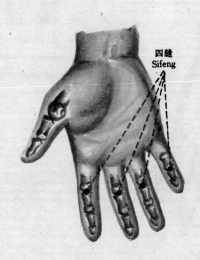

四缝
Sifeng

〔取穴法〕仰掌伸指,在第 2～5 指掌侧,近端指关节的中央,一侧 4 穴,两手共 8 穴。

〔功效与主治〕消积化痰,和中健脾。小儿疳积,消化不良,百日咳。

〔操作〕速刺 0.1寸,挤出少量黄白色透明样液体或出血为度。

Method of locating the point:

With the palm upwards and the fingers stretched out, these points are located on the dorsal aspects of the 2nd and the 5th fingers, at the midpoint proximal to the phalangeal joints, four points on one hand, 8 points in all.

Actions and indications: Promote digestion, dissolve phlegm, regulate function of the middle-jiao and strengthen the spleen, used to treat infantile malnutrition, indigestion and whooping cough.

Manipulation: Puncture quickly 0.1 cun, squeeze out a small amount of yellow-white viscious fluid or prick to cause bleeding.

十宣 Shíxuān（EX-VE11）

〔取穴法〕仰掌伸手，手十指尖端，距指甲 0.1 寸处。

〔功效与主治〕清热，开窍，醒神。主治昏迷，癫痫，高热，咽喉肿痛。

〔操作〕浅刺 0.1～0.2 寸，或点刺出血。

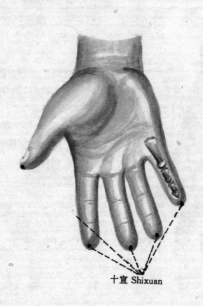

十宣 Shixuan

Method of locating the point: Ask patient to extend his or her fingers with the palm facing upwards, locate the point at the tips of the ten fingers, 0.1 cun distal to the nails.

Actions and indications: Clear away heat and restore resuscitation, used to treat coma, epilepsy, high fever and sore throat.

Manipulation: Puncture superficially 0.1—0.2cun, or prickly with a three edged needle to cause bleeding.

鹤顶 Hèdǐng (EX-LE2)

〔取穴法〕屈膝，在膝上部，髌底的中点上方凹陷处。

〔功效与主治〕舒筋活络，通利关节。膝肿痛，下肢无力。

〔操作〕直刺 0.3～0.5寸。

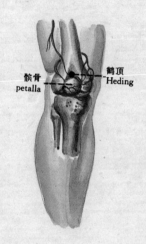

髌骨
petalla

鹤顶
Heding

Method of locating the point: When the knee is flexed, the point is located in the upper portion of the knee, in the depression superior to the midpoint of the lower boder of the patella.

Actions and indications: Relax muscles and tendons, activate flow of Qi and blood in the channels and collaterals, and benefit movement of the joint, used to treat swelling and pain of the knee, and flaccidity of the lower limbs.

Manipulation: Puncture perpendicularly 0.3－0.5 cun.

百虫窝 Bǎichóngwō (EX—LE3)

〔取穴法〕屈膝，在大腿内侧，髌底内侧端 3 寸，即血海穴上 1 寸处取穴。

〔功效与主治〕解毒杀虫，祛风止痒。虫积，风湿痒疹。

〔操作〕直刺 0.3～0.5 寸。

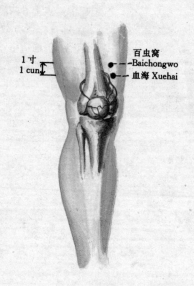

1 寸
1 cun

百虫窝 Baichongwo
血海 Xuehai

Method of locating the point: When the knee is flexed, this point is located 3 cun lateral to the medial end of the lower border of the patella, or 1 cun just above Xuehai (Sp 10).

Actions and indications: Detoxicate, destroy parasites, expel wind and relieve itching, used to treat parasitosis, itchy skin rashings due to wind-damp.

Manipulation: Puncture perpendicularly 0.3—0.5 cun.

膝眼 Xīyǎn (EX—LE5)

〔取穴法〕屈膝，在髌韧带两侧凹陷处，在内侧的称内膝眼，在外侧的称外膝眼。

〔功效与主治〕祛风湿，利关节。膝肿痛，下肢无力。

〔操作〕斜刺 0.3～0.5 寸。

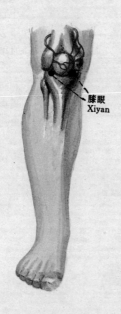

膝眼
Xiyan

Method of locating the point: When the knee is flexed, these two points are located in the two depressions lateral and medial to the patellar ligament. That in the medial side is also called Neixiyan (internal Xiyan) and that in the lateral side is called Waixiyan (external Xiyan).

Actions and indications: Expel wind-dampness, benefit articulations, used to treat swelling and pain of the knee, weaknees of the lower limbs.

Manipulation: Puncture obliquely 0.3—0.5 cun.

胆囊 Dǎnnáng（EX—LE6）

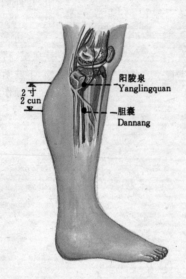

阳陵泉
Yanglingquan

2寸
2 cun

—胆囊
Dannang

〔取穴法〕正坐或侧卧，在小腿外侧上部，当腓骨小头前下方凹陷处（阳陵泉）直下2寸处。

〔功效与主治〕利胆通络。急、慢性胆囊炎，胆石症，胆道蛔虫症。

〔操作〕直刺0.5～1寸。

Method of locating the point: Ask patient to take a sitting position or lie on one side, locate the point in the upper portion of the lower leg, 2 cun inferior to the depression (Yanglingquan, GB 34) anterior and inferior to the head of the fistula.

Actions and indications: Benefit gallbladder and activate flow of blood and Qi in the channels and collaterals, used to treat acute and chronic cholecystitis, cholelithiasis, and biliary ascariasis.

Manipulation: Puncture perpendicularly 0.5—1 cun.

阑尾 Lánwěi（EX—LE7）

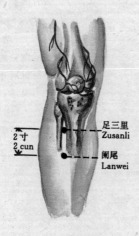

足三里
Zusanli

2寸
2 cun

阑尾
Lanwei

〔取穴法〕（1）正坐或仰卧,在小腿前侧上部,当犊鼻穴下5寸,胫骨前缘旁开一横指处。

（2）正坐或仰卧,于足三里与上巨虚之间压痛最明显处,约在足三里下2寸处。

〔功效与主治〕调肠止痛,通经活络。单纯性急性阑尾炎。

〔操作〕直刺1～1.5寸。

Method of locating the point：

(1) Ask patient to take a sitting position or a supine position, this point is located in the upper part of the anterior aspect of the lower leg, 5 cun directly below Dubi (St 35), a finger-width lateral to the anterior border of the tibia.

(2) Ask patient to take a sitting position or a supine position, locate the point in the area where the tenderness is most evident, about 2 cun below Zusanli (St 17).

Actions and indications：Regulate the movement of the bowel to relieve pain, promote blood flow in the channels and collaterals, used to treat acute simple appenditis.

Manipulation：Puncture perpendicularly 1—1.5 cun.

八风 Bāfēng (EX—LE10)

〔取穴法〕正坐或仰卧,在足背侧,第1～5趾间,趾蹼缘后方赤白肉际处,一侧4穴,左右共8穴。

〔功效与主治〕活血祛瘀,清热解毒。足趾麻木、疼痛、活动不灵活,足背肿痛。

〔操作〕斜刺0.3～0.5寸。

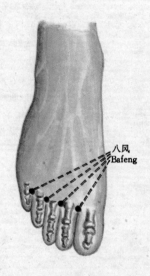

八风
Bafeng

Method of locating the point: When patient takes a sitting position or a supine position, these points are located on the dorsum of the foot, between the first and the fifth toes, at the junction of the red and white skin posterior to the webs, four points on one foot, 8 points in all.

Actions and indications: Activate blood flow and remove blood stasis, clear away heat and remove toxic materials, used to treat numbness, pain and difficult movement of the toes, swelling and pain of the dorsum of foot.

Manipulation: Puncture obliquely 0.3—0.5 cun.

常用针灸取穴汉英对照图解

张登部　王金玲　编著

*

山东科学技术出版社出版发行

（济南市玉函路　邮政编码 250002）

山东新华印刷厂印刷

*

850mm×1168mm 1/32 开本 11 印张 4 插页 234 千字

1997 年 3 月第 1 版　1997 年 3 月第 1 次印刷

印数：1—6000

ISBN7—5331—1723—9

R・498 定价 88.00 元